$15.0

Unlike statistical decision theory,
tive modeling tas

Models of Economic Systems

A Theory for Their Development and Use

The MIT Press
Cambridge, Massachusetts, and
London, England

Models of Economic Systems

A Theory for Their Development and Use

Arnold H. Packer

HD
82
.P17
1972

Contents

List of Figures   viii

List of Tables   ix

Preface   xi

**1
The Problem: Bridging the Gap between
Quantitative Analysis and Decision Making**   **1**

1.1
Introduction   1

1.2
Terminology and Basic Concepts   8

1.3
Previous Work   16

**2
Adaptive Modeling**   **26**

2.1
Adaptive Decision Processes   26

2.2
The Adaptive Modeling Procedure   30

2.3
Models and the Empirical Reality   40

2.4
Tacking Auxiliary Models onto the Primary Model   45

2.5
The Scientific Nature of the Formal Models   48

**3
Objective Functions**   **53**

3.1
Objective Functions for Choosing among Alternatives   53

3.2
Objective Functions for Microeconomic Decision Making   57

3.3
Objective Functions for Macroeconomic Decision Making   67

**4
Allocating Resources: The Static Case under
Uncertainty**   **76**

4.1
The Allocation Problem   76

4.2
The Primary Model   78

4.3
The Other Components of the Adaptive Procedure   87

4.4
A Numerical Example of the Static Case   100

5
Allocating Resources: The Dynamic Case   **110**

5.1
Growth Models and Production Functions   110

5.2
The Extended Primary Model for the Dynamic Case   117

5.3
The Decision-Making Algorithms for Investment   120

5.4
The Macrolevel Investment Decision   132

5.5
The Adaptive Procedure for the Combined Case   139

5.6
Conclusions   143

6
A Pilot Procedure for the Stabilization Problem   **147**

6.1
The Primary Model of the Pilot Procedure   147

6.2
The Four Other Components of the Pilot Procedure   155

6.3
Mechanics of the Pilot Procedure   167

7
The Certainty Components of a Prototype
Procedure for the Stabilization Problem   **172**

7.1
The Primary Model for the Prototype Procedure   174

7.2
The Monetary Auxiliary Model   176

7.3
The Decision-Making Roles   178

7.4
The Objective Function   181

7.5
The Information System   183
7.6
The Dynamic Environment   187

8
The Exogenous-Event Library and Auxiliary Models   195

8.1
The Library   195
8.2
Auxiliary Models for International Shocks   202
8.3
Auxiliary Models for Domestic Strikes   207

9
**An Appraisal of the Procedure and Its
Potential Applicability   210**

9.1
Models, Games, and Their Relationships   210
9.2
Appraisal of the Adaptive Modeling Procedure   217

Bibliography   220

Index   233

List of Figures

1.1 Formal and informal models in the decision-making process 12

2.1 The dynamic decision problem with a single instrument having two possible values and a three-period planning horizon 42

2.2 Relationships of model to reality 43

3.1 Cost-effectiveness alternatives 58

3.2 Typical Phillips curve 72

4.1 The final demand (B) matrix 82

4.2 Stipulation functions and demand curves for a typical final demand category 92

4.3 Inventory evaluation vs. inventory/sales ratio 94

4.4 Output and price coefficients 96

4.5 Primary model for the static case 98

4.6 Output and program value for two categories of goods 109

5.1 Classical production function 113

5.2 Production functions (constant technology; changing scale) 114

5.3 Production functions (changing technology; constant scale) 114

5.4 Possible production functions in period $t + 1$ 116

5.5 Fixed-proportion production functions 116

5.6 Typical flow of investment 123

5.7 Investment algorithms 124

5.8 Relaxing constraints in a two-good, three-constraint economy 136

5.9 The adaptive procedure 140

5.10 The primary model and the corresponding decisions 142

5.11 The dynamic environment for the resource allocation problem 144

6.1 General shapes of the scoring functions 156

6.2a Typical output from Version A 160

6.2b Typical output from Version B 161

6.3 The pilot procedure 166

6.4 Pilot procedure flow chart 168

8.1 Changes in supply curves resulting from an international shock 205

9.1 Possible relationships between theory, models, and policy 211

List of Tables

3.1 Estimated Case-Months Resulting from Five Alternative Programs 66

3.2 Estimated Change in Purchasing Power Resulting from Five Alternative Macroeconomic Policies 75

4.1 Producing Sectors 84

4.2 Final Demand Categories 84

4.3 Symbols for Static Primary Model 99

4.4 1958 (I— A) Matrix 100

4.5 Sector-Labor Coefficients 101

4.6 1958 B Matrix of Final Demand Expenditures 102

4.7 1958 P Matrix of Final Demand Pattern Coefficients 103

4.8 Tableau for Sample Linear Programming Problem 104

4.9 Constraints of the Sample Problem 104

4.10 Target Expenditures Stipulated for Sample Problem 105

4.11 Instrument Values of the Sample Problem 106

4.12 Shadow Prices on the Deficits (Runs 2 and 3) 108

5.1 Shadow Prices of the Sample Static Problem 122

5.2 Tableau for the Sample Parametric Programming Routine 125

5.3 1958 B Matrix of Final Demand Expenditures 127

5.4 1958 P Matrix of Final Demand Pattern Coefficients 128

5.5 Constraints in the Sample Parametric Programming Problem 128

5.6 Solutions to the Sample Parametric Programming Problem 129

5.7 Shadow Prices in the Sample Parametric Programming Problem 130

5.8 Additional Output from the Sample Parametric Programming Problem 131

6.1 Definitions of Pilot Model Variables 148

6.2 Pilot Model Equations 149

6.3 Maximum Range and Frequency of Instrument and Parameter Changes 154

6.4 Scoring Functions for Each Round 157

6.5 Scoring Functions for End-of-Game Bonuses and Penalties 158

6.6 Suggested Target Values and Weights for the Scoring Functions 159

6.7 Initialization File to Begin Play in 1969 164

7.1 The Short-Term Scoring Function Equations 182

7.2 The Long-Term Scoring Function Equations 184

7.3   Standard Quarterly Output Data   185

7.4   Noninstrument Exogenous Variables of the
          Wharton-EFU Model   188

8.1   Shocks Considered for the Exogenous-Event Library   198

8.2   Information Required by the Referee to Report
          Shocks to Players   199

8.3   Information Required from the Referee for Shock
          Auxiliary Models   200

8.4   Economic Models for Shocks That Effect
          International Trade   206

8.5   Exogenous Variables for the International Shock
          Auxiliary Models   208

9.1   Comparison of Game and Model Terminology   215

Preface

This book describes a general procedure for using computerized models of socioeconomic systems. Though the examples are drawn primarily from economic and fiscal policy, the procedure is equally applicable to other areas of public decision making.

The procedure attempts to exploit computer technology so as to bring the theoretical framework of decision analysis and the empirical methodology of econometrics to socioeconomic policy making. The goal is to make more effective use of our knowledge about social systems by facilitating the process by which such information is brought to bear on the solution to social problems.

Since the early drafts of this book were completed, I have had the unusual opportunity of observing, at close hand, some of the policy-making processes. Though I would undoubtedly make some changes if I were to begin the book now, I do not believe that I would alter the major ideas.

The fiscal policy-making process has changed in the last two years.

There has been substantial technological progress as time-sharing computer systems have come of age. There were no computers in The Executive Office Building until the spring of 1969. But by June 1971 there were approximately fifteen consoles, connected via telephone lines to large computers in Philadelphia and Cambridge, and plans were being made to install a major computer system in the building during the year. The new computer system may have not only the remote typewriter consoles described in the book but also two cathode-ray tube input-output devices—capable of being extended to the White House—that are much more appropriate for use by top policy makers.

There has been progress in making modern concepts and techniques part of the decision-making process. The presentation of quantitative economic forecasts by the President's Council of Economic Advisers was an innovation of the 1960s. Ten years later, the Council was introducing the concept of optimum feasible economic paths to public discussion where the comparative merits of Keynesian and monetarist models were already being debated.

The President's Budget and Economic Report provided the first official detailed analysis of the long-range (five-year) budget and its implications for the allocation of the nation's resources.

This progress increases the likelihood that procedures quite similar to those described in this book will become part of the policy-making process.

I would not be at all surprised to see them an integral part of the process by the early 1980s.

The text is divided into three parts: Chapters 1 to 3 describe the adaptive modeling procedures; Chapters 4 and 5 illustrate its application to the resource allocation problem; and Chapters 6 to 8 illustrate its application to the macroeconomic stabilization problem. Chapter 9 is an appraisal of the developed procedures.

Chapter 1 defines the problem, and the terms and concepts necessary to the adaptive modeling procedure. The adaptive modeling components are related to the theoretical development of decision analysis, advances in computer technology, and the development of economic planning models.

Chapter 2 describes the components of the adaptive modeling procedure. The chapter begins by formally defining the decision-making problem and points out the weaknesses of current approaches to the problem; the new problems raised by the suggested procedure are also identified.

Econometricians have typically left the definition of an appropriate welfare or objective function to the welfare theorists, who have generally ignored the problems of definition and measurement that are essential for making the concepts operationally useful. The subject of Chapter 3 is the objective functions for socioeconomic decision making; it is shown that the general insolubility of the "welfare problem" does not necessarily imply that measures cannot be obtained for important special cases. Chapters 4 and 5 describe an adaptive modeling procedure designed to deal with the problem of resource allocation and economic growth. The procedure applies mathematical programming to allocate resources so as to maximize an adaptively defined objective function.

The core model is a system of input-output equations of the Leontief type. At the beginning of each period, the policy maker can change capacity, technology, and prices. Linear programming is applied to the short-run problem of allocating resources. Next, parametric methods are used to program investment and to obtain efficient growth. This procedure does not explicitly recognize two important aspects of the real policy-making problem: the high degrees of uncertainty resulting from random events and the joint nature of the decision-making processes. Since these aspects are more evident in stabilization planning, another adaptive modeling procedure was developed to illustrate the capability of adaptive procedures to deal with them.

Chapters 6, 7, and 8 comprise the third part of the text and describe a pilot and a prototype procedure for dealing with the economic stabilization problem. Keynesian macroeconomic models serve as the core models for this second illustration, which emphasizes the multiplicity of decision-making roles and the highly stochastic nature of the economic environment.

These procedures are cast in game form; roles are defined for two or more decision makers, one decision maker is responsible for monetary policy and the other for fiscal policy. Exogenous changes (for example, international conflicts, strikes, or changes in investor confidence) are introduced into the environment. A series of plays—that is, exogenous events, player responses, and model solutions for determining the new economic state—traces the dynamic path taken by the economy during a particular game. The computer solves the model and provides the players with variable amounts of data (including conditional forecasts based on alternative assumptions regarding exogenous events). Thus, in the play of game, the image of the real world proceeds through time as the players adjust their policy instruments.

The greater portion of this book was written while I was in attendance at the University of North Carolina and employed as a research analyst at the Research Triangle Institute (RTI). During that period, a number of individuals at both institutions provided considerable assistance, which is gratefully acknowledged. Among those at RTI to whom I am indebted are R. L. Collins, for his help with mathematical programming, and J. A. Zwerneman and A. L. Cruze for their ideas on the stabilization game. Juanita Daber wrote a number of computer programs and J. C. Wright created the software that made the conversational-mode computing possible. A. Bencvic, G. E. Gearing, and R. W. Pfouts, my dissertation advisers at the University of North Carolina at Chapel Hill, provided invaluable technical suggestions and advice. I also owe a great deal to Kay Marr, Sandra Stouffer, and Cynthia McTyre, of RTI, for their help in translating illegible drafts into an earlier version of this work. To those mentioned, and to all the others whose assistance is not specifically acknowledged, I am extremely grateful.

Finally, I express my appreciation to my wife, Marcia, and to all the others whose love and sympathy made this work possible.

Arnold H. Packer
Washington, D.C.
May 1971

1

1.1

Introduction

The objective of this work is to define and demonstrate a procedure for
developing and using models of socioeconomic systems. The primary
hypothesis is that the procedure can be used effectively by individuals who
have a decision-making responsibility for all or part of the modeled
system.

The goal is to perform decision analyses by placing core models in a
decision-analysis framework. This is accomplished by simulating in a conversational mode and creating a man-machine system with a time-sharing
computer, by introducing uncertainty concerning the exogenous variables
and/or the model, by providing an information system that generates conditional forecasts as well as other data, and by employing an objective
function for limited purposes. The result is that decision makers engage in
ncertainty. In contrast to statistical
mizing technique, adaptive modeling
e that employs the users' knowledge
number of investigated alternatives.
ls as an aid to decision making is the
evident that the procedure is potenti-
etting.[1] The reference to education is
in which learning takes place. The
naker will learn about the response of
em to a variety of conditions. Another
h an experimental device for learning
objective functions and for capturing
he economic system.

deling Procedure

ribes the procedure. At the most basic
se its core model can be dynamically
staff) to reflect alternative representa-
t a more abstract level, the core model

e Trenary Dolbear, Richard Attiyeh, and
ame for Teaching Macroeconomics," *American*
pp. 458–468. There are a number of differences
e and the simulation policy game; perhaps
, or conversational mode, of the adaptive pro-

evolves from an extremely simplified to a more realistic and complex representation of the real system and, in the process, helps both the model builder and the user to better understand the reality. Finally, at the operational level a socioeconomic system is itself adaptive not only in the same way as a biological or engineering control system but also because the improved model frequently alters the way the real system operates.

The proposed adaptive procedure uses a man-machine system. Human beings contribute knowledge of the system being modeled and of the decision-making process; computers (which contain a core model) contribute calculating speed and accuracy to insure that conclusions are consistent with the incorporated hypothesized relationships. Hopefully, such processes can avoid many of the limitations of current procedures and can make greater contributions to the decision-making process.

1.1.2
The Nature of Social System Planning

The extent to which socioeconomic systems are being consciously manipulated is steadily increasing. This is shown by governments throughout the world—even by the United States with its "least-government-is-the-best" tradition—as they rapidly increase social planning at various levels. One result of this trend is the demand for better knowledge of the systems, especially better knowledge of the consequences of alternative policies.

Historically, economic planning has been the most prevalent manifestation of social planning; however, it is thought that the adaptive modeling process can be extended to systems planning that embraces more than the traditional economic considerations (for example, to educational, urban, and transportation systems).

ECONOMIC PLANNING

Jan Tinbergen, famous for his work in developing both the theory and practice of planning, surveyed the current state of the art in nineteen Communist, Western, and developing nations (excluding the United States and Russia).[2] All respondents have a central planning agency that develops national economic plans and most have a historical or ideological bias in favor of centralized planning, or at least no contrary tradition.[3] (At

[2] Jan Tinbergen, *Central Planning* (New Haven, Conn.: Yale University Press, 1964), pp. 104–142.
[3] The questionnaire was sent to 51 governments; the 19 replies were from Bulgaria, Burma, Ceylon, Chile, Czechoslovakia, Ecuador, France, Hungary, Iran, Japan, Federation of Malaya, Morocco, Netherlands, Norway, Poland, Puerto Rico, Turkey, United Kingdom, and Yugoslavia.

that time, he did not find that detailed economic models were widely used.[4]) Even in the United States, central planning of economic and social systems has become widely accepted; the U.S. government's formal responsibility for macroeconomic affairs dates back to the Employment Act of 1946, which states:

The Congress declares that it is the continuing policy and responsibility of the Federal Government to use all practicable means consistent with its needs and obligations and other essential considerations of national policy, with the assistance and cooperation of industry, agriculture, labor, and State and local governments, to coordinate and utilize all its plans, functions, and resources for the purpose of creating and maintaining, in a manner calculated to foster and promote free competitive enterprise and the general welfare, conditions under which there will be afforded useful employment opportunities, including self-employment, for those able, willing, and seeking to work and to promote maximum employment, production, and purchasing power.[5]

The U.S. government intends to use its fiscal and monetary policy instruments to promote goals of stabilization and growth. It is apparent that federal economic policy no longer relies on the automatic stabilizers built into our system or waits for a serious recession or inflation to occur before countermeasures are taken.[6]

Examination of economic data illustrates the relative importance of the government sector in the United States. About one-fifth of the nation's income passes through the federal government's hands. The annual rate of government (federal, state, and local) purchases of goods and services in 1970 was approximately $220 billion, almost 23 percent of the gross national product (GNP) and more than 1.6 times as great as gross private domestic investment. Total government employment approached 12.8 million by the end of 1970, or more than 16 percent of total employment. Because it generates such a large share of the national economic activity, the U.S. government's actions determine, to a great extent, the macroeconomic variables of output, employment, and general price levels.

Presumably, Communist planning guides the production process in detail, while Western planning is limited to guiding only macroeconomic variables. However, an examination of the U.S. Federal Budget shows that federal economic planning is not restricted to macroeconomic variables.

[4] Tinbergen, *Central Planning*, p. 39.
[5] U.S. Congress, Joint Economic Committee, *Twentieth Anniversary of the Employment Act of 1946: An Economic Symposium*, 89th Congress, 2nd Session, February 23, 1966.
[6] *1968 Economic Report of the President*. Washington, D.C.: U.S. Government Printing Office, February 1968, p. 7.

The Special Analyses of the Budget[7] discuss federal programs in manpower training, education, income security, housing, health, and environmental control; each are a part of a complex system that must be understood if effective policies are to be established. Policy makers are becoming more aware of the need for comprehensive planning and resource allocation and are determined that government expenditures be "based on an objective comparison of goals, alternatives, benefits, and cost."[8] Thus, "there is an imperative need for more systematic procedures for comparing alternatives as to their costs and benefits and for establishing priorities on this basis."[9] "There is also a need for a Comprehensive Approach to Community Redevelopment [which will] undertake a coordinated and simultaneous attack on all the problems in a particular locality."[10] Recent legislation in health, transportation, model cities, and regional development (such as that concerned with Appalachia and the coastal plains region of North and South Carolina and Georgia) are other examples of conscious federal attempts to manipulate the operation of large, complex socioeconomic systems.

Enumeration of the federal government's direct attempts can not adequately describe its effect. Fiscal 1971 serving as an example, the government's purchases of $98 billion worth of goods and services was crucially important to those individuals, firms, and industries that were the major suppliers. The federal tax structure that generated almost $200 billion and the dispersal system that distributed almost $70 billion of transfer payments strongly affected the distribution of disposable income. The cost functions of firms were partially determined by government regulations, controls, guidelines, foreign trade control, government education and retraining programs, highway building, government-sponsored research, and so forth, as well as the government's use of its monetary and credit instruments.

The government also effects, directly and indirectly, the composition and distribution of the nation's population. "In most cases, the Federal

---

[7] *Special Analyses Budget of the U.S. Government, Fiscal 1972* (Washington, D.C.: U.S. Government Printing Office, 1971).

[8] *1968 Joint Economic Report. Report of the Joint Economic Committee, Congress of the United States, on January 1968 Economic Report of the President Together with Statement of Committee Agreement, Minority and Other Views*, Senate Report No. 73, 90th Congress, 1st session. (Washington, D.C.: U.S. Government Printing Office, 1967.)

[9] *Ibid.*, p. 11. Similar statements can be found in the 1971 Joint Economic Report (p. 44).

[10] *1968 Economic Report of the President*, p. 161.

Government does not deliberately seek to influence the pattern of locational decisions. But there are nevertheless important impacts. Indeed, it is hard to conceive how Federal affairs might be conducted in a way that was 'neutral' with respect to locational decisions."[11] There is increasing recognition that migration and the nation's demography are influenced by the location of federal installations and the provision of federal funds for sewers, water supply, recreation facilities, housing, highways and other transportation facilities, and urban renewal facilities. For example, President Nixon's special revenue-sharing program for rural development attempted to influence migration. Furthermore, antipoverty programs, especially those concerned with family planning, have a direct (and often politically sensitive) impact on the population's composition.

These are only a few examples of the federal government's influence upon the socioeconomic system; others could be given for state and local governments. Inside and outside the United States, decision makers grapple with complex problems of economic development, population control, and international and regional cooperation.

DECISION MAKING AND UNCERTAINTIES

For each system noted above, policy makers are faced with the classical problem of dynamic decision making under uncertainty; that is, they must, over a period of time, make a series of decisions, or adjust policy instruments, to maximize an objective function under a set of uncertain constraints.

However, the real problem, in many respects, is more complex than the classical one, because, instead of maximizing their own objectives, policy makers are asked to maximize a social welfare function for a segment of society. Thus, the objective function is extremely difficult to state and, in general, there is no completely satisfactory way to evaluate alternative outcomes. Furthermore, it is generally a group decision-making process (for example, the case of fiscal and monetary policy) in which policy makers have interrelated but different objectives and in which perfect coordination is unlikely (at least in part because of their different appraisals of uncertainty).

The uncertainty that decision makers must face comes from two sources: First, the system is imperfectly known because it is complex and its basic

---

[11] *Ibid.*, p. 39. For a more recent example, see the report of the National Goals Research Staff, *Toward Balanced Growth Quantity with Quality* (Washington, D.C.: U.S. Government Printing Office. July 4, 1970) pp. 39–62.

structure is not well understood; second, it is subject to unexpected random technological, political, and natural events. Even though the dividing line between these endogenous and exogenous uncertainties is not exact or fixed (for example, a technological change may become predictable), both types will be problems to face in the foreseeable future.

1.1.3
Limitations of Current Procedures
The fact that many decisions are being made concerning the socioeconomic system has attracted the attention of not only the social scientists—economists, statisticians, demographers, and so forth—but also the physical scientists and engineers who have realized that the most severe constraints on human welfare are no longer, or at least not purely, technological. As a result, traditional techniques (such as economics and descriptive statistics) and newer approaches (such as decision theory, econometrics, operations research, management science, and the systems approach) have been tried with varying degrees of success.

The fact that few governments are using models in their planning process is evidence of dissatisfaction with current efforts.[12] Some of the dissatisfaction relates to specific models; as a paper introducing a major macroeconomic model of the U.S. economy states, "In our opinion, the existing models do not satisfactorily serve the needs of those charged with responsibility for stabilization policy, in the sense that they do not adequately incorporate explicit policy instruments . . . ." This led a group of economists to construct an entirely new model.[13]

There is also dissatisfaction with model-building procedures. Lawrence Klein is one of the principal architects of the large-scale Brookings-SSRC model, which was "based on the assumption that twenty heads were better than one in generating ideas for model construction."[14] Yet his most recent effort, the Wharton-EFU model, suggests that he feels a two-man team is more efficient.

Others criticize the macroapproach to model building. Guy Orcutt is one of the most outspoken critics. He claims that because predictions based on estimated relationships among economic time series have not proved

---

[12] See Note 3 earlier.
[13] Robert Rasche and Harold Shapiro, "The FRB-MIT Econometric Model: Its Special Features," *American Economic Review* (May 1968), p. 123.
[14] Michael Evans and Lawrence Klein, *The Wharton Econometric Forecasting Model*) Pittsburgh, Pa.: University of Pennsylvania, 1967), p. 3.

very successful, there is a need for microanalysis of the economy's fundamental decision-making units.[15]

The entire procedure of model construction, whether macro- or microanalysis, is often criticized by institutionalists as indicated by the dialogue
between Koopmans and Vining.[16] The controversy is not restricted to pure
economics as indicated by another dialogue on implementation in *Management Sciences* and, a third, between King and Machol in *Operations Research*.[17]

From the standpoint of this book, a paper by Holt appears to be the
best statement of the problem; in fact, its title states the basic question:
"Quantitative Decision Analysis and National Policy: How Can We
Bridge the Gap?"[18]

Holt's answer is that quantitatively oriented economists can best contribute to the decision process by making conditional forecasts of the outcomes of alternative courses of action.[19] But he adds that if economists wish
to assist in the decision process, there needs to be a "different way of
relating the work of economists to it"; he suggests several ways:[20]

1.

Formulation (not just evaluation) of alternatives;

2.

Building decision analyses for specific classes of problems that are important in national economic policy;

3.

Relating to the political decision process;

4.

Determination of welfare objectives based on the preferences of elected
officials and citizenry.

Thus, according to Holt, if the economist is to help officials achieve their
objectives and understand the implications of the actions they are taking,
then the economists must learn to understand the officials and the constraints on them. The officials must also obtain a basic understanding of

[15] G. Orcutt et al., *Microanalysis of Socioeconomic Systems: A Simulation Study* (New York,
N.Y.: Harper & Row, 1961), pp. 5, 7.
[16] Tjalling C. Koopmans, "Measurement without Theory," *Readings in Business Cycles*
(Homewood, Ill.: Richard Irwin, 1965), p. 186–231.
[17] *Management Science*, vol. 12, no. 2 (October 1965), pp. 1–42; *Operations Research*, vol. 15,
no. 6 (November–December 1967), pp. 1177–1188.
[18] Charles C. Holt, *Quantitative Planning of Economic Policy*, B. C. Hickman ed. (Washington,
D.C.: The Brookings Institution, 1964), p. 252.
[19] *Ibid.*, p. 254.
[20] *Ibid.*, p. 263.

the economist and his tools.[21] The premise of this book is that adaptive modeling procedures are one way of achieving this mutual understanding and thus bridging the gap between research and policy.

1.1.4
Delimitation of the Study

Tinbergen, in describing economic planning, discusses the "actors" and their tasks, activities, procedures, and organization.[22] This book is solely concerned with one aspect, the model building procedure and its implementation into the policy-making process, and with only a part of that procedure, that of the form of model construction—not with the statistical tasks of data collection, parameter estimation, or model validation.

Though it is felt that adaptive modeling procedures are applicable to planning for any major socioeconomic system, this book concentrates on two types of planning: long-run sectoral planning to achieve growth (the economic-growth problem) and short-run macroeconomic planning to achieve stabilization (the stabilization problem).

The adaptive modeling procedure used for the economic-growth problem employs an input-output model as its core. Some of the data are extracted from the 1958 U.S. input-output study; others are crudely estimated from published figures. The remainder are guesses at reasonable numbers. The two adaptive modeling procedures used for the stabilization problem employ macroeconomic models. One of these is a pilot procedure that is operational; it uses a 23-equation textbook model whose parameters are reasonable but not empirically estimated. The second is a design for a prototype procedure; it employs the Wharton-EFU model. In summary, this book is concerned with the form of the models and not with the statistical problems involved in estimating their parameters. In fact, a major advantage of the procedure is that it is able to accept alternative core models and thus benefit from the growing body of econometric studies. The aim is not to develop another macroeconomic model but, rather, to develop a procedure in which available knowledge can be used more effectively.

1.2
Terminology and Basic Concepts

An adaptive modeling procedure attempts to synthesize the abstract concepts of decision analysis with the empirical results embodied in models of

---

[21] *Ibid.*, p. 263.
[22] Tinbergen, *Central Planning*, pp. 6–31.

economic systems. Section 1.2.1 establishes a consistent set of definitions for the case of joint dynamic decision making under uncertainty. The elements of this decision-making problem have been defined many times in the literature; in instances where alternative terminology has been applied to similar concepts, the terminology of economists (rather than statisticians or management scientists) is used. A discussion of static decision making under uncertainty with one decision maker is followed by a discussion of the more complicated cases of dynamic and multiple decision making. Section 1.2.2 defines the concepts of socioeconomic systems and their models.

1.2.1

The Concepts of Decision Analysis

The actors in the decision-making process include decision makers, planners, and policy makers. For the remainder of this book, the decision makers are defined as those who have the authority to set values for the instruments and thus to choose among alternatives; the planners are those who formulate alternatives for the planning horizon; and the policy makers are those who determine the objective function. The same individual may be both a policy maker and a decision maker and, less often, a planner as well; all three types of actors function in a socioeconomic system.

A decision maker, given a set of information on "world states," attempts to maximize the policy maker's objective function under uncertainty. He executes his plan, or selects from a set of alternatives, by assigning values to his set of instruments.

STATIC DECISION MAKING

The "state of the world" is defined by a set of *uncontrollable variables*, for example, the rates of unemployment or inflation. The decision maker can control a set of *instruments*, or controllable variables—for example, the money supply, government spending, or tax rates. A *decision* determines the value for any element of the set of instruments; a *plan* is a set of decisions that establishes the value for the entire set.

Most real decision making is done under uncertainty; that is, more than one state of the world is possible. The decision maker also has a choice among alternative plans. The policy maker's *objective function* evaluates the conjunction of realized world states and executed plans (for example, unemployment and inflation rates *and* monetary and fiscal actions).

The decision maker receives *information* from which he assesses the likelihood that each of the alternative world states may be realized. The particular plan he executes is, therefore, a function of his information set.

DYNAMIC DECISION MAKING

The dynamic case is a sequence of static cases under uncertainty; a decision maker executes a series of plans and experiences a series of world states as information becomes available. At any time within the planning horizon, the decision maker will have the initial *data* and the *reports* he has received up to that point in time.

A *strategy* can be defined as a first-period plan followed by a series of contingent plans.

The objective function, in the dynamic case, is used to evaluate the sequence of outcomes and plans.

In the simplest case, the utilities of the intertemporal outcomes are independent and additive; since this is unnecessarily restrictive, a more general form may be used.

Thus, the problem of dynamic decision making under uncertainty is to maximize the utility of the sequence of events, employing a transformation function. The *transformation function* is whatever cognitive process (or model) the decision maker uses to predict outcomes; the model may undergo structural changes over time and may include the various sources of uncertainty involved in the prediction.

MULTIPERSON DECISION MAKING

Multiperson decision making, the most complicated type considered here, takes a number of forms: (a) the chief-subordinate case, in which the chief's objective function is decisive and his subordinates make their decisions accordingly; (b) the team case, in which all members share a common objective function and each member is responsible for a subset of instruments; and (c) the committee case, in which members may have different objective functions but share responsibility for all instruments.[23]

The joint decision-making case considered here is a combination of team and committee cases. Each member is not only responsible for a subset of instruments but may also have different objective functions. The set of instruments is composed of a number of not necessarily exclusive subsets. Each of the decision makers is responsible for one of these instrument-subsets; each may have his own objective function and his own transformation function (i.e., model).

---

[23] These are described in Henri Theil, *Optimum Decision Rules for Government and Industry* (Chicago, Ill.: Rand McNally, 1964), pp. 322–356.

1.2.2
The Concepts of Systems and Models
SYSTEM CONCEPTS

A *system* (for example, a solar or digestive system) is defined as a "regularly interacting or interdependent group of items forming a unified whole: as a group of interacting bodies under the influence of related forces . . . ."[24]

In a socioeconomic system, the individuals, families, firms, and institutions that interact under the influence of economic and social forces are defined as *elements*. A group of elements is defined as a *component;* for example, the group of firms that constitute the steel industry is a component of the economic system. A *subsystem*, or system within the system, is a component that fits the definition given above for the word system; each subsystem contains elements and components and may even contain subsystems of more limited scope.

The *state* of the system is defined by the value of a set of variables that describe the state of specific elements (for example, per capita income, personal taxes, investment in new plant and equipment, imports, and so forth).

The *structure* of the system is defined by a set of *parameters* (for example, the marginal propensity to consume) that are relatively stable. Some variables and most parameters are *coefficients* that relate two or more of the system's variables (for example, income tax rates are variable coefficients that relate two variables, tax revenue and personal income).

System variables (for example, tax rates) that can be controlled by the decision maker were defined previously as instruments; other variables and parameters that are not controllable are defined as *constraints*. The responsibilities and the time frame of the decision maker determine whether a variable (or parameter) is a constraint or an instrument. For example, the stock of capital will be a constraint to the decision maker responsible for economic stabilization and an instrument to the decision maker.

A change in any variable (if it assumes a new value) alters the state of the system. A *configuration change* is defined as a change in state achieved by the decision maker's manipulation of instruments; a *structural change* is caused by an alteration in a parameter.

[24] *Webster's Seventh New Collegiate Dictionary* (Springfield, Mass.: G. & C. Merriam, 1965), p. 895.

Generally, the decision maker is concerned with a subset of variables (these are the arguments of the objective function defined previously) with which he evaluates system performance.

SYSTEM MODELS

The decision maker uses a transformation function or abstraction of reality (that is, of the socioeconomic system) to predict system performance. This function may contain one or more *formal models* composed of mathematical and logical symbols which stand for variables and parameters of a real system and *informal models* based on the decision maker's subjective concepts. Both the formal and informal portions of the function generally vary over time and among decision makers.

A *model solution* is defined as a single use of a transformation function for a given set of constraints and decisions; it is an estimate of observable consequences that will follow if certain assumptions are realized.

Figure 1.1 illustrates where the informal and formal models fit in the decision-making process. The decision maker attempts to employ his instruments so as to maximize the policy maker's objective function under the set of constraints specified by the set of uncontrollable variables and the system structure. First the decision maker applies the informal model to the reports or information he receives from the real system in order to estimate values for exogenous uncontrollable variables. Then he uses the formal model to transform the conjunction of instrument and uncontrollable variable settings to the resulting value of the objective function. That is, the formal model estimates the implications of alternative decisions under varying assumptions.

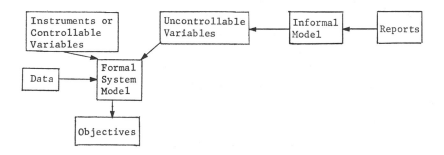

Figure 1.1.   Formal and informal models in the decision-making process.

THE SCOPE OF THE MODEL

Because there must be a limit to the scope of any model, it is necessary to categorize uncontrollable variables as endogenous or exogenous. While comprehensiveness (a systems approach) is a desirable quality in any analysis of socioeconomic systems, the analysis can be too comprehensive and lack the detail necessary to provide answers to specific questions. For example, in an analysis of the educational system of a metropolitan area, shall the model include all factors that influence manpower requirements of the city (for example, economic conditions of the nation, or influences of world trade and the balance of payments on levels and distribution of employment opportunities)? Obviously not. Isolation of the system may proceed in two dimensions: one extensive (for example, no consideration of the nation's economy) and one intensive (for example, no consideration of noneconomic factors in an economic model). An example of an intensive limitation of relevant variables is to assume that population growth is determined outside the modeled system.

Two alternatives for reducing the scope of the model are to ignore (or assign to an error term) the considerations to be eliminated or to include these as exogenous variables and establish their values arbitrarily. In the formal model, the line between *endogenous* variables (explained by the model) and *exogenous* (not explained by the model) is well defined; however, in the informal part of the transformation function, the demarcation is less clear. For example, labor force growth is exogenously determined in many formal models of the U.S. economy; however, the decision maker's transformation function must include either a second formal model or, more likely, an informal model to estimate the size of the labor force.

UNCERTAINTY

Both endogenous and exogenous variables are subject to uncertainty. Two synonymous phrases—varying assumptions and assuming a set of uncontrollable variable values—imply that the decision maker is uncertain about the true state of the system. Among the many types of uncertainties, only two basic ones are considered in this study; they are statistical and subjective uncertainty. Statistical, often called probabilistic, uncertainty is the type to which the theorems of certainty equivalence can be applied because the probability distribution is more or less well known.[25] In general,

---

[25] Knowledge of the probability distribution may come from empirical or intuitive sources; the prime requisite is that the distribution be well defined. See Henri Theil, *Optimum Decision Rules*, pp. 52–59, for the theorems.

all variables that are endogenous to a formal model and some, but not all, that are exogenous are subject to statistical uncertainty. However, subjective uncertainty is concerned exclusively with those variables of formal models whose probability distributions are unknown and cannot be empirically determined. For example, it is impossible to test a hypothesized probability that a war will occur in the next twelve months; thus forecasts of econometric models depend (or are conditional) on a set of specified exogenous variable values.

In addition to appearing in the model variables, uncertainty appears in the objective function if either the decision maker is uncertain of the relevant policy maker's objective function or if the policy maker uses a secondary objective function. The first condition cannot be ignored unless the same individual is both the policy maker and the decision maker. The problem of secondary objectives is discussed in Chapter 3.

Because problems created by uncertainty in the objective function are similar to those created by uncertainty in the model variables, they will not be considered separately. However, the effects of uncertainty are discussed further in the next section and in other parts of this book.

THE INFORMATION SET

The decision maker's (formal) *primary model* provides conditional estimates of endogenous uncontrollable variables for specified values of instruments and exogenous uncontrollable variables. Thus, it provides a conditional estimate of the world state described by the union of the exogenous and endogenous uncontrollable variables. Generally, the parameters are estimated from the initial information or data collected before the planning period and used according to a statistical maximum-likelihood technique (ordinary least squares, two-stage least squares, and so forth); in this way, the parameters are chosen to maximize the likelihood function.

The values of the exogenous variables depend on unpredictable occurrences or events such as a strike, a war, or the weather. Values of the exogenous variables are given by either informal or other formal *auxiliary models*. The arguments in these auxiliary models is the variety of information (defined as reports) available to the decision makers.

Thus, the information set includes two subsets: a subset of data for the primary model, and a subset of reports for the auxiliary models. These need not be exclusive; some of the data may be used in auxiliary models and some of the exogenous events may appear in the primary model. Nor will the sets be exhaustive; some information will not be used in the decision-making process.

OPTIMUM STRATEGY

A *planning function* establishes a strategy by relating a sequence of plans to a particular subset of reports. The *optimum strategy* maximizes the expected value of the policy maker's objective function, given the decision maker's primary and auxiliary models and the information available.

Since the argument of the strategy selection function contains the objective function and the auxiliary models, *decision making is ultimately subjective*.

The decision-making process depends on the decision maker's understanding of the functional relationships among the system variables and his knowledge of the policy maker's objective function. The decision maker is faced with two or more alternative configurations; his choice is implemented by the setting of his instruments. Combinations of configurations and world states define the system states; these are evaluated by the policy maker's objective function.

The planning function establishes decision rules that relate the elements of the set of information to instrument settings. A *decision rule* is a conditional imperative of the form: "If the Vietnamese conflict ends, we will suspend the tax increase." It is meaningful to have one decision rule on taxes and another on expenditures. A cohesive group of such decision rules is a *contingent plan*. In addition to the set of available configurations, there is a set of strategies from which the decision maker can choose.

The decision maker requires a transformation function that uses the information available from empirical observations to estimate the implication of alternative plans on the true state of the world. His transformation function is composed of two parts: the set of auxiliary models that provide values for the exogenous variables of the primary model and the primary model that estimates the state of the world, given the plan and the exogenous variables. In this way the decision maker, given his information set, attempts to maximize the policy maker's objective function.

It is the dynamic case under uncertainty that describes most real situations of planning for socioeconomic systems and makes the concepts of strategies truly meaningful. In the dynamic real world situation, plans in one period must be executed (that is, decisions made) before the next period's reports are received; thus the development of alternative plans whose execution is contingent on the realization of one of a number of possibilities. A sequence of contingent plans is a *strategy*, and the selection of the optimum strategy may include alternatives such as restudying the situation or even reestimating the primary model if its predictions appear inaccurate.

1.3
Previous Work

The purpose of this book is to synthesize two bodies of knowledge that have been developed in the management and economic sciences. The first body is the logical theory of decision making; the second is represented by econometric models that are based on empirical data. The remainder of this chapter notes some of the contributions from these two fields that are most pertinent to the ideas developed in this book.

1.3.1
Decision Analysis

Twelve years ago Chernoff and Moses wrote: "In recent years, statistics has been formulated as the science of decision theory under uncertainty."[26] At that time, the statisticians and mathematicians seemed to have made the major contributions to decision theory.

The primary concepts (which have already been used in this chapter) are: alternative world states, information, alternative plans, and maximizing an objective function. The primary tool was Bayes' theorem:

$$\text{prob (hypothesis} \mid \text{datum)} = \frac{\text{prob (datum} \mid \text{hypothesis) prob (hypothesis)}}{\text{prob (datum)}}$$

where prob (datum) is greater than zero. To use the theorem, decision makers are supposed to have a priori knowledge of all possible reports or data and thus know the three probability distributions on the right-hand side of the equation.

Before this time, the theorem, which was almost 200 years old, had been ignored because of the philosophical reservations about the personal evaluation view and general acceptance of the frequency view of probability. Much attention was given during the development of decision theory to transforming what was previously defined as subjective uncertainty into statistical uncertainty by accepting personal intuition as a valid estimator of probability parameters.[27]

[26] H. Chernoff and L. E. Moses, *Elementary Decision Theory* (New York: John Wiley & Sons, 1959), p. vii (preface).
[27] See L. J. Savage, "Bayesian Statistics," *Recent Developments in Information and Decision Process* (New York, N.Y.: The Macmillan Co., 1962), pp. 161–194.

According to the frequency view, the probability of an event is based on observations of empirical situations (for example, flips of a coin or births); a random event is defined as one with a relative frequency of occurrence which approaches a stable limit, and the limit value is defined as the probability of the random event.

Keynes was one of two leading advocates (the other was Carnap) of a half-way position between the frequency and the personal view.[28] They held what has become known as the necessary view: information (other than observation of a situation) may determine probability, but only one estimate is justified by any body of evidence. This concept has been essentially discarded because philosophically oriented statisticians embraced the Bayesian view that it is permissible to "guess" the probability distribution if appropriate information is not available.[29]

More recently, psychologists and information scientists related the Bayesian ideas to their work and developed experimental designs for empirically testing the validity of these concepts.[30]

Generally the experimenters fed information sequentially to two groups of individuals who were presented a set of hypothetical world states for their evaluation. One group repeatedly evaluated prob (datum | hypothesis) for each hypothesis and used Bayes theorem to calculate prob (hypothesis).

A control group estimated prob (hypothesis) directly, and the experimental results showed: "With respect to the design of diagnostic systems, the present research tends to confirm the notion that automated Bayesian hypothesis selection on the basis of expert human estimation of the conditional probabilities may well prove useful in systems with a diagnostic mission."[31] By 1959, the Bayesian concepts were accepted as part of scientific business management.[32] At that time, the major area of application was investment analyses (for example, to explore for petroleum and natural gas).

[28] J. M. Keynes, *A Treatise on Probability* (2nd ed., 1929) (London: The Macmillan Co., 1921); and R. Carnap, *Logical Foundations of Probability* (Chicago, Ill.: University of Chicago Press, 1950), as referenced in Savage, "Bayesian Statistics," p. 168.
[29] Savage, "Bayesian Statistics," p. 168.
[30] R. J. Kaplan and J. R. Newman, *Studies in Probabilistic Information Processing* (Santa Monica, Calif.: Systems Development Corp., October 1964); see also, D. A. Schum, *et al.*, *The Influence of Experience and Input Information Fidelity upon Posterior Probability Estimation in a Simulated Threat-Diagnosis System* (Columbus, Ohio: Ohio State University, April 1965); see also, W. Edwards and P. Stovic, *Seeking Information to Reduce the Risk of Decisions* (Ann Arbor, Mich.: The University of Michigan, August 1962).
[31] Schum, *et al.*, *The Influence of Experience*, p. 49.
[32] For example, see R. Schlaifer, *Probability and Statistics for Business Decisions* (New York, N.Y.: McGraw-Hill Book Co., 1959), p. 17–18.

In the popular literature, decision analyses have been described by the decision tree approach.[33] The primary difficulty with this approach is the near infinity of potential "branches" or alternative information and world states in any realistic decision problem.

Bellman's solution is dynamic programming, which he applied to multistage decision problems such as maximizing an integral, finding the shortest path through a network, and replacing equipment.[34] Dynamic programming is essentially a computational technique based on what he calls: "*The Principle of Optimality*: An optimal policy has the property that whatever the initial state and the initial decision are, the remaining decisions must constitute an optimal policy with regard to the state resulting from the first decision."[35] At each stage in a dynamic program, an essentially mechanical comparison is made of all alternatives; the alternatives are evaluated by functional equations (that is, the values are computed each time) and the "curse of dimensionality" is removed.[36]

Bellman also investigated the adaptive case, defined as a situation in which learning takes place. In the adaptive two-armed bandit problem, the gambler faces two slot machines.[37] The payoff probability of only one of the machines is known and the gambler tries to learn the unknown probability distributions during the gambling process. His decision problem is to place the bets so as to maximize the expected value of the winnings under the constraint of his initial stake.

A recent paper by Koichi Miyasawa illustrates a number of difficulties that restrict the applicability of decision analysis to real decision-making problems.[38] He assumes the system is essentially Markovian; thus the state of the world at any time is a function of the previous period's state and plan, and a random disturbance. He also assumes that total utility is evaluated by an objective function whose arguments are the world states and plans for all previous periods, and this period's world state.

[33] J. F. Magee, "Decision Trees," *Harvard Business Review* (July–August 1964), pp. 126–129; and "How to Use Decision Trees in Capital Investment," *Harvard Business Review* (September–October 1964), pp. 79–97.
[34] R. Bellman and R. Kalaba, *Dynamic Programming and Modern Control Theory* (New York, N.Y.: Academic Press, 1965), pp. 39, 40, 50–54, 66–70.
[35] R. Bellman, *Adaptive Control Processes, A Guided Tour* (Princeton, N.J.: Princeton University Press, 1961), p. 57.
[36] *Ibid.*, pp. 90–95.
[37] R. Bellman and R. Kalaba, *Dynamic Programming*, pp. 86, 99–101.
[38] "Information Structures in Stochastic Programming Problems," *Management Science*, vol. 14, no. 5 (January 1968), pp. 275–291.

The decision-making problem is to choose a sequence of plans that maximizes the objective function. Miyasawa investigated the information the decision maker had concerning the random variable at $t = 0$ and the other information available at time $t = 0, 1, 2, \ldots, T$. This dichotomy is similar to that concerning data required for the formal models and reports used in the informal models. He defined an information structure as a subset of information available characterized as to whether information is remembered, delayed, etc. Then, using the functionals of the model and the objective function, he could compare the values of alternative information sets.

Two difficulties in applying formal decision analysis can be shown by examining Miyasawa's two assumptions. The first assumption is that the set of equations expressing the transformation and the objective functions can be written in a form that can be solved for the maximum; the second assumption is that the prior probability of each world state and the joint probability of the random variables are known. With the second assumption, he proved that decision-making problems under subjective uncertainty (the adaptive case) can be reduced to statistical uncertainty (the stochastic case) and the optimum strategy can be calculated.

Miyasawa's assumptions about the form of the model and the decision maker's knowledge of the probability distributions seem untenable in most real complex decision-making situations; in other words, the reduction of the adaptive case to the stochastic is generally not possible. This central point of adaptive modeling is referred to again in Chapter 2.

Henri Theil, though he restricts his analysis to statistical uncertainty, confronted the practical problem of formulating an objective function and model that is both realistic and able to be optimized.

Theil's objective function is quadratic in the state and instrument variables, his model is linear.[39] Thus classical calculus can be used to maximize the quadratic objective function under the linear constraints; the first- and second-order conditions (disappearance of first derivatives and alternating signs of the appropriate minors of the matrix of second-order derivatives) define the optimum policies. An optimizing technique makes it possible to find a best solution immediately if it exists. A number of other advantages can be gained if optimization is possible; Theil illustrated what these can mean in real decision-making situations.

[39] H. Theil, *Optimum Decision*, p. 34.

One benefit of being able to evaluate outcomes cardinally (that is, having a unidimensional objective function) is the ability to define a function to measure losses due to suboptimal decisions. If a loss function can be specified, a value can be assigned to each constraint. Under certainty, this function assigns a shadow price to each constraint; under uncertainty, it can also assign a value to imperfect knowledge; as an example of the latter, Theil measured the loss due to specification errors in the coefficient matrices of his linear models.[40] The loss function is basic to his example of a multiperson decision maker—that of a research manager trying to maximize the improvement in the entrepreneur's objective function within a research budget.[41] The loss function makes it possible to put a value on a reduction in uncertainty and to provide a guide for the allocation of research resources; the loss function is a viable concept that is independent of the ability to solve for a system optimum (as shown in the adaptive modeling procedure described in Chapter 2).

Theil's social welfare function reflects Tinbergen's concepts of meaningful policy targets and is developed as a quadratic function of the deviation between actual and target values.

Restricting uncertainty to statistical uncertainty with the probability distributions known and the variances of the disturbances assumed finite and independent of the instruments, Theil proves certainty equivalence—substituting the expected value for the probability distribution of the random variable does not alter the optimum decision.

A significant aspect of Theil's contribution is that he used realistic models of real economies—the Klein Model I of the United States and a 40-equation econometric model of the Netherlands. Further, he attempted to build a joint objective function that is truly representative of the Social and Economic Council of the Netherlands. Not only did he examine the mathematical characteristics of the optimal and suboptimal strategies, he worked out the numerical values for each. Theil accomplished, in many respects, what this book hopes to do—to bring the concept of decision theory to practical use by using realistic models of concrete situations.

The obvious limitations of Theil's approach are the restrictions that the model must be linear and that the objective function must be quadratic for the prescribed mathematical techniques to be applicable. A more subtle but important limitation is that uncertainty is restricted to the

[40] *Ibid.*, pp. 59–68.
[41] *Ibid.*, pp. 323–324.

statistical type in which each coefficient is subject to an explicit probability distribution that is either empirically estimated or subjectively postulated (as in the Bayesian case); thus the certainty equivalence theorems can be employed.[42] *The point of view taken in adaptive modeling is that the decision-making situation is not so well structured.*

When Keynes published his *General Theory* in 1935, he introduced a revolution in the economist's theory, focus, and methodology. The Keynesian model was capable of solving problems in the real world because it contained a great deal of the conceptual framework required for decision analysis. The model identified the important constraints, the instruments, and the elements of the objective function, and it provided a reasonably good transformation function so that decision makers could estimate the effects of alternative decisions on their objectives.

The dependent variables in his model have become accepted by policy makers as the determinants of their objective function; he stated: "Our dependent variables are the volume of employment and the national income (or national dividend) measured in wage-units."[43] Eleven years later, in 1946, the U.S. Employment Act stated that it was the responsibility of the federal government to "promote maximum employment, production, and purchasing power"[44] Keynes also stated the constraints in modern terms:

We take as given the existing skill and quantity of available labour, the existing quality and quantity of available equipment, the existing technique, the degree of competition, the tastes and habits of the consumer, the disutility of different intensities of labour and of the activities of supervision and organization as well as the social structure including the forces, other than our variables set forth below, which determine the distribution of the national income. *This does not mean that we assume these factors to be constant; but merely that, in this place and context, we are not considering or taking into account the effects and consequences of changes in them.*[45]

Keynes was aware of the need to isolate instruments: ". . . to select those variables which can be deliberately controlled or managed by central authority in the kind of system in which we actually live."[46] Thus his primary purpose was to create a model that would establish required relationships between the conjunction of constraints and instruments and the

---

[42] *Ibid.*, pp. 52–59.
[43] J. M. Keynes. *General Theory of Employment, Interest, and Money* (New York, N.Y.: Harcourt, Brace & World, 1936), p. 245.
[44] U.S. Congress, *1946 Employment Act.*
[45] J. M. Keynes, *General Theory*, p. 245. (Italics added).
[46] *Ibid.*, p. 247.

elements of the objective function so that rational policy making would be possible: "Our present object is to discover what determines at any time the national income of a given economic system and . . . the amount of its employment; which means . . . the factors whose changes *mainly* determine our *quaesitum*."[47]

Admittedly, the Keynesian model is primitive by current standards; however, it does predict the result of a fiscal policy (increased output ≥ 2.5 times the expenditure-generated deficit) financed so that the money supply would increase at least as rapidly as income (interest rates maintained near the minimum level).

Each component of Keynes' crude model has since been dis-aggregated and its parameters estimated to yield a more sophisticated model. For example, to the consumption function, Duesenberry added the ratchet effect which occurs as individuals attempt to maintain previous maximum consumption; Modigliani, the concept of maintenance of one's place in the income distribution; Friedman, the permanent-income hypothesis.

However, it can be argued from the decision maker's point of view that the value added by improvements is relatively small; for example, a 2.5 multiplier is still frequently used to evaluate decisions.

Also, though considerable effort has been directed to improving Keynes' monetary function, at the moment the causal relationship between the monetary and the real sector is still not understood.

This discussion of Keynes is meant to indicate the potential of crude, but theoretically sound models that are consistent and have a decision analysis framework.

1.3.2

Econometric Models

The initial developments of quantitative econometrics were essentially confined to single markets. Of these developments, the most significant was, perhaps, Shultze's studies of supply and demand in agricultural markets.[48] Then, publication of the *General Theory* directed attention to complete macroeconomic systems. In 1939, Tinbergen completed his classic research on business cycles by producing a complete aggregative

---

[47] *Ibid.*
[48] H. Shultze, *Statistical Laws of Supply and Demand* (Chicago, Ill.: Chicago University Press, 1928); and *The Theory and Measurement of Demand* (Chicago, Ill.: Chicago University Press, 1938).

macroeconomic model of the U.S. economy for the League of Nations.[49] Later, development of the National Income Accounts provided data consistent with the model of the *General Theory*, and in 1950 Lawrence Klein at the Cowles commission developed his first macroeconometric model[50] of the United States—the first in a series of Klein models. It was followed by the Klein-Goldberger model in 1955[51] and the Wharton-EFU model in 1967.[52] Klein was also one of the major architects of the Brookings model of the U.S. economy[53] and instrumental in the creation of macroeconometric models for Great Britain and Japan.[54]

Klein's approach is decision oriented; in his recent textbook, in a section entitled "The Goals of Aggregative Economics," he describes multiplier analysis as a technique ". . . which shows the current effect of policy decisions on variables representing economic activity."[55] We must also be able to forecast what *would be* (under alternative economic policies) as well as what *is to be* under the selected policy.

Klein's models include exogenously specified instruments (primarily fiscal) and uncontrollable variables which represent economic activity that presumably are elements of the policy maker's (unspecified) objective function.

Another well-known, widely used U.S. macroeconomic forecasting model is the 32-equation annual model developed by Suits at the University of Michigan; the policy instruments range from federal and state taxes, deductions, and transfer payments to the interest rate ceilings on federally insured financing for residential construction.[56]

[49] J. Tinbergen, *Statistical Testing of Business Cycle Theories, Business Cycles in the United States of America 1919–1932* (Geneva, Switzerland: League of Nations, 1939), as referenced by K. Fox and E. Thorbecke, "Specification and Data Requirements in Policy Models," *Quantitative Planning of Economic Policy*, B. G. Hickman, ed. (Washington, D.C.: The Brookings Institution, 1964), p. 61.

[50] L. R. Klein, *Economic Fluctuations in the United States 1921–1941* (New York, N.Y.: John Wiley & Sons, 1950).

[51] L. R. Klein and A. Goldberger, *An Econometric Model of the United States 1929–1952* (Amsterdam: North-Holland Publishing Co., 1955).

[52] M. Evans and L. R. Klein, *The Wharton Econometric Forecasting Model* (Philadelphia, Pa.: University of Pennsylvania Press, 1967).

[53] J. S. Duesenberry et al., *The Brookings Quarterly Econometric Model of the United States.* (Chicago, Ill.: Rand McNally, 1965).

[54] L. R. Klein, *An Introduction to Econometrics* (Englewood Cliffs, N.J.: Prentice-Hall, 1962), pp. 229–235; also see Klein et al., *An Econometric Model of the United Kingdom* (Oxford: Basil Blackwell, 1961); see also Klein and Y. Shinkai, "An Econometric Model of Japan 1950–59," *International Economic Record* (January 1963), pp. 1–26.

[55] Klein, *An Introduction of Econometrics*, p. 132.

[56] D. B. Suits, "Forecasting and Analysis with an Econometric Model," *American Economic Review* (1962), pp. 104–132.

Suits, in a manner similar to Klein, uses both impact (short-run) and dynamic (long-run) multiplier analysis to examine alternative policies.[57] Conceptually, there is no difference between the multiplier analysis of simultaneous equation models and the simple Keynesian multiplier; however, in simultaneous-equation models, the multiple interdependencies and feedback between variables must be considered.[58] Also, simultaneous-equation analysis applies to all policy instruments and to many dependent variables of the model and defines multiplier dynamics more explicitly than Keynes did in the *General Theory*. Whereas the Keynesian multiplier estimates change in a single variable—national income—as a result of a dollar change in (exogenous) investment, the simultaneous-equation multiplier estimates the change in any dependent variable as a result of a unit change in any of the policy instruments (or even any predetermined variable). For example, Suits computes impact multipliers, or changes in GNP, employment, tax receipts, social insurance, and government surplus as a result of an increase (typically $1 billion) in investment, federal purchases, federal employment, and federal personal income taxes.[59]

Development of the Brookings Quarterly Econometric Model is the most ambitious macroeconomic model-building effort yet undertaken.[60] This attempt to build a model by committee took 13 investigations to develop important subsector models before they could be put together as a complete model containing over 400 equations.

One purpose of the model is policy simulation "for evaluating the total impact of alternative policy measures."[61] A few who were involved in developing the Brookings model (Holt, in particular) view the policy process in terms of decision analysis.[62]

Gary Fromm used a condensed version (176 equations) of the Brookings model to investigate monetary policy instruments. He used the familiar multiplier technique to compute both impact and dynamic multipliers on

[57] *Ibid.*, pp. 109–111. (Suits provides a simple numerical example of the concept with a three-equation model.) See also A. Goldberger, *Econometric Theory* (New York, N.Y.: John Wiley & Sons, 1963), pp. 369, 374–376. (Goldberger provides a more analytical treatment.)

[58] Technically, the desired current period impact multipliers are given by the reduced form coefficients β_{km} which may be interpreted as the partial derivative of X_k with respect to Y_m where X_k is the endogenous variable explained by the kth reduced form equation and Y_m is the exogenous policy variable.

[59] Suits, "Forecasting and Analysis," p. 128.

[60] Duesenberry, *et al.*, "The Brookings Quarterly Econometric Model."

[61] *Ibid.*, p. 11.

[62] *Ibid.*, pp. 643–4.

real GNP and real consumption and to compute the impact multipliers on many endogenous variables for six exogenous changes (for changes in durable expenditures, income tax, discount rate, time deposit reserve requirement, demand deposit reserve requirement, and open market operations).[63] He discussed the need for an objective function "to evaluate outcomes," but he did not make the concept operational in that paper.

Gary Fromm and Paul Taubman published a monograph, *Policy Simulations with an Econometric Model*. Of special interest for the concept of adaptive modeling is the development and use of an objective function with a model which cannot be optimized.[64]

Many countries have developed macroeconometric models to assist in their planning processes.[65] The Netherlands, for instance, has attempted to develop an operational planning model by using interview techniques to obtain an objective function in terms of employment, prices, income distribution, and balance of payments; this work, carried out by van de Boggard and Barten, is described by Theil.[66]

The majority of current models are short-term forecasting models used primarily for stabilization policy; however, some attempts have been made to create development (growth) models. Extending the time horizon is not sufficient to create useful long-term models; these models must relate sets of long-term policy instruments and constraints to long-term objectives. Thus, growth models that emphasize production functions and capacity concepts are generally more neoclassical than the Keynesian models.

Macroeconomic model building is the basis of the stabilization model presented in Chapters 6 and 7, and input-output techniques are the basis of the growth model in Chapters 4 and 5.

[63] G. Fromm, "An Evaluation of Monetary Policy Instruments." Unpublished paper presented at the Annual Econometric Society Meeting, San Francisco, Calif., December 1966.

[64] G. Fromm and P. Taubman, *Policy Simulations with an Econometric Model* (Washington, D.C.: The Brookings Institution, 1968).

[65] For a review of a number of such models, see: B. Hickman, ed., *Quantitative Planning of Economic Policy*, Washington, D.C.: The Brookings Institution, 1964; E. S. Kirschen, et al., *Economic Policy in Our Time*. Amsterdam: North-Holland, 1964; and M. Nerlove, "A Tabular Survey of Macro-Economic Models," *International Economic Review*, vol. 7, no. 2 (May 1966).

[66] Theil, *Optimum Decision*, pp. 256–280.

2.1
Adaptive Decision Processes
2.1.1
Definitions

Depending on whether uncertainty is present and whether it is of the statistical or subjective type, decision processes may be categorized as deterministic, stochastic, or adaptive. Richard Bellman distinguishes the three according to the assumptions of the models.[1]

A *model of a deterministic process* assumes that at each stage or time period in the process the following characteristics of the system are known: the system state, the set of possible decisions, the effect of each of the possible decisions, the duration of the process, and the objective function. A *model of a stochastic process* relaxes one or more of these assumptions by replacing known variables of the deterministic process with known probability distribution functions. For example, unknown values of uncontrollable variables for the current time period are given by a known distribution. Finally, a *model of an adaptive process* assumes that the probability distributions of the uncontrollable variables are unknown; thus the decision maker must learn and perform simultaneously.

Bellman identifies three possible sources of the uncertainty that creates adaptive processes; each is characterized by a basic premise:

Source I:

The process is deterministic, but the mechanism is not understood.

Source II:

The process is stochastic, but the probability distribution (or the parameters of a known distribution class) is unknown.

Source III:

Within the process are hidden variables (for example, the decision makers may be unknown or the question of whether or not Source I or II is being encountered may be unanswered).

Bellman, Theil, and others have shown (for example, by the certainty equivalence theorems referred to in Chapter 1) how deterministic and stochastic processes can be treated by similar mathematical techniques. The adaptive process can be reduced to the stochastic if certain conditions

---

[1] Richard Bellman, *Adaptive Control Processes, A Guided Tour* (Princeton, N.J.: Princeton University Press, 1961), p. 198.

are met;[2] these conditions generally require that the source of uncertainty be a special case of Source II; that is, the class of the underlying probability distribution (that is, Gaussian, binomial, and so forth) is known but the parameters are not. Thus, to optimize the adaptive process, it must be assumed that an a priori distribution is known and a mechanism (usually based on Bayes' theorem) can be applied to incoming information. The mathematically treatable adaptive processes are thus characterized by what amounts to statistical uncertainty; the probability distribution can be defined but the parameter values are determined subjectively and not as the limiting values of the frequency of the events.

More formally, adaptive decision processes can be reduced to stochastic processes by using Bayes' theorem to transform the subjective uncertainty to statistical uncertainty. If X^i denotes the ith world state (out of n possibilities) and R denotes the received report, then the theorem states that

$$\text{prob } (X^i \mid R) = \frac{\text{prob } (R \mid X^i) \text{ prob } (X^i)}{\sum_{i=1}^{n} \text{prob } (R \mid X^j) \text{ prob } (X^j)} \tag{2.1}$$

for each of m possible reports.

Adaptive processes characterized by subjective uncertainty are quite new mathematically; they may never yield to complete mathematical solutions. The purpose of this chapter is to formulate a modeling procedure for untractable adaptive decision processes characterized by subjective uncertainty. For these processes it is generally *not* possible to do one or more of the following: (1) state an a priori probability distribution for unknown variables or parameters; (2) enumerate the information possibilities; or (3) know the conditional probabilities that alternative information sets will exist for each of the possible world states. For these adaptive processes, the prob (X^i) are unknown and the prob $(R \mid X^i)$ cannot be stated objectively for many reports; in fact, neither can all possible Xs and Rs be enumerated. Adaptive processes of this nature will be referred to as adaptive decision processes under subjective uncertainty.

The premise of the proposed procedure is that, at present, significant economic decision-making problems may fruitfully be explored by *man-machine systems;* the human element can cope with the subjective uncertainty and the computer can cope with the computational part of the

[2] *Ibid.*, pp. 203–218; for the Miyasawa proof see Koichi Miyasawa, "Information Structures in Stochastic Programming Problems," *Management Science,* vol. 14, no. 5 (January 1968) p. 276.

problem. Thus, both parts of the problem can be reduced to manageable size, either for computer manipulation or for human decision making.

The suggested procedure is adaptive in Bellman's sense; that is, it is one in which learning takes place. First, the decision maker learns in each exercise, or simulation, about the state of the world represented by the imbedded primary and auxiliary submodels. Second, he learns more about the underlying reality in the real world through participating in the simulation exercises in which he explicitly recognizes the system interactions. Third, he improves the imbedded models as he reflects and criticizes the formulations in this realistic setting.

2.1.2
Advantages and Disadvantages of Previous Approaches

The previous chapter traced two streams of thought: the *decision-analytic approach* to maximizing utility under uncertainty and the *econometric approach* to developing empirical models of socioeconomic systems. Adaptive modeling attempts to synthesize these two and to gain the advantages and eliminate the disadvantages of each, but the attempt cannot be completely successful, because not all of the advantages of decision analysis and econometrics can be simultaneously retained.

To review the decision analysis approach, the problem is to maximize the utility of the sequence of outcomes, subject to uncertain constraints, where in the adaptive process under statistical uncertainty, a priori knowledge of prob $(R \mid X^i)$, prob (X^i), and the possible set $\{R\}$ is assumed for all t. If we assume that the constrained maximization problem can be solved by classical calculus techniques or by linear or nonlinear programming, the solution provides

1.

An optimum strategy, or strategies in the case of multiple optimums. (Thus, a search process is not needed.)

2.

An evaluation of shadow prices for each constraint.

3.

A loss function that measures the suboptimality of nonoptimal decisions to determine the value of information sets.

4.

An evaluation of flexibility in a first-period plan that permits alternative contingent plans in the future depending on the receipt of alternative information sets.

The three disadvantages of the decision-analytic approach are

1.

The difficulty of obtaining an acceptable objective function.

2.

The restrictions on the mathematical form of the objective function and constraints that are necessary for solving a constrained maximization problem.

3.

The restrictive assumptions (discussed previously) about a priori knowledge of prob $(R \mid X^i)$, prob (X^i), and $\{R\}$.

The advantages of econometric model building are (1) it avoids the three disadvantages of the decision-analytic approach, (2) it is based on empirical data, and (3) it provides answers in concrete terms (for example, fiscal and monetary multipliers) that are immediately useful to decision makers. On the other hand, the four advantages of the decision analysis are lost.

The proposed adaptive modeling procedure surrenders the optimizing techniques (Advantages 1 and 2) of the decision-analytic approach and some of the rigorous statistical tests of the econometric approach. However, the statistical tests applied to econometric models are frequently less rigorous than they seem. Generally, a priori information does *not* tell with certainty which variables belong in any particular equation, or which set of data is the best measure of each desired conceptual variable, or what form the equation has (for example, linear in variables, linear in logarithms of variables, etc.). Therefore, economists often formulate several forms of an equation, all plausible in the light of the available a priori information. After all the alternative forms have been estimated and the numerical estimates of the coefficients are examined, the equation form that appears best is accepted. The process of trying *several* alternatives and choosing the one with the highest correlation coefficient will generally lead to seemingly more significant coefficients when the null hypothesis is true for all alternatives than will the process of choosing *one* equation form on a priori grounds. "Therefore the tests of significance · · · will be too likely to reject the null hypothesis, if they are applied to an equation that has been chosen because of having the highest correlation coefficient among a set of alternative equations."[3]

[3] Carl Christ, *Econometric Models and Methods* (New York, N.Y.: John Wiley & Sons, 1966), pp. 537–538.

The problem is that no maintained hypothesis can be stated with sufficient precision and confidence before examining the empirical data, while at the same time the data are insufficient for beginning again each time an hypothesized model is abandoned. Therefore, the "cut-and-try" procedure is likely to be used as long as econometricians continue to be faced with a large choice of mathematical forms, data sources, lag structures, and so forth. In fact, the gains achieved by abandoning the procedure (even if it were possible) are not likely to be worth the loss of the model builder's intuition.

2.2
The Adaptive Modeling Procedure

This section discusses adaptive modeling procedures that will permit those who are not necessarily econometricians but who are familiar with the socioeconomic system to contribute knowledge in a systematic manner to the model building process.

2.2.1
Characteristics of the Procedure

Model builders should use an adaptive modeling procedure when the following conditions exist:

1.

The primary purpose is to aid in the development of strategies for situations in which planners are faced with the problem of dynamic decision making under subjective uncertainty;

2.

The subject matter is complex socioeconomic systems for which objectives cannot be easily stated; and

3.

The subject system is characterized by considerable uncertainty arising because the relationships among the system variables are imperfectly known and because random exogenous events are extremely significant to system performance.

Models developed for adaptive modeling procedures are structured to represent the actual decision-making environment as realistically as possible and to take maximum advantage of the principles of decision analysis. The models are intended to be modified and extended as they are used; they are not restricted to empirically derived relationships. They will accept the judgement of those familiar with the system's operation concerning imperfectly known parameters and relationships; however the model's conclusions must be empirically testable. The models are designed to facilitate the most efficient interaction between the users and the model by using computers in a conversational mode (that is, the computer executes one or more instructions, the user views the output and inputs new data or instructions, the computer responds to the new input, and so forth; in effect a responsive "conversation" is carried out between user and computer). More specifically, the procedure will have at least some, and perhaps all seven, of the components described in Section 2.2.2.

2.2.2

Components of the Procedure

The adaptive modeling procedure can be created with the following components: (1) a primary model, (2) a definition of the roles of the decision makers, (3) an objective function, (4) an information system, (5) a library of exogenous events, (6) a set of auxiliary models, and (7) a dynamic environment.

THE PRIMARY MODEL

A primary model is generally formal and explicitly stated so that a numerical solution can be found; this implies that a computer program can be written. The primary models used in the two procedures developed in this study are an input-output model and a 23-equation Keynesian macroeconomic model. Given specific values for exogenous uncontrollable variables X_t^* and for instruments Y_t, the primary model F, which contains the parameters Π, provides conditional estimates of the state of the world; thus

$$X_{t+1}^e = F(\Pi \mid X_t^*, Y_t). \tag{2.2}$$

DECISION-MAKING ROLES

The second component of adaptive modeling is the definition of the decision-making roles. Since the primary objective of an adaptive modeling procedure is to aid in the decision-making process, it is necessary to define clearly roles within the model that correspond to decision-making roles in the socioeconomic system. Thus, if Y is the set of all instruments defined in the primary and auxiliary models, it is necessary to specify the instrument subsets $\{y^a\}, \{y^b\}, \ldots, \{y^r\}$ corresponding to the decision makers $a, b, \ldots, r$. Constraints on the manipulation of instruments within which the decision makers may act (for example, tax rates cannot be changed more than once annually; tax increases cannot exceed 10 percent) must also be defined. Furthermore, the definition of roles also depends on the information set available to a decision maker. All decision makers need not receive all available information at the same time or with the same degree of accuracy.

The amount of communication permitted among decision makers must also be defined. Experiments with alternative organizations of the decision-making apparatus can be devised by changing the roles and by then observing whether performance is improved or not. The objective function Φ^a and the transformation function G^a (where G denotes the composite of primary and auxiliary models—i.e., the complete transformation function) must be defined to complete the role of decision maker a. Within this study, the primary and auxiliary models, objective functions, and information system are described as if they are all identical for all decision makers engaged in the procedure; but that is not necessarily the case. The clearly defined decision-making roles of the adaptive modeling procedure are not an accurate representation of the real-world situation. In the real situation, fiscal policy makers do not frequently hesitate very long before giving advice to the monetary authorities; nor is the flow of information and advice undirectional. While the procedure permits experimentation with organization structures, it is unlikely that it can ever accurately capture the complex interrelationships among policy makers and their advisors as they really exist.

THE OBJECTIVE FUNCTION

The third component is an objective function for measuring the performance of the system:

$$\Phi = \Phi(\{\phi\})_t;$$
$$\phi_t = \phi_t(X_t^i, Y_t^j). \tag{2.3}$$

If an optimizing procedure is used, the objective function determines the instrument values in a formal way—that is $Y = G[\Phi, F(X,Y)]$. In an adaptive modeling procedure, the objective function provides a comparative measure to be used for limited heuristic purposes. When it is used to compare outcomes, the decision maker may either modify or ignore the value assumed by Φ or ϕ; the function remains useful for measuring such things as the value of information (that is, reduction in uncertainty) or the value of changes in the decision-making organization. Also, by the observing of actual or potential decision makers, it may be possible to determine empirically the objective functions which are the basis of their reactions.

What is required for an objective function to be usable is discussed in Chapter 3; requirements for its use in an optimizing procedure are shown in Chapters 4 and 5 on the growth model.

THE INFORMATION SYSTEM

The information system provides the set $I = D, R_1, R_2, \ldots, R_t$; the data D are used to build the primary and auxiliary models and the reports R_t provide information on the performance of the system during the simulated period. The reports fall into three categories: descriptions of past performance of the system, formal forecasts of future performance, and reports concerned with random exogenous events. The latter are contained in the report library, described in the following section.

THE REPORT LIBRARY

The fifth component, the report library, may be formal, informal, or mixed, depending on the way in which the random exogenous events are established. The reports simulate the information that precedes, occurs simultaneously with, or comes after the event. Thus, the report library contains the set of possible shocks or exogenous events the system may face and the sequence of reports associated with the possibility or occurrence of each event; it generates reports as a function of exogenous events: $R_t = (E_{t+\tau})$; $\tau = -2, -1, 0, 1, 2, \ldots$. For example, if the occurrence of a steel strike is a random exogenous event occurring in period t, reports may be generated in $t - 1$ concerning the progress of negotiations, in t indicating that the strike has occurred, and in $t + 1$ describing the settlement.

THE AUXILIARY MODELS

Auxiliary models connect the primary model with the outside world—the relevant parts of the socioeconomic system not explicitly represented in the primary model. If an auxiliary model is frequently used and acquires the same level of confidence as the primary model, it may become part of a new and more comprehensive primary model; that is, when the separation between primary and auxiliary model is no longer useful, it disappears. Three categories of auxiliary models are described below. The categorization depends on the part of the outside world represented by the auxiliary model.

Auxiliary models in the first category link the primary model with exogenous events; the events and their reports generally affect either the exogenous variables X^* or the error terms u of the primary model. By denoting the exogenous event auxiliary models as f', one obtains

$$(X^*, u) = f'\{R(E)\}. \tag{2.4}$$

If the primary model contains a dummy strike variable with a value of one or zero, depending on whether or not a steel strike is in progress, the auxiliary model would only provide the value for the strike variable: one when there is a report of a current steel strike and zero otherwise. If the primary model does not contain a strike variable, the strike presumably affects an error term: for example, if the primary model contains an equation such as

$$\text{INV}_t = \Sigma_i \Pi_i z_{it} + u_t \tag{2.5}$$

where INV = inventory investment, Π = a nonzero parameter, z = an explanatory variable, and u = the error term. The auxiliary model might be u_t equals \$10 million if there were a report that a steel strike was expected within 6 months, $-\$10$ million if a steel strike was in progress, or \$5 million if a steel strike was settled last month; otherwise, u_t equals zero.

Auxiliary models in the second category link the primary model with instruments available to the decision maker but omitted from the primary model. For example, a macroeconomic model that does not contain instruments available to a monetary decision maker may contain secondary variables that are influenced but not controlled by monetary policy. This situation is described in Chapter 7; there the primary model contains free reserves in the banking system as an exogenous variable, but not open market operations of the Federal Reserve Board (FRB). In this case, a useful auxiliary model would define a relationship between open market operations and net free reserves. Denoting the omitted instrument category of auxiliary models as f'', one obtains

$$X^* = f''(Y^*) \tag{2.6}$$

where X^* are exogenous variables in the primary model (for example, free reserves) and Y^* are instruments omitted from the primary model.

Generally, whatever the level of aggregation in the primary model, decision makers are interested at some time in specifics that can only be discerned in a more disaggregated model. If the primary model is macroeconomic, the performance of specific sectors (for example, housing or steel) enter the decision maker's objective function at some time (that is, he is interested in balanced performance or balanced growth). If a primary model is an input-output type, the decision maker may seek knowledge about a geographic region of the country or about a specific investment within a sector. The latter is similar to an omitted instrument auxiliary model; however, disaggregated auxiliary models are categorized on the basis of relevant variables in the primary model as follows: Auxiliary models in the third category link the endogenous variables of the primary model to other uncontrollable variables; that is, the variables X^{**} are the explanatory variables of the auxiliary model. An auxiliary model in this category is denoted as g; values of variables W that are excluded from the primary model are given by

$$W = g(X^{**}). \tag{2.7}$$

A model created by grafting one or more (formal or informal) auxiliary models onto a primary model is referred to as a composite model; the composite model embedded in the computer program is the core model. Whether the primary model is affected by, and should be modified as, a result of grafting one or more auxiliary models onto it is a complex problem that will not be answered here, but Section 2.2.4 discusses topics that may lead to a meaningful answer.

DYNAMIC ENVIRONMENT

The final component of the adaptive modeling procedure is the dynamic environment in which it is used; that is an environment in which

$$X_{t+1} = G_t(X_t, Y_t, u_t) \tag{2.8}$$

where G denotes the complete transformation function and where the plan, the exogenous variables, and the error term need only be specified one period at a time after the results for the previous period have been determined. The dynamic environment is created by using a computer in a conversational mode and employing discrete period models as the primary and auxiliary models. Most econometric models are of this type; generally t is not continuous but assumes discrete values—quarters of a year or entire years.

The adaptive modeling procedure differs from the usual approach to simulation with econometric models in many respects; two very important differences are treatment of uncertainty and development of strategies. These differences are discussed in the following sections.

2.2.3

Treatment of Uncertainty

Random events are the most significant elements of uncertainty faced by the decision maker; an example was the extended controversy over the reliability of Vietnam expenditure forecasts between the executive branch and Congress, which was part of the debate concerning the 1968 surtax.[4]

The decision maker, over a period of time, faces a number of such exogenous events under subjective uncertainty; many can be foreseen to have a finite probability of occurrence, but the amount of foresight depends inversely on how far into the future a decision maker is looking and how precisely the events are defined. For example 10 years ago the probability of continued U.S. military involvement in Southeast Asia may have been foreseen, but it is doubtful that the policy makers foresaw the possibility of a conflict in Vietnam involving 500,000 U.S. troops. The true state of the Vietnamese situation is only one aspect of the world state; to completely describe the world state for decision-making purposes, it is necessary to examine all the categories of exogenous events that significantly influence the system. Assume that the decision maker faces uncertainty in 10 important categories—foreign events requiring military action, foreign events affecting trade or financial markets, technological change, domestic labor disruption, and so forth. Assume also that, on the average over a planning horizon of 5 years, 10^2 possibilities exist for each of the 10 categories; for example, if labor disruptions can occur simultaneously at one of three levels of intensity in one or two of five major industries then there are 75 possibilities in this single category. Assume further, that each may occur in one of 10 time periods; then the number of alternative world states (assuming events in each category are independently determined) is conservatively on the order of 10^4.

The Bayesian approach of asking the decision makers to provide a priori estimates of the probability for each of 10^4 world states is impractical; it is especially so because, in addition, the decision maker must estimate the conditional prob $(R^k \mid X^i)$ for $i = 1, 2, \ldots, 10^4$ where k may, very conservatively, be on the order of 100. The current, or conventional planning procedure, is to use econometric models to provide a few conditional estimates based on alternative ad hoc assumptions about plans and exogenous events.[5]

A compromise, created in the adaptive modeling procedure, is to determine and define specific exogenous events and, in a sense, to create

[4] See *Economic Outlook and Its Policy Implications*, Hearings before the Joint Economic Committee, June 27–29, 1967; and the *Report of the Joint Economic Committee on the 1967 Economic Report* and . . . *on the 1968 Economic Report* (Washington, D.C.: U.S. Government Printing Office, 1967 and 1968).
[5] Lawrence R. Klein and Michael Evans, "Wharton Economic Newsletter," *Wharton Quarterly*, Winter 1968, pp. 17–18, illustrates the current procedure.

alternative world states by permitting combinations of events to occur and to generate reports likely to be associated with the realized world state. Thus the report library is developed on the decision-theoretic basis of alternative world states that may occur with a finite probability and generate alternative report sets. The decision maker may then investigate those situations that he finds likely or interesting.

The selection of random events and their reports from the library creates a gaming structure as illustrated in Chapters 6 to 8 by the stabilization model. Random events and associated reports represent "nature's move" in the game; the move may be simulated by a random-number generator operating with some probability distribution, a game referee operating in some heuristic fashion, or a combination of both.

2.2.4
Development of Strategies

An adaptive modeling procedure not only differs from current simulation procedures in its treatment of uncertainty but it differs in its approach to the development of strategies or sequence of plans. The decision maker works with the adaptive model in a dynamic fashion—making decisions and receiving information sequentially over time. The procedure corresponds to Bellman's adaptive process; the decision maker simultaneously performs and learns about the system being simulated. The adaptive approach may be described in terms of improvements in computer technology: The development of high-speed, mass storage, electronic equipment in the 1950s made it possible to solve large econometric models and input-output tables; these computers are batch processors, that is, the program and the data are entered sequentially into the main processing unit, which executes the program and generates output. With the batch processing procedure, values for exogenous variables and for instruments $X_0^*, Y_0, X_1^*, \ldots, X_T^*, Y_T$ of the entire period to be simulated are the essential data the program uses to solve the model T times and to generate conditional estimates of endogenous variables $X_1^{**}, X_2^{**}, \ldots, X_T^{**}$ as output for the planning period. The sequence of plans $Y_1, Y_2, \ldots, Y_T$ must be made at simulated time $t - 0$; this is a rigid strategy: The plan executed in each period does not depend on the results of the previous period. Batch processing is perfectly adequate for simulation of deterministic or stochastic processes; any learning, however, must take place before or after, not during, a simulation.

One of the most significant recent developments in computer technology is conversational mode processing which permits communication between the computer and one or more users. This feature is common to most third-generation equipment; it has been available in special situations with older computers such as the Project MAC at M.I.T., which is the best known and which uses IBM-7094s. The conversational mode makes it possible to prepare data—exogenous variables and instruments—period by period after receiving information on the previous period; thus the adaptive process can be simulated. Also, each decision maker may operate at a console, receiving a specific set of information and supplying values for the specific instruments under his control.

Hypothetically, it would be possible to develop strategies covering each possible situation and to solve the model with a batch processing mode; this, however, again brings up the problem of having to enumerate every possible condition. Martin Shubik describes the approach of defining every possible alternative as an extensive form of the game.[6] The extensive form of chess is a problem too large for even the largest computers; on the other hand, the adaptive form, in which decisions are made dynamically on the basis of the current state of the board, is relatively simple. A reduction of this magnitude in the size of the computational problem is what is sought in the proposed adaptive modeling procedure; it is an attempt to develop a man-machine system in which man and machine individually perform the tasks each can do best.

Conversational mode computing capacity, in a time-sharing arrangement, is not necessary to adaptive modeling in the same way that large-scale computers are not necessary to solve econometric models. In both situations however, the technology makes the procedure economically feasible.

2.2.5

Modifications

The adaptive procedure should encourage continuous modification of its components. Auxiliary models, objective function, information processing, decision-making roles and organization, etc., may be modified considerably within and between simulations. It should also be possible to employ alternative primary models to compare their effectiveness in similar situations. The remainder of this subsection briefly categorizes some modifications.

---

[6] Martin Shubik, *Strategy and Market Structure: Competition, Oligopoly and the Theory of Games* (New York, N.Y.: John Wiley & Sons, 1959).

The simplest modifications are procedural changes that can be effected through changes in the rules within or between simulations. For example, the amount of communication permitted between fiscal and monetary decision makers may be altered, or the number of forecasts allowed the decision maker may be changed as described in Chapters 6 and 7 for the stabilization model.

Data modifications are also simple and can be made within or between simulations through an input device such as a console typewriter. The model may also be changed in this way; the better the program, the more flexible it will be. Modification of parameters (for example, input-output coefficients, or marginal propensities to consume, or weights in the objective function) are possible in the procedures developed for the growth and stabilization problems described in later chapters. More elaborate changes call in complex subroutines such as alternative auxiliary, or even alternative primary, models; both may be stored and used as instructed from the console keyboard.

Programming changes, the next in order of complexity, can only be made between simulations; these may affect the form of the model or perhaps only certain parameters that cannot be changed by data modifications. The effort required varies from the simple case, in which a few instructions need to be modified, to the extremely complex case in which extensive programming is needed.

The final and most complicated changes are the organizational modifications; these may arise if the decision-making function is disaggregated or if revisions are requested for the input or output routines that change the number of remote terminals.

The full range of the variety of anticipated modifications that may be needed is difficult to foresee; thus it seems wise to begin simply and build flexibly as demonstrated in the stabilization model (see Chapters 6 and 7).

The procedure is adaptive in the short run, during a simulation, and in the long run, between simulations. The short-run changes, made in response to the results of the previous periods' activity, are those in the instrument values (the plans), in the weights applied to the elements of the objective function, in the value of parameters or dummy variables, in the probabilities assigned to exogenous events, and in the values assigned to exogenous uncontrollable variables.

The long-run changes are made in response to the experience gained in previous simulation exercises or from experience with the real system. In addition to the short-run changes, these may include changing the structure of the primary and auxiliary models and the objective function, redefining the decision-making roles or the information system, adding new events to the report library, and adding new auxiliary models.

2.3
Models and the Empirical Reality

A model is a simplified representation of reality that is more easily understood and more amenable to manipulation than reality. For example, a set of architectural plans is a model of a house; because of the diminutive size and the ease with which lines may be erased and redrawn, an architectural planner can easily (and inexpensively) evaluate and modify the plans and thus try alternative configurations.

2.3.1
Model Differences

Models that represent the economy are considerably more difficult to construct than models that represent house plans. For example, the way in which beams react to stress is known and can be represented with a high degree of certainty; furthermore, the stresses the beam will have to bear in the future can be predicted with relative confidence; finally, it is reasonable to assume that the relationships between the beam and its loads will remain constant. On the other hand, the way consumers react to changing prices or incomes is not known with a great deal of certainty. Thus, it is difficult to predict price or income changes that a consumer may experience in the future or whether observed consumer reactions to the changes will be the same even if the identical situation is repeated.

2.3.2
Model Similarities

Despite very real differences between these two models of reality, many similarities do exist. With the economic model, the planner, like the architect, manipulates instruments within imposed constraints in order to decide on an optimum, or at least a favorable, result. To build a model, each seeks a function that maps a conjunction of two sets—a set of assumptions about uncontrollable variables and a plan, or set of values for controllable variables—into the objective function. Both planners must also have a way of evaluating the calculated results (that is, an objective function) so that alternative configurations can be compared.

Some aspects of the results (or objectives) may be easily quantified (for example, the square feet of living area or the GNP); others may be more subjective (for example, aesthetic considerations or composition of output) and difficult to quantify. Both planners operate within constraints (for example, number of bedrooms and kind of terrain or resource availability and production functions) that are more or less rigid. Finally, both have a number of instruments, or controllable variables (relative location of rooms or the tax rate and structure), that they manipulate.

2.3.3
Goals of Adaptive Modeling
Adaptive modeling is an attempt to provide the economic planner with a procedure that is as flexible (or adaptable) as the one used by the architect. The result is a man-machine system made possible by current computer technology. The man may have a high-ranking planning position, or he may be the actual decision maker or policy maker; the machine may contain an extremely complex cluster of formal models. The human element copes with the subjective uncertainty and the machine handles the computations of the decision-making problem.

Figure 2.1 illustrates what adaptive modeling attempts to accomplish with a decision tree of an extremely simple problem. A decision-making problem under certainty with only a three-period planning horizon and a single instrument that takes on one of two values has eight possible solutions. A simultaneous search, which examines all eight solutions, requires that the simulation be run eight times; since each simulation requires three solutions of the transformation function G, 24 solutions of G are necessary. However, if one can *try* the possible moves and choose *go* with the correct alternative, only six solutions of G are necessary. If a simple form of uncertainty is introduced into the decision problem, for example allowing two possible states of the world at each stage, 192 solutions (3×64) are needed to examine all alternatives, but only 12 solutions (6×2) are necessary if the correct choice can be made at each stage.

If a more realistic problem is confronted, one with a half dozen instruments and sources of uncertainty, each of which can take on four or five values, and if the planning horizon contains 10 or more periods, the problem becomes unmanageably large. If it is necessary in this situation to investigate each path, the problem is computationally insoluble. The implicit assumption of the adaptive procedure is not that a decision maker can choose the optimum path at each stage but that he can correctly

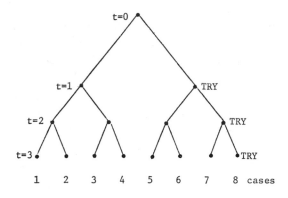

a.   The case under certainty.

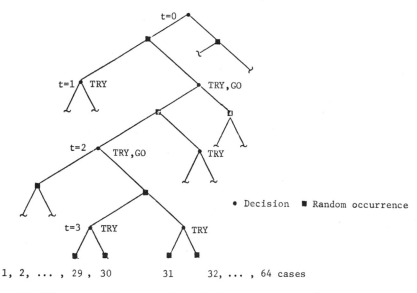

b.   The case under uncertainty with two possible world states.

Figure 2.1. The dynamic decision problem with a single instrument having two possible values and a three-period planning horizon.

eliminate many of the dominated paths. The adaptive modeling procedure, like the architect's planning procedure, is heuristic and "satisficing" because there is no assurance that the optimum path will not be overlooked.

The rationale of the adaptive approach is an attempt to be more realistic and to permit more play for economic judgement than is usually the case with most models. Ultimately, there are two sources of subjective uncertainty where rational analyses are inadequate: One is exogenous events and the other is the basic underlying objective (welfare) function. In the final analysis, these must be left to specific individuals charged with responsibility for the socioeconomic system: the duly elected political officials. The most analyses can do is push these ultimates as far back as possible by showing the implications (or range of implications) of alternative exogenous events and objective functions and/or plans. These points are illustrated with the resource allocation problem (Chapters 4 and 5), in which the objective function is adaptable, and in the stabilization problem (Chapters 6, 7, and 8), in which the uncertainty of exogenous events is emphasized. While the resource allocation problem uses well-known mathematical programming algorithms, the stabilization problem is discussed in terms of games rather than models.

2.3.4
The Reality, Models, and the Computer Programs

One possible schema of the interrelationship between reality and its models is illustrated in Figure 2.2.

An observer of the empirical reality abstracts to create a theoretical model whose structure is mathematical. One possibility at this point—that is not of interest in this work—is to solve the mathematical model (for example, solve for the optimizing conditions) and draw implications for

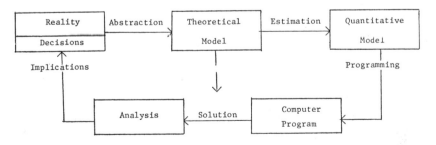

Figure 2.2. Relationships of model to reality.

the real world. This work is concerned with the other option, in which numerical values are estimated—subjectively or statistically, or through some combination of both—for the model's parameters. If a computer program is written to represent the model, it becomes convenient frequently to solve it under alternative assumptions about its structure, the exogenous variables, and the plan. The solutions may be analyzed, and the implications drawn for the real world may then be used as a basis for decisions.

None of the relating functions of Figure 2.2 are unidirectional; feedback loops interconnect all of them. Further, the abstracting process and the drawing of implications for the real world require creative acts that, so far, have not yielded to analytical treatment.

The adaptive modeling procedure is more concerned with connecting all the entities shown in Figure 2.2 (for example, reality, theoretical model, and so forth) than with how any single one of the relating functions (for example, abstraction, estimation, etc.) is performed.

In this book, existing theoretical models are used and the numerical parameters are either obtained from the literature or arrived at in a nonrigorous manner. The two illustrative problems (that is, the growth and stabilization problems) indicate the type of conversational-mode computer program that facilitates the adaptive procedure. The following section briefly suggests how the solutions might be used to draw implications and affect the real world; this is made somewhat clearer by the illustrative problems of the later chapters.

2.3.5
The Adaptive Modeling Procedure in the Real World

The adaptive modeling procedure is a man-machine simulation of a real-world process. The real-world process contains policy makers who establish objective functions, planners who define alternative courses of action, and decision makers who specify plans to be implemented. In the real world, individuals or groups of individuals may assume one or more of these roles simultaneously. Most frequently the roles are ill-defined and tend to overlap. The objectives and the transformation functions the decision makers use may be informal; the reports may be quite diverse (newspapers, formal staff reports, expert advice, and so forth). The real world is unstructured and chaotic; some decisions are made after careful study, others are immediate responses to special situations. The adaptive modeling procedure simulates and structures this real situation. Within the procedure, individuals assume well-defined roles that correspond to real roles in the system.

The place of the adaptive modeling procedure in the real world depends on a number of factors such as the relationship of the individuals participating in the procedure to those who fulfill these roles in the real system, and the correspondence between the primary and auxiliary models and the real system, and between the library of exogenous events and the events the real decision maker must face.

The procedure may be used by real planners to study alternatives, by real decision makers as an aid in making decisions and in communicating their reasons to policy makers, by policy makers to better define their objectives, by researchers in developing more relevant and accurate models, and by analysts to study alternative governmental organizations or information. For example, the adaptive modeling procedure can be used to create a laboratory in which alternative information systems can be investigated by scrambling, delaying, or presenting data in alternative ways and by noting the effect on the decision-making procedure.

The remainder of this chapter digresses from the primary purposes of this work to discuss the problem of tacking auxiliary models onto a primary econometric model and to consider the question of whether the adaptive modeling procedure can be considered scientific.

2.4
Tacking Auxiliary Models onto the Primary Model

Attaching one or more auxiliary models to a primary model leads to the crucial question: Do the parameters Π of the primary model F lose their validity in the composite model G which is composed of primary and auxiliary models?

To state the problem more formally, the composite model G may be statistically estimated as a single model G' or it may be created for the adaptive modeling procedure by adding auxiliary models to a primary model F. This applies to any of the three categories of auxiliary models f', f'', or g. Consideration of exogenous-event auxiliary models $(X^*, u) = f'(R_t, E_t)$ makes the discussion more concrete; however, the remainder of this section is applicable, with minor modifications, to auxiliary models in any of the three categories.

When considering a composite model consisting of a primary and a typical auxiliary, exogenous-event model, the choice is between

$$\hat{X}'_t = G'_t(X_{t-1}, Y_{t-1}, u_t \mid Y_t, X^*_t) \tag{2.9}$$

and

$$\hat{X}_t = G_t[F(X_{t-1}, Y_{t-1}, u_t \mid Y_t f'(R_t, E_t))]. \tag{2.10}$$

Examination of the parameters that are common to both F and G' provokes two more specific questions: Is the set of parameters Π_g of G' likely to be different from the set of parameters Π_F of F? If so, how significant will the changes be? The answers are relatively simple if models F and f' are independent; then G can be estimated in block recursive fashion and Π_g equals Π_F and Equations 2.9 and 2.10 are identical. Alternatively, if R or E is dependent on any endogenous primary model variable in the set X^{**}, then $\Pi_g \neq \Pi_F$ and the estimate $\hat{\Pi}_F$ of the true parameter Π_g would be biased and inconsistent.

Examination of the parameters provokes a third, more complex question about the practical significance of using $\hat{\Pi}_F$ instead of $\hat{\Pi}_g$. The answer most likely depends on the particular model used, the sample size, and the size of error terms in the particular equation involved, and on other factors.

The simplest situation arises when the primary and the auxiliary model each consist of a single equation; then the choice is between simultaneous estimation of two equations (estimating G' in equation 2.9) or ordinary least squares of each equation (estimating G in equation 2.10).

A number of investigators have used Monte Carlo experiments to test the accuracy of ordinary least squares and a variety of simultaneous equation estimators. Their general procedure was to generate data from a model with known coefficients and variances and to estimate these parameters by alternative procedures for a number of different circumstances, including misspecified models.[7] The mean square error of the coefficient and the predictive ability of the model were generally used as criteria. Ordinary least squares generally has a larger bias but a smaller variance than alternative procedures; it may perform better if mean square error (rather than bias) is used as the relevant criterion. Overall, the results are not conclusive; however on the basis of recent econometric work, two-stage least squares appears to be the best.

Lawrence Klein's paper, perhaps the classical treatment of the subject,[8]

---

[7] John Johnston, *Econometric Methods*, pp. 275–294, and Carl Christ, *Econometric Models*, pp. 464–481, report work of Basmann, Summers, Quandt, Nagar, Wagner, *et al.*
[8] Lawrence Klein, "The Efficiency of Estimation in Econometric Models," *Essay in Economics and Econometrics*, R. Pfouts, ed. (Chapel Hill, N.C.: University of North Carolina Press, 1960), pp. 216–232.

points out that it is the reduced form parameters Π and the forecasts $\hat{X}$ (which are functions of Π) that are significant for decision makers. Simultaneous estimation procedures provide maximum-likelihood estimates of Π and of the functions of Π (that is, the forecasts). He proves that the efficiency of ordinary least squares (relative to simultaneous estimation methods) is not preserved under the transformation to the reduced form and that the bias is magnified.[9]

Klein, testing the small sample properties of various estimators in a Monte Carlo study, found that the data supported his thesis. In summary, Klein's theoretical analysis and his Monte Carlo studies seem to indicate that simultaneous estimation performs well for reduced form parameters and forecasts in overidentified models.[10]

Thus, the problem created by linking primary and auxiliary models is complicated analytically. Even in the simple case of single equation primary and auxiliary models, one must trace the effect of bias and variance on parameter values, the effect of a parameter error on the forecasts, and the effect of forecast errors on the decision maker's objective function.

However, the real problem is that the primary model is frequently a set of equations that have been simultaneously estimated by two-stage least squares or similar procedures. To proceed from bias and variance in the parameters to forecast errors and from there to losses in the objective function is much more complex if a simultaneous equation (rather than a single equation) primary model is used. Even the first step—analyzing the bias in parameters of a simultaneous set of equations when each equation may contain many variables—is extremely difficult.

An optimistic viewpoint might hold that as the primary model is used and improved, the important exogenous events will be endogenized and the error terms reduced. Nevertheless, the adaptive procedure is likely to be an improvement over current ad hoc methods of linking exogenous events (or omitted instruments or disaggregated variables) to econometric models.

If the adaptive modeling procedure is used, the number and kinds of auxiliary models will constantly change as researchers develop new models in auxiliary areas and as new instruments, or exogeneous events, or other variables become important. Furthermore, if certain auxiliary models continue to be useful in changing economic conditions, more comprehensive primary models will be developed to include them.

[9] *Ibid.*, pp. 220–223.
[10] Carl Christ, *Econometric Models*, p. 481.

2.5
The Scientific Nature of the Formal Models
2.5.1
The Scientific Content of the Primary and Auxiliary Models

The heart of decision analysis and the basis for all "scientific" decision-making procedures is the model used to represent reality. If the adaptive modeling procedure is to be successfully used, the decision maker must have some confidence that the model used is a relatively accurate representation of reality; that is, that the model has been scientifically constructed. This is the reason that empiricism has been emphasized in the previous discussion.

SCIENTIFIC METHOD

There is still considerable controversy as to the necessary characteristics of a scientific model. The following premises are implicit in the adaptive modeling procedure. Braithwaite states: "The function of a science · · · is to establish general laws covering the behavior of empirical events · · · to enable us to connect together our knowledge of the separately known events, and to make reliable predictions of events as yet unknown."[11]

Karl Popper suggests falsifiability as the criterion of demarcation between science and metaphysics; that is, a scientific statement is capable of being tested.[12] This definition is almost identical to Samuelson's definition of a *meaningful theorem*: "A hypothesis about empirical data which could conceivably be refuted."[13]

The scientific method is one of experience; thus, it must be possible for scientific systems to be refuted by experience. Scientific progress is a consequence of scientific methodology. "The distinguishing characteristic of empirical statements is their susceptibility to revision—in the fact that they can be criticized and superseded by better ones · · · [thus] the characteristic ability of science to advance."[14]

Empiricism is necessary to test hypotheses but not to state them; that is, a statement is "scientific" if it predicts empirical events that can be either affirmed or contradicted by experience, but the source of hypotheses

[11] R. B. Braithwaite, *Scientific Explanation* (New York, N.Y.: Harper and Brothers), 1960. p. 1.
[12] K. Popper, *Logic of Scientific Discovery* (New York, N.Y.: Harper Torchbooks, 1965), p. 49.
[13] P. Samuelson, *Foundations of Economic Analysis* (New York, N.Y.: Atheneum, 1965), p. 49.
[14] K. Popper, *Logic of Scientific Discovery*, p. 49.

is not necessarily empirical. More concretely, an empirically estimated parameter is not necessarily "better" than one based on informed judgement. For example, if an empirically estimated parameter of a variable is not significantly different from zero, it is not necessarily unscientific to keep the variable in the model. The variable may be retained because no single source of knowledge is authoritative.

Karl Popper published a paper entitled "Three Views Concerning Human Knowledge."[15] One view—essentialism—holds that science aims at ultimate explanation and that the scientist can succeed in finally establishing truth beyond all shadow of a doubt. A second view holds that scientific theories are nothing but computational algorithms or inference rules and that objective truth is a myth. A third view—the one taken here—assumes that objective truth does exist even though it can never be grasped with certainty. In other words, scientific theories are "genuine conjectures—highly informative guesses about the world—which although not verifiable can be submitted to severe critical tests; they are serious attempts to discover the truth."[16]

2.5.2
Evaluation of Alternative Models

Acceptance of the third view requires a means of evaluating alternative models. Abstractly, evaluation criteria do exist; they are, however, frequently difficult to apply in specific cases. For example, in a relatively simple case of a single-equation linear model in which the explanatory variables are assumed to be known, the selected model (that is, parameter values of the variables) minimizes the sum of the squared deviations between estimated and observed values for each explained variable if the typical Gauss or LaPlace criterion is used.

Even for this simple linear model the selection criteria may be controversial. Is it more important to predict turning points in a business cycle or to have the best "fit" (prediction within a specified range) or a prediction that can be tested for periods other than the one which provided data; or is it more important to use only explanatory variables with parameters that are significantly different from zero?

Expanding the list of explanatory variables and permitting multiple

---

[15] K. Popper, *Conjectures and Refutations: The Growth of Scientific Knowledge* (New York, N.Y.: Basic Books, 1962), pp. 97–119.
[16] *Ibid.*, p. 115.

equation models would eliminate, for all practical purposes, the possibility of objectively evaluating alternative models by traditional methods.

According to Braithwaite, the fundamental difference between a theory and a model is the order in which the various statements in the deductive system are developed.

A scientific theory is a deductive system in which observable consequences logically follow from the conjunction of observed facts with the set of fundamental hypotheses of the system.[17]

In developing a theory, the consequences are observed before the hypotheses (the higher level statements containing theoretical terms) are induced from the data; using a model, the hypotheses are established before the observable consequences are deduced.

The typical procedure is to develop a theory from observations, then to develop a model representing the theory that is finally used in practical applications. Braithwaite pointed out that the inherent danger of this procedure is projecting the empirical or logical model features onto the theoretical concepts:

Thinking of scientific theories by mean of models is always *as if* thinking; hydrogen atoms behave (in certain respects) as if they were solar systems . . . . But hydrogen atoms are not solar systems; it is only useful to think of them as if they were such systems if one remembers all the time that they are not. The price of the employment of models is eternal vigilance.[18]

His remarks are especially appropriate for models of socioeconomic systems because these are built on assumptions that simplify reality in order to reduce the mathematical and statistical problems.

2.5.3

Scientific Method and Adaptive Modeling Procedures

The adaptive modeling procedure suggested here is scientific according to the definitions supplied by Braithwaite and Popper. The procedure assumes that no one source of knowledge is authoritative. Also, though the composite model may be subjectively constructed and evaluated (via an objective function), the conclusions derived from its deductive system must permit empirical testing against subsequent data.

A true statement must correspond with facts; a false statement may also correspond with some facts but it can be disproved by other facts (that is,

---

[17] Braithwaite, *Scientific Explanation*, p. 22.
[18] *Ibid.*, p. 93.

new empirical tests). Progress is made by testing and refuting theories and developing new theoretical systems that correspond to more of the known facts. Popper makes the following analogy:

The status of truth may be compared to that of a mountain peak which is permanently, or almost permanently, wrapped in clouds. The climber may not merely have difficulties in getting there—he may not know when he gets there, because he may be unable to distinguish, in the clouds, between the main summit and some subsidiary peak. Though it may be impossible for the climber ever to make sure that he has reached the summit, it will often be easy for him to realize that he has not reached it. Similarly, there will be cases when we are quite sure that we have not reached the truth. Thus while coherence, or consistency, is no criterion of truth, incoherence or inconsistency do establish falsity; so, if we are lucky, we may discover inconsistencies and use them to establish the falsity of some of our theories.[10]

2.5.4
Special Characteristics of the Social Sciences

According to many observers the differences between the physical and social sciences are less significant than their similarities, and, in fact, social sciences (particularly economics) are at a point that corresponds to an early stage of development in the physical sciences. Koopmans, for example, compares the empirical work of the National Bureau of Economic Research to the "Kepler stage" of celestial mechanics and the more theoretical basis of the econometric work of the Cowles commission to the "Newton stage."[20] The reference to celestial mechanics by the economists and the examples drawn from astronomy by Popper and Braithwaite are particularly appropriate for a discussion of the social sciences since experimentation is difficult in both economics and astronomy. Einstein's hypothesis that light waves are subject to gravitational forces had to wait for the appropriate astronomical event before it could be tested; Keynes' theory that government manipulation of gross investment was possible and could stabilize the economy had to wait for the appropriate economic and political event before it could be tested. Thus, a comparison of methodologies indicates that one "essential difference" between physical and social sciences—that is, the ability to experiment in the one and the general inability in the other—can be eliminated.

A comparison of the differences in the subject matter of the physical and

[19] Popper, *Conjectures and Refutations*, p. 187.
[20] Koopmans, *Readings in Business Cycles*, pp. 186–231.

social sciences is as important as a comparison of the differences in the applicable methodologies. Large socioeconomic systems have two distinctive characteristics: they are adaptive and they are unique.

Social science is more closely related to biology than physics because social systems are adaptive. Among the natural sciences, human psychology is probably a better analogy than general biology because the object under observation changes in response to the research performed; however, the fact that the single, long-lived subject and the researcher (economist) are part of the same system creates a special situation for the economic sciences. For example, knowledge resulting from observation of the monetary crunch of the summer of 1966 unalterably changed the economic system. In this case, neither the Federal Reserve Board nor the housing industry would react in the same way if a similar situation were to arise;[21] immediately after the economists discovered and accepted new knowledge, the system was no longer the same.

Experiments on social systems cannot be truly replicated because the systems are unique. Thus the special difficulty in economic research—compared to biological studies—is that there is only one specimen.

[21] Indeed, they did not in 1969.

3

The objective function is used by the decision maker to choose among outcomes associated with alternative economic policies. Creating the objective function has been defined as the role of the policy maker; we must investigate the means by which a policy maker may explicitly express his preferences and thus provide guidelines for the decision maker.[1]

Traditionally, objective functions for socioeconomic systems are discussed in terms of welfare theory; however, the direct relationship of welfare theory to economic decision making is not readily apparent. Welfare theory does provide a rationale for certain fundamental viewpoints,[2] but its reliance on immeasurable concepts (such as individual or community welfare functions) frequently makes it useless when practical decisions have to be made. However, Holt[3] suggests that the concepts should be studied and can be made useful. While noting the economist's usual skepticism, he points out that "the goal structures of most societies are sufficiently cohesive to keep the societies from falling apart," and concludes that there is "a body of shared values that are relevant to economic policy choices."

The purpose of this chapter is to relate welfare and utility theory to obtainable data so that policy makers may specify an objective function that is useful to decision makers.

3.1
Objective Functions for Choosing among Alternatives
Recall that the decision-making problem is

$$\max \Phi = \Phi(X, Y)$$

subject to

$$X = G(\Pi \mid Y)$$

where Φ is the value of the objective function, X is the set of uncontrollable

[1] Roles of the decision maker, planner, and policy maker are defined in Chapter 1.
[2] Example viewpoints include: perfect competition and marginal cost pricing are optimal conditions; income taxes are preferable to excise taxes; and marginal cost pricing policies should be used by regulated industries. See the seminal work of Harold Hotelling, "The General Welfare in Relation to Problems of Taxation and Railway and Utility Rates," *Econometrica*, vol. 6 (1938) pp. 242–269; see also, Richard G. Lipsey and Kelvin Lancaster, "The General Theory of the Second Best," *Review of Economic Studies*, vol. 24 (1956), pp. 11–32.
[3] Charles C. Holt, "Quantitative Decision Analysis and National Policy: How Can We Bridge the Gap?" *Quantitative Planning of Economic Policy*, B. G. Hickman, ed. (Washington, D.C.: The Brookings Institution, 1965), p. 256.

variables, Y is the set of instruments or controllable variables, and Π is the set of parameters in the transformation function G.

It is important when developing a model to identify whether each variable and parameter in the model is an instrument (controllable variable) or a constraint (uncontrollable variable) and also to determine if it occurs in the objective function. Furthermore, the role of the decision maker must be specified (to a greater extent than is usually possible in the real world) because a variable that is a constraint to one decision maker may be an instrument to another.

Also, there is a difference between the objective function and the model which predicts its value. A model that is to be used for decision analysis requires an objective function, but an objective function can be developed before specifying the model or defining the decision-making roles; thus it is possible to distinguish between policy-making and decision-making roles. The policy-making role and function takes precedence in the organization and in the process. In fact in certain circumstances (illustrated in Chapters 4 and 5 by the growth model), decisions automatically follow once the objective function is explicitly stated.

3.1.1
Constructing Objective Functions

Models of consumer behavior (which attempt to explain or predict decisions, not to help make them) generally take the form

$$U = f(q_i, p_i, w). \tag{3.1}$$

In this case, the value of the objective function is U, the utility of the individual consumer; the instruments are q_i, the quantities of each good purchased; the parameters are p_i, the prices of each good (which relate quantities to expenditures); and the constraint (that is, the independent variable in the constraint equation) is w, the consumer's income.

Economists use models of the firm to explain its behavior; managers of the firm use them to help make operating decisions. These models frequently take the form

$$P = F(x_i, q, r_i, p). \tag{3.2}$$

In this case, the value of the objective function is P, the profit of the firm; the instruments are x_i, the input requirements per unit output (that is, the manager can choose his production function) and q, the output quantity; the factor prices r_i are the parameters (assuming a competitive economy) and the constraint is p, the selling price.

In both cases, the decision maker seeks a system configuration—that is, an optimum setting of the instruments—that maximizes the value of the model. Thus, in the first example the consumer equates the marginal rates of substitution of each pair of goods to the price ratio, and in the second example the manager of the firm equates marginal revenue to marginal costs (assuming the corresponding functions are differentiable).

The value of the objective function, in both examples, is given by complex functions of all the model variables in Equations 3.1 and 3.2. However, generally the objective function can be evaluated by a subset of the model's elements. Thus for the utility-maximizing consumer, utility is evaluated by

$$U = U(q_1) \tag{3.3}$$

and for the profit-maximizing manager of the firm, profit is measured by

$$P = P(x_i, q, r_i, p) = pq - \Sigma x_i r_i. \tag{3.4}$$

Equation 3.3 contains only the instruments of the corresponding Equation 3.1; in contrast Equation 3.4 contains both the instruments and the constraint of Equation 3.2.

By definition, the evaluating function (Equations 3.3 and 3.4) is the objective function. There is a basic difference between these two objective functions (it may be argued that profit maximizing is a special, simpler case of the general utility function). Most economists agree that individual utilities cannot be measured; thus these cannot be compared or added to obtain an aggregate quantity. Profit, however, is a measurable quantity that can be computed (by using the right-hand side of Equation 3.4); thus if the appropriate cost-accounting data are available and the same basic computational procedures are used by all firms, then the profits of different firms can be compared, added, and so forth.

3.1.2

Alternative Approaches

A review of the theory of utility shows three approaches for choosing alternatives corresponding to three types of objective functions—the cardinal, the ordinal, and the vector choice. The domain of each is the n-dimensional space formed by n elements (for example, collection of n goods). The range of the cardinal function is the measurable (in the sense that it is meaningful to compare distances) real line. The range of the ordinal function is again the real line (one point of which corresponds to each indifference surface), but the line is unitless and elastic. The range of the vector-choice function is a set of feasible alternatives.[4]

Solutions to cardinal objective functions are one-dimensional; that is, a single number is obtained each time the function is evaluated. The alternative that maximizes the value of the number is the best choice.

Solutions to ordinal objective functions are one-dimensional but cannot be measured. If, however, the objective function and the constraining functions are differentiable and well-behaved (it is assumed, throughout this work, that all functions are real-valued functions of real variables), the usual procedure is (1) to use Lagrangean multipliers in each inequality to obtain strict equalities and to insure that the solution is at an extreme point of the feasible set, (2) to differentiate with respect to the controllable variables, and (3) to determine the marginal conditions or relationships between the instruments and the constraints required to obtain the first- and second-order conditions for maximizing. (This procedure is also applicable to cardinal objective functions if the equations of the model are differentiable and well behaved.)

Solutions to a vector-choice objective function are multidimensional. The basic premise is that the objective function is not differentiable (thus, equating marginal utilities is impossible) but that rational individuals can make consistent choices among alternative outcomes or collections of goods.

Kenneth Arrow gives two theorems of social choice that show (Theorem 1) that democratic social choice is possible if only two alternatives exist, but the choice must be imposed (Theorem 2), or dictated if there are more than two alternatives.[5] Theorems 1 and 2, taken together, are the logical foundation for a political system that allows the majority to select one of two alternative political parties and then empowers representatives of the elected party to impose their choice on the society. That is, a social choice based on individual preferences is obtained through the selection of the elected party, while the elected policy maker provides the objective function that guides specific decisions. It is assumed, in this book, that the policy maker's objective function is rational but also that it generally corresponds to Arrow's social choice function (that is, the policy maker seeks to represent the interests of society).

[4] This approach assumes that the set of alternatives at any stage in the decision-making process is finite and small; for most real decision making this is true.
[5] K. Arrow, *Social Choice and Individual Values*, Cowles Foundation Monograph No. 12 (New York, N.Y.: John Wiley & Sons, 1951), p. 59.

The policy maker provides the required transformation from the large group of preference functions, held by individuals within society, to the single social choice function; this transformation is the subject of this chapter. The policy maker's objective function (that is, social choice) is analogous to the consumer's utility function; the vectors representing the alternative collections of goods in the consumer's utility function are replaced by the vectors representing the alternative sets of social goods that are the elements in the policy maker's objective function.

Whether the objective function is of the cardinal, ordinal, or vector type will determine if it can be evaluated numerically (if indifference curves can be constructed) or if the policy maker can only rank specific alternatives.

Let us look at the types of objective function that should be used for the specific problem of allocating public health expenditures as an example. A cost-effectiveness technique is used to allocate expenditures for public health programs;[6] thus the value of the objective function is one of program effectiveness rather than one of personal utility or profit.

3.2
Objective Functions for Microeconomic Decision Making
Recently there has been an attempt to apply cost-effectiveness analysis to the allocation of government expenditures for programs (for example, defense, public health, urban renewal, and so forth).[7] The problem facing the government decision maker is analogous to that facing the consumer and the manager; however, the value of the objective function in this situation is program effectiveness rather than utility or profit.[8] Assuming that the budget is fixed, the decision maker attempts to maximize effectiveness under the budget (and other) constraints.

3.2.1
The Concept of Cost Effectiveness
For each budget level and specific set of constraints, there is at least one system configuration that will maximize the objective function. Each

[6] For a fuller discussion, see Arnold H. Packer, "Applying Cost-Effectiveness Concepts to the Community Health System," *Operations Research*, vol. 16, no. 2 (March–April 1968), pp. 227–253.
[7] See *Program Budgeting*, David Novick, ed. (Cambridge, Mass.: Harvard University Press, 1965); especially A. Smith's "Conceptual Framework for the Program Budget," pp. 24–60 and G. Fisher's "The Role of Cost-Utility Analysis in Program Budgeting," pp. 61–78.
[8] Bert G. Hickman, ed., "Introduction," in *Quantitative Planning of Economic Policy* (Washington, D.C.: The Brookings Institution, 1965), p. 2.

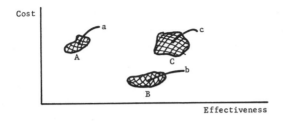

Figure 3.1.   Cost-effectiveness alternatives.

configuration is the result of a program; thus if the most effective program is implemented, the most effective configuration will be achieved.

If effectiveness is measurable, analysis can provide ratios of effectiveness to cost and indicate the marginal effectiveness of additional expenditure.[9] Interval, rather than point, estimates of cost and effectiveness are made if uncertainty exists. In Figure 3.1, the crosshatched areas (A, B, C) indicate the predicted bivariate cost-effectiveness interval for three alternative system configurations. (More complete information will reduce uncertainty and diminish the areas A, B, and C surrounding the expected values.) Points a, b, and c within the areas represent the expected value of the cost and effectiveness variables.

Even if effectiveness is not measurable, some choices can be made; for example, since System A is dominated, under all circumstances by System B, it need not be considered further. (System A is less effective and more costly than B.) Assuming the budget is a controllable variable, the policy maker may choose between Systems B and C.

3.2.2

Approaches to Evaluating Effectiveness

Corresponding to the three theories of utility, there are three approaches for evaluating effectiveness. The first, in accord with the cardinal theory, is to derive a cardinal utility function that assigns a numerical value to each alternative outcome;[10] this approach places a numerical scale on the abscissa of a cost-effectiveness graph such as that shown in Figure 3.1.

[9] Peter D. Fox, "A Theory of Cost-Effectiveness for Military Systems Analysis," *Operations Research*, vol. 13, no. 2 (March–April 1965), pp. 191–202.
[10] These are often referred to as von Neumann–Morgenstern functions; see John von Neumann and Oskar Morgenstern, *Theory of Games and Economic Behavior* (Princeton, N.J.: Princeton University Press, 1944); see also P. C. Fishburn, *Decision and Value Theory* (New York, N.Y.: John Wiley & Sons, 1964).

The second approach, in accord with ordinal utility theory, would not assume that a numerical value can be assigned to each effectiveness vector but rather that vectors can be continuously ordered—that is, one vector is better than, worse than, or equivalent to another. Thus the scale of abscissa would become indeterminate (that is, unitless and elastic) and a statement could be made about relative, not absolute, effectiveness. For example, the system configuration represented by Point c is more effective than Point b, and Point b is more effective than Point a; however, there is no way to measure or even compare these differences. Whether additional effectiveness is worth the additional cost must be left to the policy maker's subjective value judgement. Thus, with ordinal utility theory, the concepts of marginal effectiveness and cost-effectiveness ratios lose their meaning.

The third approach is to present the policy maker with an effectiveness vector corresponding to each alternative system configuration and allow him to make his own choice. This approach is used for most evaluations of complex systems.

Let us now apply the three approaches (cardinal effectiveness, ordinal effectiveness, and vector choice) to evaluate public health programs within that part of the socioeconomic system directly related to the health of its members.

EVALUATING ALTERNATIVE HEALTH PROGRAMS

Expenditures for health and medical care services in 1969 was approximately $59 billion, or 6.4 percent of the Gross National Product (GNP); public expenditures amounted to more than $23 billion, or almost 40 percent of this amount. Since 1955, annual expenditures have increased 260 percent; this increased the percentage of GNP expended for health and medical care by more than half.

Public expenditures have risen more rapidly than the total; its share has increased from 23.4 percent in 1955 to 39.9 percent in 1969.[11] By 1969 the per capita total expenditure was approaching $300; it had almost doubled in 14 years. It has been estimated that by 1975 expenditures for the goods and services of the health industry will be greater than for any other U.S. industry and that 3.8 million people will be employed in health occupations.[12] It is prudent to use cost-effectiveness procedures to allocate resources of this magnitude.

[11] Budget of the U.S. Government, Fiscal 1972 (Washington, D.C.: U.S. Government Printing Office, 1971), pp. 62, 63.
[12] U.S. Dept. Health, Education, and Welfare, *Reference Facts on Health, Education and Welfare* (Washington, D.C.: U.S. Government Printing Office), January 1966, p. 6.

A necessary precondition to the development of measures of effectiveness required for cost-effectiveness analysis is an acceptable, qualitative statement of basic goals. The statement must be sufficiently comprehensive so that alternative programs, whose specific aims are often strikingly diverse, may be evaluated against basic goals.

For example, the goals of communicable disease, vector (insects, rodents) control, and accident prevention programs are to reduce the incidence of specific health problems. Hospitals, diagnostic and treatment centers, ambulances and other emergency equipment, and chronic disease and rehabilitation programs attempt to ameliorate the effects of specific diseases. Health education, environmental control (sanitation, noise abatement, and air, water, and land pollution control), and certain preventive health programs are aimed at a broad spectrum of health problems. Mental and emotional health activities and social welfare programs (economic development, general education, health insurance, housing, poverty alleviation) often require a complete restatement of basic objectives. If the yardstick—whether a general qualitative statement of goals or a precise measure of effectiveness—is to be universally applied, it must be able to cope with the diversity of goals in the health field.

One approach has been the development of a health index—an index of community health that could measure the effectiveness of alternative programs. However, an acceptable index that is both sensitive to the effectiveness of health programs and composed of measurable components has proven elusive.

Indices of crude and age-adjusted death rates have been used. However since 1956, the death rates in the United States have been relatively constant; thus greater attention has been paid to morbidity. Since increased morbidity is often the result of reduced mortality (for example, the longevity of diabetics has increased morbidity but decreased mortality), the evaluation of any combination of mortality and morbidity rates must be interpreted.

D. F. Sullivan suggested classifying morbidity by four categories of disability: confined, limited mobility, limited activity, and restricted activity.[13] C. L. Chiang proposed an index composed of age-specific components derived from the death rate and incidence and duration of

[13] National Center for Health Statistics, USPHS, *Conceptual Problems in Developing an Index of Health* (Washington, D.C.: U.S. Government Printing Office, 1965).

illness.[14] B. S. Saunders suggests measuring health rather than illness and uses a concept of the individual's "adequacy to fulfill a social role."[15] In no case has the development progressed to the point of producing an operationally useful index.

Effectiveness should be a function of measurable variables so that the degree of attainment of the basic goal (community health) can be measured. For instance, the stated goal may be to maintain community health; a secondary goal, derived from the primary one, is to maintain adequate health resources. To obtain a measurable variable, health officials may attempt to maintain a minimum, per capita, number of hospital beds, or practicing physicians. In the following discussion, variables for measuring effectiveness will be applicable, in a primary sense, to many health programs, but in certain instances, they will be related to the basic goal in a secondary or tertiary manner.

The basic goal, or objective, of public health programs may be stated as the absence of ill health. Thus the objective function would measure ineffectiveness; effectiveness would be complementary.

A Cardinal Objective Function: As viewed by an individual, ineffectiveness is some weighted sum of his chance of being in any state of ill health for a finite time period. If m discrete states of impairment are defined to represent various disability levels (and ultimately death), then ineffectiveness is

$$I^p = \sum_{i=l}^{m} c_i t_i \tag{3.5}$$

where I^p is the individual's measure of ineffectiveness, c_i is the weighting factor, and t_i is the duration of stay in state i. The value of I^p must be obtained from an analysis of each potential hazard the individual faces; one of m disability states is assigned to each definable stage of each disease or accident, and then the time in each state is estimated. To avoid double counting, a single disability state is assigned when multiple diseases and/or accidents are involved; that is, the measure of ineffectiveness aggregates all diseases and accidents to which a single individual is simultaneously vulnerable. A reasonable starting point for determining m, the number of disability states, might be to use the four morbidity levels suggested by

[14] U.S. Public Health Service, *An Index of Health—Mathematical Models* (Washington, D.C.: U.S. Government Printing Office, 1965).
[15] B. S. Saunders, "Measuring Community Health Levels," *American Journal of Public Health*, vol. 54, no. 7 (July 1965), pp. 1063–1070.

Sullivan and to add two states: an initial state (controlled disease—minor disability) and a terminal state (premature death); that is, m would be six. (The duration of stay in the terminal state is defined as the actuarially estimated reduction in life span as a result of bad health.)

How can individual ineffectiveness be aggregated to obtain a measure for the community? A function is needed to relate the community's measure of ineffectiveness to the number of individuals in each state of impairment. Every individual in each disability state burdens the community by demanding additional health resources and, at the same time, diminishes the community's capacity to cope with the burden since the individual is less productive and because the facilities may become saturated. Thus, the ineffectiveness function should be monotonic and should have a derivative that increases as the number of ill persons increases.

One possible aggregation scheme is to multiply the individual measures of ineffectiveness by a ratio of the form:

Number of people in disability state i

Total population — number in disability state i

Another possible aggregation scheme is the exponential form that expresses ineffectiveness as

$$k_i = c_i t_i e^{\alpha x_i} \tag{3.6}$$

where for each disability state, k_i is the community's measure of the health system's ineffectiveness, x_i is the number of individuals in the state for time t_i, α is an appropriate constant (α can be replaced by α_i to permit assignment of a second constant to each state), and c_i is the policy maker's evaluation of the disutility attached to the state. The expected value of system effectiveness under these assumptions is given by

$$\bar{S} = 1 - \sum_{i=1}^{m} c_i \exp (t_i) \exp (e^{\alpha x_i}).$$

Admittedly, since the policy maker must choose the appropriate value for c_i, effectiveness remains partially dependent on subjective value judgements. Initial insight may be obtained by estimating the weights implicitly assigned by current health programs. (It would be interesting to compare the weights currently assigned various programs. For example: Is the implicit value of an extra year's life implied by kidney disease or cancer programs equivalent to that implied by accident prevention or preventive health programs?) Also, individuals reveal preferences by their expenditure decisions; demand (income-expenditure) studies might indicate the relative value or disutility implicitly assigned to certain health problems by individuals in the marketplace.

The results obtained from a cardinal effectiveness measure would be invariant under any linear transformation; however, if the policy maker's effectiveness function is ordinal, the results would have to be invariant under any monotonic transformation. This implies that the results obtained under an ordinal ranking would be independent of the values assigned to the disutility weights c_i, c_2, . . . , c_6; that is, the problem of comparing alternative disability states could be avoided.

An Ordinal Objective Function: The ordinal approach assumes the policy maker is indifferent to the combination of results represented by any of the points on an m-dimensional indifference surface ($m = 6$ if effectiveness can be described by Sullivan's four states plus the two other suggested disability states).

Theoretically if effectiveness is measured by an ordinal function, an optimum is achieved when the ratio of marginal utilities is equated to the ratio of marginal costs; that is, effectiveness is maximized at the point where the m-dimensional hyperplane, representing the budget restraint, is tangent to the indifference surface. Thus, an optimum configuration would be obtained if

$$\frac{\dfrac{\partial E}{\partial x_i}}{\dfrac{\partial E}{\partial x_j}} = \frac{\dfrac{\partial B}{\partial x_i}}{\dfrac{\partial B}{\partial x_j}} \qquad \begin{array}{l} (i = 1, 2, \ldots, m) \\[2ex] (j = 1, 2, \ldots, m) \end{array} \tag{3.7}$$

where for each state i, $\partial E/\partial x_i$ is the rate of change in effectiveness relative to the number of disability man-months[16] and $\partial B/\partial x_i$ is the (perhaps variable) expenditure required per unit decrease in disability man-months (that is, cost of improvement).

If the relevant budget hyperplane and indifference surface are known, the c_i do not need to be estimated to determine the optimum point for a given expenditure level. However, because the abscissa of Figure 3.1 is unitless and elastic, there is no way to evaluate alternative expenditure

---

[16] The integrability assumption is necessary to obtain the results shown; if a disability man-month unit is too large to maintain the assumption, a man-day or man-hour could be used.

levels, because neither computation of cost-effectiveness ratios nor comparison of alternative cost-effectiveness levels is possible. Furthermore, each time a new budget level is evaluated, a new indifference surface and budget hyperplane must be defined.

The ordinal approach does permit elimination of dominated (more costly and no more effective) solutions; however, a vector-choice function eliminates them without requiring definitions of the indifference surfaces or budget hyperplanes.

A Vector-Choice Objective Function: Assume that effectiveness can be related to a finite list of elements; the list might include age-specific death rates, incidence and prevalence of disease, indications of mental health, and so forth. If the elements are numbered $1, 2, \ldots, n$, the list can be represented by an n-dimensional effectiveness vector where the elements take on different values for alternative system configurations. For example, the vector $\mathbf{x}' = (x_1', x_2', \ldots, x_n')$ would denote the results of program X, and $\mathbf{y}' = (y_1', x_2', \ldots, y_n')$ would denote the results of program Y.

The assumption that a policy maker can only choose between distinct alternatives seems to imply that the analysis is complete when the alternative vectors have been specified, however, this is not the case. If each of the n elements of the vector is placed into one or more (not necessarily mutually exclusive) sets $A, B, \ldots, M$, then m measurable utility (or subobjective) functions can be defined as follows:

$$x_1 = \phi_A(x_1') \qquad \text{where } i \text{ is an element of } A;$$
$$x_2 = \phi_B(x_j') \qquad \text{where } j \text{ is an element of } B;$$

$$\vdots$$

$$x_m = \phi_M(x_k') \qquad \text{where } k \text{ is an element of } M.$$

In this way the basic vector $(x_1', x_2', \ldots, x_n')$ can be replaced by a new vector $(x_1, x_2, \ldots, x_m)$.

If in general, x_i is more directly related to the program's basic goals than x_i' and if m is less than n, then the transformation is useful. For example, six disability states can define the effectiveness vectors $\mathbf{x}, \mathbf{y}, \mathbf{z}$ that result from alternative programs X, Y, Z even when the basic data denoted by vectors $\mathbf{x}', \mathbf{y}', \mathbf{z}'$ are in different terms. A typical element x_i of $\mathbf{x}$ is case-months in disability state i, while a typical element x_i' of $\mathbf{x}'$ is number of inoculations, hospital beds, and so forth.

Making vector transformations from inoculations to case-months ($\mathbf{x}'$ to $\mathbf{x}$, $\mathbf{y}'$ to $\mathbf{y}$, etc.) does not provide a general solution to the problem of comparing alternatives, because any attempt to aggregate individual utility functions (for example, Equation 3.5) requires interpersonal welfare comparisons. Values assigned to each c_i may vary among individuals at any point in time or for a single individual among different points in time. The problem is generally insoluble because the solution requires a social indifference curve or a preference function for interpersonal comparisons of welfare. The general insolubility does not indicate that solutions are not possible or that reasonable approximations cannot be made for important particular cases. In fact, the vector function can provide an unambiguous choice for many real decisions if the situation is analogous to the conditions of Pareto optimality. (The choice is made from alternatives with known consequences; uncertainty, which is ignored in this discussion, complicates the analysis but does not alter basic conclusions.) Under these conditions, a feasible alternative to the "optimal" decision creates additional case-months in some disability state without offsetting reductions in another state.

Another possibility for further extending the area of unambiguous choice is to assume that the disability states can be strictly ordered (for example, limited mobility is strictly preferred to confinement). In this case, any feasible alternative to the optimal decision creates at least one more case-month in a less preferred state for each case-month that is eliminated from a more preferred state.[17]

These two concepts—Pareto optimality and optimality under strict ordering—may be illustrated by a simple example: Assume that the decision maker must choose one of five alternative disease control programs (A, B, C, D, E) and that, for each program, the case-months in each of six disability states are known (Table 3.1). Examine the proposition that Program C is the optimum program. It is unambiguously superior to A on the basis of the analog with Pareto optimality; for each disability state, the number of case-months associated with Program A equals or exceeds the number for C. Program C is unambiguously superior to B under the assumption of strict ordering; under Program B, a reduction in the number of case-months in the more preferred State 4 is offset by the increase in case-months in the less preferred State 5. A comparison between Programs C and D is only a more complicated case of C and B; Program C

[17] The strict ordering conditions specify that for all individuals, if $i < j$ then $c_i < c_j$.

Table 3.1 Estimated Case-Months Resulting from Five Alternative Programs

Disability State	Disease Control Program				
	A	B	C	D	E
1. Minor Disability	1000	1000	1000	900	1000
2. Restricted Activity	1100	1000	1000	1100	0
3. Limited Activity	1200	1000	1000	900	1000
4. Limited Mobility	1000	900	1000	900	1000
5. Confinement	1000	1100	1000	900	1000
6. Premature Death	1000	1000	1000	1300	1001

is unambiguously superior since reductions in more preferred states are at least offset by increases in less preferred states. A comparison between Programs C and E illustrates that no general solution can be found; comparing 1,000 case-months of restricted activity to one additional case-month of premature death is subjective—either C or E could be the optimum program. Whether the outcomes of feasible alternatives are ambiguous or whether they can be clearly ranked is a question that can be answered only for specific cases.

An advantage of the vector-choice function is flexibility; the length of the vector may be expanded arbitrarily and unevenly (that is, length of $\mathbf{x}$ may differ from that of $\mathbf{y}$). Flexibility may be necessary, because it is frequently impossible to relate changes in the number of case-months to effects of alternative actions; that is, the functional relationships between disability state changes and controllable variables or parameters are not known for all programs. For example, while the beneficial emotional and physical effects of comfort care are recognized, it is difficult to quantify the relationship or to establish the point at which comfort no longer serves a useful purpose. In this instance, the choice vectors can be expanded to include terms measuring availability and quality of care. In other instances, the relationships are known from laboratory experiments or case histories. For example, the effectiveness of immunization programs designed to control communicable diseases such as smallpox, diphtheria, influenza, and so forth, may be measured by the probability distribution of secondary cases following one or more initial cases. Also, the effectiveness of detection and treatment programs for controlling communicable diseases (for example, venereal disease, tuberculosis) could be measured directly in terms of the probability distribution of case-months in each disease (disability) state.

This section indicates that welfare theory concepts are useful for health planning—a highly complex discipline that abounds with value judgements concerning the most personal aspects of individual behavior. This conclusion can be extended beyond health planning to other areas of government decision making where the problem is effectively allocating funds among alternative programs. Thus welfare economics is relevant for resource allocation, the microeconomic problem of government.

The next section examines the relevance of welfare theory to constructing objective functions for macroeconomic decision making—the process of determining the fiscal and monetary policy that will maximize total economic welfare through efficient utilization of all resources.

3.3
Objective Functions for Macroeconomic Decision Making
The previous section illustrated the usefulness of welfare theory for microeconomic problems of resource allocation. Whether cardinal, ordinal, or vector-choice objective functions are most appropriate depends on the characteristics of the policy maker, his objectives for the program, and his knowledge of the system. This section extends these concepts to the macroeconomic problems of total resource utilization.

3.3.1
Alternative Approaches
Two objective functions—one using a cardinal approach and the other a vector-choice approach—are suggested in this section. The first is a quadratic function of deviations between actual (predicted) and target values of specific macroeconomic goals; the second relates alternative policies to changes in purchasing power for identifiable subgroups of the population.

A cardinal approach to quantitative analysis can be achieved if a single-valued function of deviations of actual performance from target goals is used; in this case, determining which weights to assign to each target is a problem that must be solved. Otherwise, a vector-choice approach, which extends as far as quantitative analysis can go without omitting considerations that cannot be combined or aggregated, may be adequate. In this case, welfare concepts should be used to obtain the shortest (with the fewest elements) meaningful choice vector.

Questions of who gains from a particular growth rate, who loses by unemployment, who benefits, and who is hurt by price increases can be answered without ethical judgements.[18] If economists can reduce the general welfare function (with its almost infinite number of elements) to a six- to ten-element choice vector, they will perform a valuable service for policy makers—those who must make social policy.

3.3.2
Welfare Criteria

The theory of welfare economics deals with the production and distribution of goods and services. Lerner distinguishes four separable problems—two in production and two in distribution:

1.

Determining the optimum output mix: ". . . the optimum division of a factor among different products so that we do not produce too much of one product and too little of another."[19]

2.

Determining the optimum allocation of input factors (efficiency): ". . . the combination of the factors used in the production of each good."[20]

3.

Determining the optimum distribution of goods: ". . . distributing the available goods among the individuals . . . ."[21]

4.

Determining the optimum division of income: ". . . how much money [income] shall be given . . . [to each individual]."[22]

The analyses given by "new welfare" economists (assuming ordinal and differentiable utility functions) provide solutions, in marginal terms, to Lerner's four problems and thus establish the four solution criteria described by Bergson.[23]

---

[18] Perhaps compensation can be paid to the losers (for example, tie social security, interest rates, and pension payments to the cost-of-living index) for any general welfare-increasing policy that is detrimental to particular population groups.

[19] Abba P. Lerner, *The Economics of Control* (New York, N.Y.: The Macmillan Co., 1946), p. 117.

[20] *Ibid.*

[21] *Ibid.*, p. 7.

[22] *Ibid.*, p. 23.

[23] A. Bergson, "A Reformulation of Certain Aspects of Welfare Economics," *Quarterly Journal of Economics*, vol. 52 (1938), pp. 310–334.

The solution to Lerner's Problem 1 requires that the marginal welfare per "dollar's worth" be equal for all commodities. The solution to Problem 2 (Bergson refers to these as "Lerner conditions") insures that the input factors are optimally allocated so that no alternative allocation could produce more of all goods;[24] the solution requires that wages for each type of labor equal their marginal value productivity. The solution to Problem 3 (Bergson refers to these as "Pareto conditions") requires that marginal rates of substitution for all commodities (including leisure) be equal for all individuals. The solution to Problem 4 (Bergson refers to these as the "Cambridge conditions") requires that the distribution of income shares (not necessarily money) be equal.

The last condition, concerning the distribution of income, is not generally considered as part of macroeconomics, the subject of the following sections.

3.3.3
Current Macroeconomic Goals and Welfare Criteria

The most explicit statement of United States macroeconomic goals is contained in the Employment Act of 1946; it states that it is the responsibility of the Federal Government to "promote maximum employment, production, and purchasing power."[25] Twenty years later it was possible to add, ". . . the new concerns of price stability and growth into the act by identifying maximum production with growth and maximum purchasing power with price stability."[26]

The connection between the macroeconomic goals and the welfare criteria are tenuous at best. A primary reason may be that welfare models are static (for example, optimum distribution and allocation of fixed quantities), while the problems of growth are dynamic.[27]

The goals of maximum employment and growth can, however, be related to the solutions to Lerner's four welfare problems. For example, reducing involuntary unemployment tends to equate the marginal utility

---

[24] Neither Bergson nor Lerner distinguishes between constraints and instruments in the welfare function. If the community welfare function is the sum of individual utility functions, it is evaluated by the labor inputs and the commodities and services consumed; if the production function constraint is included, the problems of encouraging technological change, etc., should also be investigated. (Then, perhaps, pure competition will not be so readily identified with maximum welfare.)

[25] *Employment Act of 1946*, U.S. Congress, Sec. 2, "Policy Section," 1946.

[26] U.S. Congress, Joint Economic Committee, *Twentieth Anniversary of the Employment Act of 1946; An Economic Symposium*, 89th Congress, 2d sess., Feb. 23, 1966.

[27] For example, what happens to the welfare function as population increases? Should welfare be summed over the current or some future population?

of leisure with its marginal social product (Problem 1); growth, whether its source is technological change or more extensive use of a fixed production function, implies a more efficient allocation of input factors (Problem 2).

In contrast, the goal of price stability is difficult to relate to welfare criteria; in fact, in some instances price stability is adverse to the satisfaction of the criteria. For example, equating price ratios with marginal utility ratios to solve Problem 1 requires competition in the selling markets and rapid price adjustment in response to changes in demand or supply; if institutional resistance to downward price movements is strong, a rising price level is required to achieve flexibility in relative prices. Another example is that of achieving price stability at the expense of growth in real output; the result is a decrease in community welfare. A third example is that of obtaining price stability but causing unemployment, another social cost. On the other hand, welfare objectives can be thwarted through unstable prices. A rising price level usually implies an unequal redistribution of income (rather than solving Problem 4). Also, severe instability destroys the usefulness of prices as a resource allocation mechanism (implying failure to solve Problem 2).[28]

Evaluation of any combination of growth, unemployment, and price change is extremely difficult without cardinal utility functions; thus, as a practical matter, policy makers rarely seek the welfare implications of alternative fiscal and monetary policies except in an informal way. Henri Theil points out that the usual response is to attack this problem very informally, taking measures that, hopefully, will lead to a more satisfactory state of affairs. The apparatus of economic theory will usually be employed, of course, but intuition and feeling are frequently the more important ingredients. Theil concludes that "from the standpoint of economic analysis this situation is not satisfactory."[29]

Neither current practice nor the lack of previous success lessens the need for an acceptable objective function. Moreover, the problem is not

[28] Some observers think a changing rate of increase, not a changing price level, is necessary to impair allocation efficiency. A related consideration is the balance-of-payments problem.
[29] H. Theil, "Linear Decision Rules for Macrodynamic Policy Problems," *Quantitative Planning of Economic Policy*, B. G. Hickman, ed. (Washington, D.C.: The Brookings Institution, 1965), pp. 19–42.

hopeless; both a cardinal and a vector-choice objective function are possible solutions.

3.3.4

A Cardinal Objective Function

A cardinal objective function related to the macroeconomic goals described in Section 3.3.3 can be developed. One approach, used by Tinbergen, is to set numerical targets and to develop the objective function in terms of deviations from the targets.[30] Theil suggests the function should be quadratic; for example, if the growth, price change, and employment targets are G^*, P^*, and E^*, respectively, the objective function would take the form

$$\Phi = c_1(G^* - G)^2 + c_2(P^* - P)^2 + c_3(E^* - E)^2 \tag{3.8}$$

where the c_i are arbitrarily assigned values (thus the value judgement problem remains). The symmetrical nature of the quadratic function of Equation 3.8 implies that exceeding a target by a given amount is equivalent to falling short of the target; this result can be avoided by indirectly assigning values to c_1, c_2, c_3. That is, an asymmetric function is created by adding the following to Equation 3.8:

$$c_i = a_i \qquad \text{when } T_i^* > T_i$$

and $\tag{3.8a}$

$$c_i = b_i \qquad \text{when } T_i^* < T_i$$

where T_i are the targets (for example, growth, price change, and employment) and a_i and b_i, which are generally of opposite sign, are the new weights.[31]

Despite the difficulties (previously noted) in relating welfare gains and losses to price level changes and unemployment, target rates of 2 percent (for prices) and 4 percent (for unemployment) have often been mentioned. Use of these rates is based on the concept of the Phillips curve (see Figure

---

[30] Jan Tinbergen, *Economic Policy: Principles and Design* (Amsterdam: North-Holland Publishing Co.), 1956; see also, Charles E. Ferguson, *Macroeconomic Theory of Workable Competition* (Durham, N.C.: Duke University Press, 1964), chap. 3.

[31] The interaction terms $[c_4(G^* - G)(P^* - P) + c_5(G^* - G)(E^* - E) + c_6(P^* - P) \times (E^* - E)]$ that have been omitted to simplify the discussion can also be used to obtain a formulation that reflects the underlying asymmetrical nature of the objective function.

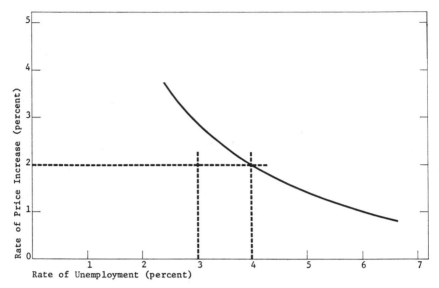

Figure 3.2.   Typical Phillips curve.

3.2), which shows an inverse relationship between the rate of change of prices (or wage rates) and the unemployment rate.[32]

If the quoted target is an optimum, then it must follow that a 2-percent annual price increase and a 4-percent unemployment rate is a point on the Phillips curve and that the marginal equality

$$\frac{\text{Change in welfare}}{\text{Change in the rate of price level increase}}$$

$$= \frac{\text{Change in welfare}}{\text{Change in the unemployment rate}}$$

---

[32] See, A. W. Phillips, "The Relation Between Unemployment and the Rate of Change of Money Wages in the United Kingdom, 1862–1957," *Economica*, vol. 25, no. 4 (Nov. 1958), pp. 283–299; Richard G. Lipsey, "The Relation Between Unemployment and the Rate of Change of Money Wage Rates in the United Kingdom, 1862–1957: A Further Analysis," *Economica*, vol. 27, no. 1 (Feb. 1960), pp. 1–31; Paul A. Samuelson and Robert M. Solow, "Analytical Aspects of Anti-Inflation Policy," *American Economic Review*, vol. 50, no. 2 (May 1960), pp. 177–194; and Lawrence R. Klein and Ronald G. Bodkin, "Empirical Aspects of the Trade-Offs Among Three Goals: High Level Employment, Price Stability, and Economic Growth," *Inflation, Growth, and Employment, Commission on Money and Credit* (Englewood Cliffs, N.J.: Prentice-Hall, 1964), pp. 367–428. See also, George L. Perry, "The Determinants of Wage Rate Changes and the Inflation-Unemployment Trade-off for the United States," *The Review of Economic Studies*, vol. 30, no. 4 (Oct. 1964), pp. 287–308; and George L. Perry, *Unemployment, Money Wage Rates, and Inflation* (Cambridge, Mass.: The MIT Press, 1966).

is satisfied at that point on the Phillips curve; only then is it an optimum point in a welfare sense.

Fromm and Taubman criticize three aspects of Theil's quadratic approach and suggest several alternatives.[33] They point out that the inter-action terms must be included because of the symmetric nature of the usual quadratic form, that the targets cannot be chosen arbitrarily since they must be on the production possibility frontier, and that the targets must be chosen so that utility is maximized when all deviations are zero. The addition of Equation 3.8a to Equation 3.8 may be a partial answer to these criticisms. The two equations are employed in the stabilization problem described in Chapter 6.

Fromm and Taubman suggested a cardinal function be used that is mathematically identical to the constant elasticity of substitution (CES) function frequently used as a production function. With appropriate parameters, a CES function exhibits diminishing marginal utilities and rates of substitution. The properties of the CES function are well known, especially in the special Cobb-Douglas form. Using a CES utility function eliminates the need for stating the targets quantitatively. (Whether this is a virtue or not is debatable.) Also, the CES form is inconvenient for such things as price changes that are inherently asymmetric about a null point.

A cardinal function based on macroeconomic goals is more difficult to relate to welfare theory than is a vector-choice function. This difficulty reflects the fact that unemployment, price stability, and economic growth are really secondary objectives.

3.3.5
A Vector-Choice Objective Function

The greatest difficulty impeding the development of a welfare function is the ultimate incomparability of individual utilities. Circumstances favorable to the farmer frequently are injurious to the urbanite; the interests of business often oppose those of labor, and so forth. If the population were homogeneous, in the sense that any particular set of economic events would affect all members in a similar way, the difficulty would be less. Unfortunately, even the large population groups themselves (farmers, urban, business, labor) are not homogeneous. For example, salaries of some wage earners are fixed, while wage rates of others are adjusted for changes in the cost-of-living index; thus, the two subgroups are affected

[33] Gary Fromm and Paul Taubman, *Policy Simulations with an Econometric Model* (Washington, D.C.: The Brookings Institution, 1968), pp. 106–110.

differently by price increases. Because the size and composition of groups and subgroups change, the analysis is more difficult; for example, an evaluation of the welfare of the aged (or unemployed) depends on the size of the group as well as the welfare of the individuals within the group.

If a vector-choice function is used, the analysis of each alternative economic strategy should produce a vector, consisting of a reasonable number of elements, which a policy maker can evaluate. The policy maker's evaluation would be based on his own ethical judgement; if the analysis is complete, the elements would be fundamental and would measure the welfare objective in a primary sense.

For example, a vector, for choosing among macroeconomic alternatives, might contain two elements for each identifiable group within the population; one element would measure the size of the group and the other the average per capita change in purchasing power that would follow from the various alternatives.

A feasible scheme could be achieved if the population were divided according to current data series (rural farm, rural nonfarm, manufacturing employees, nonmanufacturing employees, proprietors, government employees, unemployed, retired, and so forth). Conceptually, a more satisfying division (but a more difficult one for the model builder) would be income groups; it may require transformation from the first vector—that is, knowledge of the income distribution of manufacturing employees, and so forth. If the population groups are of equal size, the second subgroup of elements (indicating group size) could be omitted.

A vector of this type would be analogous to the one suggested for public health expenditures. If each element of vector **x** resulting from economic policy X is at least equal to the corresponding element in **y** and if one element is superior, then X is unequivocally superior to Y;[34] that is, if the purchasing power of one subgroup is greater under policy X than under Y and no other subgroup is better off under Y than under X, then policy X is unequivocally superior to Y. Furthermore, if improvement in the purchasing power can be strictly ordered for income classes, the area of unambiguous choice can be further extended; that is, if income equality (or purchasing power equality) is a welfare objective, then improvement for one income class is preferred to an equivalent improvement for any other higher income class.

[34] The phrase "economic policy" is the macroeconomic equivalent of "program" in the discussion of public health expenditures.

Table 3.2   Estimated Change in Purchasing Power Resulting from Five Alternative Macroeconomic Policies (Family-dollars)

Annual Family Income	Macroeconomic Policy*				
	A	B	C	D	E
1. $12,500 and over	1000	1000	1000	1100	1000
2. $9,000–12,499	900	1000	1000	900	2000
3. $6,500–8,999	800	1000	1000	1100	1000
4. $5,000–6,499	1000	1100	1000	1100	1000
5. $3,000–4,999	1000	900	1000	1100	1000
6. Under $3,000	1000	1000	1000	700	999

* Algebraic signs of the difference between C and $A, B, C,$ and E were reversed from Table 3.1, because purchasing power provides utility, but time in a disability state detracts from utility.

Table 3.2 is similar in form to Table 3.1 of the public health example. Policy C is unambiguously superior to A; by using the assumption of strict ordering, C is superior to B and D; in choosing between C and E, the policy maker must make a subjective judgement.

Adequate objective functions are extremely important to quantitative decision making. It is necessary, however, that their limits and underlying assumptions be well understood by both policy makers and decision makers and that they be subject to modification as more insight is gained into the implications of alternative functions; the adaptive modeling procedures described in the following chapters are designed to accomplish these purposes.

4

Allocating Resources: The Static Case under Uncertainty

4.1
The Allocation Problem

Chapters 4 and 5 describe an adaptive modeling procedure for allocating resources. The procedure employs—as its primary model—a growth model that is sufficiently disaggregated and realistic to be useful in economic planning; it uses mathematical programming and obtainable data to allocate resources so as to maximize an adaptively defined (one that can be repetitively changed by the policy maker as he learns the implications of his previous specification) objective function. Such a procedure is useful in a decision-making environment characterized by considerable governmental control of a closed economy. As a normative procedure, it prescribes optimum production programs and investment schedules but does not specify how optimum values are obtained nor what actual production or investment levels are expected. In a mixed economy (the current U.S. experience), prescribed optimal conditions can be useful even if the mechanism for obtaining them is not specified.

The dynamic growth model describes each yearly or quarterly period of the economy's operation with a system of input-output equations of the Leontief type. At the beginning of each period, the capacity, technology, and prices can be changed either through straightforward interperiod linkage equations or through auxiliary models. Linear programming is applied to the short-run or static problem of allocating resources to maximize the objective function, which is written in terms of net output. The shadow prices resulting from the linear programming solution are capital and labor force bottleneck evaluations for each sector of the economy; they are divided by the corresponding capital/output ratios to rank investment opportunities. Next, parametric techniques are used to program investment so that efficient growth can be obtained. Finally, a dynamic programming approach to the long-run problem of intertemporal allocation of resources is suggested.

Chapter 4 presents the procedure for the static case, and Chapter 5 describes the procedure for the dynamic case.

The resource allocation problem discussed in Chapters 4 and 5 can be separated into two interdependent problems: *the static problem* of employing existing resources to produce this period's output, and *the dynamic problem* of investing part of that output to augment the resources and thus determine the feasible output for future periods.

4.1.1
The Static Problem

The static problem is frequently covered in economics texts under the subject of multimarket equilibrium or the Walrasian system.[1] The description usually begins with a barter (or real) system in which the money market is ignored. (This simplifying assumption is maintained in both Chapters 4 and 5.) All markets are interrelated by the (aggregate) preference functions of consumers and the production functions of firms. As a result, the sets of quantities and prices that will keep all markets in equilibrium must be determined simultaneously and a shift in any function will generally change all prices and quantities. The production functions, in the procedure described in this chapter, are given by an input-output model; the consumer preference functions are given by the policy maker. The policy maker must provide the preference functions for each of m categories of final demand. Furthermore, the functions must reflect the interdependencies among the categories; that is, any particular function for one category depends upon a specific set of values (quantities) for the remaining $m - 1$ categories. Rather than ask the policy maker to specify preference functions for each final demand category in terms of the other categories an adaptively defined objective function is used. In this procedure, the policy maker defines m steplike stipulation functions to represent the m preference functions; after each iteration he may examine the resulting (from the linear programming algorithm) quantities in each of the m categories and change any of the stipulation functions that no longer reflect the underlying preference function. Thus, static problems are solved by a series of iterations; each iteration contains a solution of a linear program.

4.1.2
The Dynamic Problem

The dynamic problem is an extension of the static problem or a sequence of static problems at time t_1, t_2, . . . , T (where $T - t_1$ is the duration of the planning horizon) connected by the investment decisions. Leaving aside the question of dividing output between investment and consumption, the investment decision is one of allocating the given investment

[1] For example see James M. Henderson and Richard E. Quandt, *Microeconomic Theory* (New York,: McGraw-Hill Book Co., 1958), pp. 126–163; or M. Blaug, *Economic Theory in Retrospect* (Homewood, Ill.: Richard D. Irwin, 1962), pp. 523–531.

amount among alternative uses; in this case investing in plant and equipment in one or more of the n producing sectors and/or by training labor for one or more of the n sectors. The criterion used for the decision is the capital/output or retraining/output ratios of the $2n$ alternatives. The relevant output in this ratio is not that of the specific sector in which the investment will be made, but the output evaluated by the adaptively defined objective function of the static case. This output is evaluated by the shadow prices contained in the last linear programming iteration; however, it would be more correct to use the shadow prices of the objective functions of future periods in which the new resources are used. Because these are not known until the future periods are reached, the entire process for the dynamic case must be repeated a number of times as the policy maker learns the implications, in future periods, of each period's investment decisions. The result is two sets of adaptive iterations (in addition to the mechanical iteration of the linear programming algorithm) : one set of iterations, in which the objective function is changed, is made for each period t_i in the procedure; a second larger set (encompassing the first) as the entire procedure is repeated for $t_1, t_2, \ldots, T$. Thus, the plan for the static case is a set of production decisions; the plan for the dynamic case includes the investment allocation decisions as well.

4.2
The Primary Model

The terminology defined in Chapter 1 differs somewhat from the typical terminology used to describe linear programming; however, a correspondence can be established. The linear relationships correspond to the primary model; the linear program's solution variables, constraints, and coefficients to the primary model's instruments, uncontrollable variables, and parameters. The objective functions are similar in both cases; the linear program's function is a special case of the more general objective function described, in Chapter 3, for adaptive modeling procedures. A linear programming objective function must be a linear combination of its solution variables (instruments); its cost coefficients are the weights assigned to the variables.

4.2.1
Problem Formulation

The linear programming formulation, described here for a static case, identifies the sector outputs and the elements of final demand as solution variables; the physical capacity and labor availability as constraints (modified by inventory depletion and imports); and the elements of final demand as variables in the objective function.

A dynamic man-machine solution process, in which the man makes changes at each stage in response to new information, is an essential component of adaptive modeling procedures. Frequently, it will be the decision maker who changes the values of his instruments; in the static resource allocation problem, however, the policy maker changes the objective function as he receives information about the results that followed from the objective function he specified in the previous stage. (In the static case, the stages occur at a single point in simulated time; thus the solution process is "dynamic" even though the problem is static.)

The roles in adaptive modeling procedures have been defined as follows: the decision maker sets the instrument values; the planner develops alternatives; and the policy maker defines the objective function. For this particular adaptive procedure, the linear program is the decision maker in the static situation; that is, the algorithm uses the primary model to determine the instrument values that maximize the objective function specified by the policy maker.[2]

The true objective function is based on the vector-choice approach; the policy maker must choose among alternative vectors of final demand. However, a cardinal function that is linear in the elements of the final demand vector is used for the computations. The need to modify this function each time the model is solved indicates that the underlying function is nonlinear, contains interaction terms, and, in general, is too complex to be explicitly stated; that is, there is uncertainty in the objective function.

The problem of allocating industrial resources can be viewed in several ways. For example, if the decision maker sets market prices, one could solve for the optimum input-factor prices; alternatively, if he sets production schedules, one would directly attempt to minimize the use of scarce resources. Each alternative calls for a different primary model and linear programming formulation. Nor are the constraints unequivocally distinguished from the elements of the objective function. If the nature of a variable is such that exceeding a particular limit (for example, reducing

[2] The individual playing the policy-making role in this adaptive procedure may, in fact, be a decision maker or planner. However, since the policy-making role (defined in Chapter 1) is setting the objective function, the noun "policy maker" is used in Chapters 4 and 5 to refer to the man in this man-machine system.

inventory below a "minimum") is considered impossible (it is infinitely costly to exceed the limit), the variable is a constraint; alternatively, if the limit can be exceeded, (for example, corresponding gains are high enough to further deplete inventory), the variable is an element of the objective function.

The appropriate formulation is the one that most closely reflects reality, including the institutional arrangements, responsibilities, and authority of the real policy and decision makers.

4.2.2
Solution Variables

SUPPLY EQUATIONS

The primary model is a standard static Leontief system. An input-output system assumes that: (1) industrial sectors produce n identifiable goods or services (that is, no joint or multiproduct firms), (2) returns-to-scale are constant, and (3) output of each industrial sector is given by a fixed production function.[3]

The three assumptions may be stated mathematically as follows. Let n be the number of industrial sectors; x_i be the total output of the ith sector; y_{ij} be the interindustry output of the ith sector which is required by the jth sector; and b_i be the net output of the ith sector which is available for final demand. The total (gross) output required to satisfy both the interindustry and the final demands of the industrial sector is

$$x_i = \sum_{j=1}^{n} y_{ij} + b_i \qquad i = 1, 2, \ldots, n. \tag{4.1}$$

Required input from sector i is related to total output for sector j by

$$x_j = f^j(x_{1j}, x_{2j}, \ldots, x_{nj}, x_{n+1,j}) \qquad j = 1, 2, \ldots, n \tag{4.2}$$

where f^j is a homogeneous production function of the first degree and x_{n+1} is the nonproduced primary good or the value added. For all sectors, the fixed-proportion production function is

$$y_{ij} = a_{ij}xj \qquad \text{for all } i \text{ and } j \tag{4.3}$$

where a_{ij} is a nonnegative technological coefficient indicating the interindustry output of sector i that is required by sector j to produce a single

---

[3] The description in this book was primarily drawn from R. Dorfman, Paul Samuelson, and Robert Solow, *Linear Programming and Econometric Analysis* (New York: McGraw-Hill Book Co., 1958), pp. 487–493, and G. Hadley, *Linear Programming* (Reading, Mass: Addison-Wesley, 1962), pp. 204–264.

unit of output. If Equation 4.3 is substituted into Equation 4.1,

$$x_i = \sum_{j=1}^{n} a_{ij}xj + b_i \qquad i = 1, 2, \ldots, n. \tag{4.4}$$

Thus, for sector i, stipulation of final demands represented by the net output vector $(b_1, b_2, \ldots, b_n)$ gives a set of n simultaneous linear equations in n variables which, for a real input-output system, can be uniquely solved.

Matrix A, the input-output matrix of a_{ij} coefficients, represents the technology of the economy. Each coefficient specifies the input required from the industrial sector in row i to produce a unit of output from the industrial sector in column j, and each column represents a production function. The basic input-output relationship can be written in matrix form as:

$$\mathbf{x} \qquad - A\mathbf{x} \qquad = \mathbf{b} \tag{4.5}$$

Gross   interindustry   Net
output   demands   output

where $\mathbf{x}$ and $\mathbf{b}$ are n-dimensional column vectors and A is the $n \times n$ technology matrix. To solve for the $\mathbf{x}$ vector,

$$\mathbf{x} = (I - A)^{-1}\mathbf{b} \tag{4.6}$$

where I is the identity matrix. Thus, solving Equation 4.5 we have the gross output of a real system.

FINAL DEMAND EQUATIONS

The net output vector $\mathbf{b}$ can be divided into final demand vectors so that $\mathbf{b} = \mathbf{b}_c + \mathbf{b}_i + \mathbf{b}_g$, where the column vectors correspond to consumption, investment, and government sector expenditures, respectively. Each of the three column vectors may be further disaggregated; for example, the government component of the expenditure may be subdivided into federal, state, and local purchases.

The B matrix of final demand is formed by n vectors (Figure 4.1) numbered according to the following scheme:

$\mathbf{b}_1, \quad \mathbf{b}_2, \quad \ldots, \mathbf{b}_a \quad$ = personal consumption,

$\mathbf{b}_{a+1}, \mathbf{b}_{a+2}, \ldots, \mathbf{b}_b \quad$ = government purchases,

$\mathbf{b}_{b+1}, \mathbf{b}_{b+2}, \ldots, \mathbf{b}_{m-1}$ = investments (except inventories),

$\mathbf{b}_m \quad$ = net inventory changes.

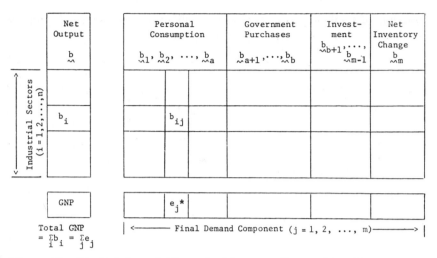

Figure 4.1. The final demand (B) matrix. (Note: $e_j = \Sigma_i b_{ij}$ and $b_i = \Sigma_j b_{ij}$).

Finally,

$$\mathbf{b} = \mathbf{b_1} + \mathbf{b_2} + \cdots + \mathbf{b}_m. \tag{4.7}$$

In the matrix, the sum of the entries in any column gives e_j, the demands of that type; that is, $e_j = \Sigma_i b_{ij}$. Each entry in the net output vector is the sum of all entries in the corresponding row; that is, $b_i = \Sigma_j b_{ij}$ (where $i = 1, 2, \ldots, n, n + 1$) where the $n + 1$ row is the sum row. The sum of the columns equals the sum of the rows:

$$\sum_i b_i = \text{GNP} = \sum_j e_j. \tag{4.8}$$

The entries in the B matrix are quantities—measured in 1958 dollars—of goods and services flowing from industrial sectors to final demand components. If these entries are normalized, a new matrix of demand coefficients is created.

NORMALIZING THE FINAL DEMAND RELATIONSHIPS

If $\mathbf{p}_j$ is a proportioning vector which distributes the e_j among the rows, then

$$e_j\mathbf{p}_j = (b_{1j}, b_{2j}, \ldots, b_{nj}) \qquad j = 1, 2, \ldots, m \tag{4.9}$$

where $\sum_i p_{ij}$ equals one. Let P be a matrix made up of the $\mathbf{p}_j$ vectors which represent final demand patterns with each element p_{ij} representing a fraction of final demand component j obtained from sector i (that is, $p_{ij} = b_{ij}/e_j$). If $\mathbf{e}$ is an m-dimensional final demand vector $(e_1, e_2, \ldots, e_m)$,

$$b = P\mathbf{e}. \tag{4.10}$$

Thus, the P matrix transforms $\mathbf{e}$, which is the disaggregated national income accounts, into a $\mathbf{b}$ vector of net output requirements; that is, p_{ij} denotes the dollars of net output required from industrial sector i to produce a dollar of GNP component expenditure e_j.[4]

The A and P matrices make it convenient to convert the final demand vector $\mathbf{b}$ into the gross output requirement vector $\mathbf{x}$; the matrix conversion is $\mathbf{x} = (I - A)^{-1}\mathbf{b} = (I - A)^{-1}P\mathbf{e}$. The next subsection describes the A and P matrices used in the development of the growth model.

DISAGGREGATION OF SUPPLY AND DEMAND

A heuristic procedure was used to develop the growth model; thus, a small-scale model was constructed with approximate data to experiment with the various concepts; those that seemed reasonable were tested computationally.

The industrial disaggregation scheme for the experimental model was based on an 8-sector economy, corresponding to an 8×8 technology, or the A matrix developed at the Brookings Institution from the 1958 Office of Business Economics (OBE) input-output study. The dimensions are 8×8 for the A matrix and 8×1 for the $\mathbf{b}$ vector. (Table 4.1 lists the producing sectors used in this study and the corresponding sectors of the OBE study.) Choosing the dimensions of the $\mathbf{e}$ final demand vector determines the dimensions of the P matrix; since a 12-element $\mathbf{e}$ vector was chosen, the P matrix is 8×12. (Table 4.2 lists the 12 elements of the $\mathbf{e}$ vector.) For the B matrix (see Figure 4.1), i goes from 1 to 8 for the sectors of Table 4.1, and j goes from 1 to 12 for the categories of Table 4.2 ($a = 7$, $b = 9$, $m = 12$). The "mechanical" relationships[5] of the primary model for the static case are now specified.

---

[4] The units of the net output vector $\mathbf{b}$ are not the same as the final expenditures in the national income and product accounts (for example, the sale of an automobile generates final demand for the manufacturing, transportation, and trade sectors). See: Gary Fromm, "Econometric Models and Defense Policy," unpublished paper presented at the Symposium on the Role of Economic Models in Policy Formulation, Washington, D.C., Oct. 20–21, 1966.

[5] "Mechanical" means that the relationships are not explanatory; they are merely a collection or network that mechanically deduces conclusions from facts. Such theories have been called "reticular." (See Ralph W. Pfouts, "Artistic Goals, Scientific Methods and Economics," *Southern Economic Journal* (April 1967), pp. 459–460.

Table 4.1   Producing Sectors

Sectors of the Model*		Corresponding Industry Numbers in the Input-Output OBE Table†
No.	Description of Sector	
1	Agriculture	1–4
2	Construction	11, 12
3	Trade	69
4	Regulated industries	65–68
5	Residual industries	5–10, 70–77
6	Durable manufacturing	13, 20–23, 35–64
7	Nondurable manufacturing	14–19, 24–34
8	Government enterprises	78, 79, 84

* Michael D. McCarthy, "On the Aggregation of the 1958 Direct Requirements Input/Output Table" (Washington, D.C.: The Brookings Institution, June 1965).
† Office of Business Economics, "The Transactions Table of the 1958 Input-Output Study and Revised Direct and Total Requirement Data," *Survey of Current Business*, September 1965, pp. 33–56.

Table 4.2   Final Demand Categories

Categories of Final Demand		
No.	Description of Expenditures	PCE Categories*
	Personal Consumption	
1	Food and tobacco	I
2	Apparel, personal care, and recreation	II, III, IX
3	Housing and household operation	IV, V
4	Medical services	VI
5	Personal business	VII
6	Transportation	VIII
7	Education and religion	X, XI
	Government	
8	Federal purchases	
9	State and local purchases	
	Investment	
10	Plant and equipment	
11	Residential construction	
12	Net inventory change	

* The personal consumption expenditures (PCE) categories are an aggregation of the 12 sectors used in the 1958 OBE table with the exception of Sector XII—Exports and Imports. See Nancy W. Simon, "Personal Consumption Expenditures in the 1958 Input-Output Study," Table I, Industrial Composition of Personal Consumption Expenditures, *Survey of Current Business* (October 1965).

After **e** has been determined, both **b** and **x** can be calculated from **b** = Pe and **x** = $(I - A)^{-1}$**b**. The technology (or A) matrix and the demand pattern (or P) matrix are assumed to be fixed within a single time period. If the final demand in any period is not drastically different from that of the previous period, the assumption of a constant P matrix is reasonable.[6]

4.2.3

Constraints

For a single time period, the output for each sector is given by a fixed-proportion production function; the function may be ten-dimensional: one for each of eight sectors from which it requires inputs and one for labor and one for capital (value added by the industry itself). The matrix algebra of the input-output relationships acknowledges the first eight dimensions and leaves only the value added by the payments to labor and capital (profit, depreciation, and interest) as true constraints.

Assuming that labor and capital for industry i are the two constraining variables of the value-added gives the constraining inequality for the sector output

$$x_i \leq \min \left[\frac{k_i}{a_{ki}}, \frac{m_i}{a_{mi}} \right] \qquad (4.11)$$

where k_i is the plant and equipment capacity, m_i is the manpower available, a_{ki} is the plant and equipment requirements per unit output, and a_{mi} is the labor requirements per unit output.

The aggregate production function of the economy, for all sectors combined, does not require fixed proportions of labor and capital; these vary with the composition of the net output vector **b** (the output mix). Thus the aggregate production function (in contrast to individual sector functions) can be represented by a classical curve which varies in shape depending on the limits on the composition of output and on the interindustry substitutability of capital and labor.

If labor and capital are both assumed to be homogeneous and perfectly substitutable among sectors, the aggregate output for a given output mix

[6] This is a strong statement of a separable demand function. See: Robert H. Strotz, "The Empirical Implications of a Utility Tree," *Econometrica*, vol. 25 (April 1957), pp. 269–278. Also see: Masazo Sono, "The Effect of Price Changes on the Demand and Supply of Separable Goods," *International Review*, vol. 2, no. 3 (September 1961), pp. 239–271.

is limited by

$$X \leq \min \left[\frac{K}{A_K}, \frac{M}{A_M} \right]. \tag{4.12}$$

(The notation of equation 4.12 is identical to that of equation 4.11 except for uppercase letters referring to aggregate rather than sector variables.) Even if the assumption of perfect substitutability is discarded, the restriction of equation 4.12 must be satisfied.

The two assumptions made concerning substitutability in a single period are that plant and equipment are not substitutable among sectors and that each sector can absorb only a limited increase in labor force. Since the increase is limited to a fixed proportion δ_i in a time period (for example, the labor force of the construction industry can only increase δ_2 percent annually), labor is assumed to be completely homogeneous in any single sector and sufficiently homogeneous among all sectors to permit the addition of δ_i labor units to sector i from any other sector.

Capital and labor constraints limit current domestic output; excess demands for output are met by importing goods or by depleting inventories. In the long run, net imports are limited by the desire to maintain a favorable balance of payments. Similarly, even in a purely technological sense, a working organization cannot entirely deplete its inventories (for example, a steel mill cannot consume all its raw material, in-process, and finished good inventories) and still function. Furthermore, a lower limit, which is substantially higher than the technological minimum, is established on inventories by economic considerations;[7] the minimum for each sector is assumed to be some multiple of last period's output—a minimum inventory-to-sales ratio.

Thus, in the single-period model, a specified set of final demands **e** is satisfied by inventory depletion $\Delta \mathbf{v}$, imports **f**, and current production **x**. Current production is given by $\mathbf{b} = (I - A)\mathbf{x}$ where **x** is limited by available manpower and capital.

4.2.4
Relationship of this Procedure to Decision Analysis
The model described in this section corresponds to the decision-analysis concepts developed in Chapter 1 in the following way: The linear model

---

[7] It can be shown that the profit-maximizing level is related to current sales volume and a number of other factors. See Richard G. Brown, *Statistical Forecasting for Inventory Control* (York, Pa.: Maple Press, 1957).

is the transformation function G; the final demand, imports, final inventory, and gross output vectors, $\mathbf{e}$, $\mathbf{f}$, $\mathbf{v}$, and $\mathbf{x}$, respectively, are the instruments $\{y\}$; the constraints specified by the vectors for capital $\mathbf{k}$, labor $\mathbf{m}$, and initial inventory $\overline{\mathbf{v}}$ are the uncontrollable variables $\{x\}$; the A and P matrices are the parameters $\{\pi\}$. The elements of the final demand and imports vectors are the variables in the objective function $\phi = \phi(\mathbf{e}, \mathbf{f})$.

This section has described the primary model component of the adaptive modeling procedure. The next section describes four other components: the objective function, the decision-making role which is defined by the linear programming algorithm, the information system which provides the data for the policy maker, and the dynamic fashion in which the policy maker modifies the objective function.

4.3
The Other Components of the Adaptive Procedure
4.3.1
Linear Programming as the Decision Maker

The primary model assumes linear relationships between fixed-proportion production functions and a series of constraints on capital, labor, and inventory; these assumptions suggest that linear programming can be used to allocate resources optimally. The general linear programming problem is: ". . . Given a set of m linear inequalities or equations in r variables, we wish to find non-negative values of these variables which will satisfy the constraints and maximize or minimize some linear function of the variables."[8]

The following paragraphs are not intended to be a description of linear programming or duality theory; they only define several related concepts.

Any nonnegative set of variables that satisfies the constraints is feasible; the set that maximizes (or minimizes) the objective function is the optimum feasible solution. A fundamental linear programming theorem states that (in the absence of degeneracy) the optimum solution to a set of m equations in r variables will have exactly m variables different from zero. The duality theorem states that each primal linear program problem has a corresponding dual problem, and if one has a solution, the other does also. The solution indicates which program (that is, the values of the variables) is needed to maximize the value of output and to minimize the

---

[8] G. Hadley, *Linear Programming*, p. 4.

value of unexploited opportunities; thus the program optimizes both the primal and the dual problems.

The duality concept can be illustrated with a simple input-output model. For example, in an economy that contains only one scarce resource (a homogeneous labor force that is perfectly and instantaneously substitutable among n industrial sectors), the model consists of $n + 1$ linear relationships: one for each sector (see equation 4.4) plus one to represent the limiting labor supply. The n production relationships are expressed in matrix notation by equation 4.6:

$$\mathbf{x} = (I - A)^{-1}\mathbf{b}; \tag{4.6}$$

and the labor constraint, by

$$[\mathbf{a}_{n+1}(I - A)^{-1}]\mathbf{b} \leq m \tag{4.13}$$

where m is the total labor supply, $\mathbf{a}_{n+1}$ is the vector of unit labor requirements for the n sectors, and the remaining notation is as defined in the previous section. If inequality 4.13 is made an equality by adding surplus labor to the left side, there are $n + 1$ equations and $n + 1$ unknowns.

If $\mathbf{b}$ is specified, the solution to the system is unique; then the system is deterministic with only a single possible solution, and the problem of resource allocation is eliminated. However, for a viable economy, an infinite set of $\mathbf{b}$ vectors representing producible net output (the production possibility frontier) is formed by the intersection of three sets: (1) the space formed by the vectors of the production functions, (2) the space formed by the nonnegativity constraints on output, and (3) the half-space formed by inequality 4.13. Selecting the "best" net output vector from the infinite set is a real opportunity for choice; linear programming can optimize the choice. The appropriate primal and dual linear programming formulations follow.

Since each element α_{ij} of the inverse $(I - A)^{-1}$ represents the total x_i needed to produce a unit of b_j, in general,

$$x_i = \sum_{j=1}^{n} \alpha_{ij} b_j \qquad i = 1, \ldots, n, n + 1. \tag{4.14}$$

By rewriting the labor supply restriction 4.13,

$$m \leq \sum_{j=1}^{n} \alpha_{n+1,j} b_j. \tag{4.15}$$

Furthermore, if p_j is the unit price of good j and w is the uniform wage rate in all sectors,

$$p_j = \sum_{i=1}^{n} a_{ij} p_i + x_{n+1,j} w; \qquad (4.16)$$

that is, in this simple model of the economy, the price of each good equals the sum of the material (interindustry) prices plus the labor cost. In matrix form,

$$(I - A)'\mathbf{p} = \mathbf{x}_{n+1} w, \qquad (4.17)$$

where the prime notation indicates the transpose of a matrix. Since the inverse of the transpose is the transpose of the inverse, the price of each good in terms of labor input (the only resource in the model) is shown by

$$p_j = \sum_{i=1}^{n} \alpha_{ij} w x_{n+1,i} \qquad j = 1, \ldots, n. \qquad (4.18)$$

A primal linear programming problem that seeks to minimize the labor input while producing at least the net output $\mathbf{b}$ is

$$(I - A)\mathbf{x} \geq \mathbf{b}, \qquad \mathbf{x} \geq \mathbf{0}, \qquad \min z = a_{n+1} \mathbf{x}; \qquad (4.19)$$

a dual problem that attempts to maximize the amount of output while assuring that the price of any good produced does not exceed the input value is

$$(I - A)'\mathbf{p} \leq a'_{n+1} w, \qquad \mathbf{p} \geq \mathbf{0}, \qquad \max Z = \mathbf{b}'\mathbf{p} \left(\frac{1}{w}\right). \qquad (4.19a)$$

The unique optimum solution to the primal problem is the program of output quantities, given by $\mathbf{x} = (I - A)^{-1}\mathbf{b}$; the unique optimum solution to the dual problem is the price of goods produced given by

$$\mathbf{p} = w(I - A)^{-1} a'_{n+1}.$$

The duality between prices and output in this simple model of the economy can be interpreted in the following ways: (1) If net output $\mathbf{b}$ is producible, a set of nonnegative prices does exist. (2) If the economy is perfectly competitive and has homogeneous production functions that provide constant returns to scale, the equilibrium market prices will equal the calculated optimum prices. (3) The dual variables p_j are imputed values, or shadow prices, which measure the contribution which one more unit of good j would make to the objective function (contribution to GNP in this case).

The simple model can easily be transformed into a model of a more realistic economy in which prices are not set competitively but are established by entrepreneurs in an imperfect market. The most elementary formulation would set prices equal to cost plus a percentage markup applied to labor input; that is,

$$p_j = \sum_{i=1}^{n} a_{ij}p_i + (1 + \mu_j)w_j x_{n+1,j} \tag{4.20}$$

where μ_j is the markup percentage and w_j is the particular wage rate for industrial sector j.[9]

The growth model developed herein uses a linear programming formulation different from these two simpler models; it optimizes the value of the economy's output subject to constraints on labor, capital, and inventory. (The aggregation scheme for the supply side and for the demand side of the economy is provided in Tables 4.1 and 4.2). A number of modifications were made to the relatively familiar technique of applying linear programming to an input-output model. One modification resulted in the development of a nonlinear objective function; another, in the incorporation of a final demand matrix so that the information system can provide the policy maker with national income account data; and a third in the incorporation of the substitutability characteristics of human resources.

4.3.2

The Objective Function

The linear program maximizes a linear function of the variables, which in this case are the elements of the final demand vector **e** and the imports **f**. If we ignore the imports at this point, the simplest form of the objective function is

$$\max \phi = c_1^* e_1 + c_2^* e_2 + \cdots + c_n^* e_n \tag{4.21}$$

where ϕ = value of the objective function, c_j^* = the relative price for each final demand component, and e_j = the final demand component ($n = 12$ in the experimental model).

However, the objective function is unsatisfactory since the marginal rate of substitution between any two components c_i^*/c_j^* is constant and independent of supply levels $e_1, e_2, \ldots, e_n$.

[9] For an analysis of the mathematical properties of the more complex model, see Charles E. Ferguson, "Inflation, Fluctuations and Growth in a Dynamic Input-Output Model," *Southern Economic Journal*. vol. 28, no. 3 (January 1962), pp. 251–264; the simple model described above is similar to one outlined by G. Hadley, *Linear Programming*, pp. 487–492. Note that the variable p in this section is unrelated to the proportioning matrix of Section 4.2.2.

A procedure for circumventing this disability is to replace the constant c_j^* with a step function (referred to as a stipulation function) for a typical demand component:

$$c_j^* = c_j + \beta_j \qquad \text{if } e_j < \bar{e}_j$$

or   (4.22)

$$c_j^* = c_j \qquad \text{if } e_j > \bar{e}_j$$

where for category j, the $\bar{e}_j$ is a target quantity, the c_j is the relative price for each unit above the target, and β_j is the relative penalty for importing each unit if domestic production is below the target quantity.[10] The policy maker adapts each stipulation function as he learns the implications (or the resulting state of the world) for each set of stipulation functions.

Thus, the objective function is formed from a set of stipulation functions. To be more explicit, the objective function should represent a set of demand curves which, in a free economy, determines the system's equilibrium conditions; each curve is represented by a stipulation function. A typical curve, which relates price and quantity for a given income, resembles the heavy line in Figure 4.2; this figure superimposes a stipulation function on a typical demand curve for a typical final demand category.

The procedure described does not require that the policy maker define a set of curves; however, for the marginal unit produced in each final demand category, he must set a single target level and two relative prices: $c^* = c + \beta$ when the target demand is not met by domestic production, and c when the target is met or exceeded. He is assured that if output is not close to the target level $\bar{e}_j$ he will be able to choose new values for $\bar{e}$, c, and β. The coefficient β_j establishes a higher priority for production to satisfy final demand in category j until the target level $\bar{e}_j$ is satisfied. Thus, the policy maker can reduce the distance between points a and b in Figure 4.2 to find an appropriate point on the demand curve.

A policy maker may stipulate a minimum (target) quantity for each final demand category (for example, food based on a minimum per capita consumption); if $\bar{e}_j$ represents such a quantity, it is desired (but not

---

[10] The avoidance of the penalty implies that a bonus, or higher price, is assigned to the domestic production of each unit until the target is met; after that no penalty is incurred and, thus, the bonus no longer exists. As a result, while $\Sigma_j \beta_j f_j$ is subtracted in the computation of the objective function, $\beta_j f_j$ is added to evaluate the production of one more unit of the jth category until the target is met.

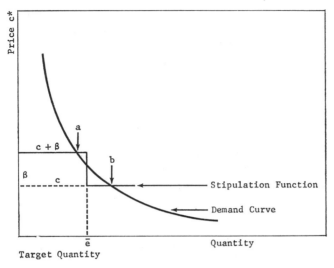

Figure 4.2. Stipulation functions and demand curves for a typical final demand category.

necessary) that

$$e_j \geq \bar{e}_j \quad \text{for all } j \tag{4.23}$$

where e_j is goods produced domestically and designated for final demand category j. In other words, the domestic supply should be at least equal to the minimum (target) domestic demand. The quantity $\bar{e}_j$ is an instrument that can be changed from run to run; it can be considered a first guess, a first approximation, or a necessary minimum. The bases for target stipulations do not have to be consistent; for example, $\bar{e}_1$ can be a necessary minimum for food consumption, while $\bar{e}_{11}$ can be, at best, a first approximation of the target for investment in new plant and equipment.

Relation 4.23 can be transformed into the following equality:

$$e_j + f_j = \bar{e}_j + e_j^* \tag{4.24}$$

where f_j represents the quantity of final demand component in category j either denied (that is, below the minimum $\bar{e}_j$ target) or imported to meet domestic demand, and e_j^* represents the quantity in excess of the minimum. Since all variables in equation 4.24 are nonnegative, f_j or e_j^* must be zero; if domestic production is inadequate, there is no excess, and vice versa; in matrix notation,

$$\mathbf{e} - \mathbf{e}^* + \mathbf{f} = \bar{\mathbf{e}}. \tag{4.25}$$

The linear programming algorithm assigns a value of c_j^* to each unit of final demand produced domestically for the jth category; repeating equations 4.22 in a slightly different form:

$$c_j^* = c_j \qquad \text{if } f_j = 0$$

or $\hspace{11cm}$ (4.22a)

$$c_j^* = c_j + \beta_j \qquad \text{if } f_j > 0.$$

For example, if the alternative is to produce one more unit of either good 1 (food) or good 2 (apparel), the algorithm computes the net change $c_1^* - c_2^*$.

The stipulation function need not be restricted to two steps. Three or more steps could be used to represent the stipulation function shown in Figure 4.2; however, the two-step arrangement is convenient. The solid lines can be brought closer to any portion of a dashed line by changing the target $\bar{e}_j$ and the value coefficients β_j and c_j. Thus, at each stage, the policy maker must: (1) set the tentative targets for the various categories of consumption, investment, and governmental expenditures, (2) set the penalties β_j for the marginal unit below the target quantity, and (3) set the relative prices c_j for the marginal unit in excess of the target quantity.

For some or all of the consumption categories, setting the price levels may be more meaningful to the policy maker than setting target consumption levels. Here, setting the values of c_j and β_j is important; the $\bar{e}_j$ value is supplementary. For government expenditures and investment, $\bar{e}_j$ may be the only relevant variable in the stipulation function; in this case, the c_j and β_j can be set to insure that the target is exactly met but not exceeded (for example, use a high β_j and a low c_j).

The information system provides the policy maker with the solution to the linear program—that is, the optimum $\mathbf{x}$ and $\mathbf{e}$ vectors for the objective function he has specified. He may view this as a forecast based on a tentative objective function; he now can change the function on the basis of this forecast. After the linear programming solution is reviewed, the stipulation functions are evaluated (e_j for the given objective function is now known) and, if necessary, modified; then the model is rerun with a new objective function. The process is repeated until a satisfactory set of targets and value coefficients (and an optimum production schedule corresponding to the finally specified function) is obtained.

The final requirement is to give the policy maker the capability of using

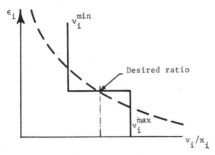

Figure 4.3.   Inventory evaluation vs. inventory/sales ratio.

the objective function to evaluate inventory changes ($\Sigma_i \epsilon_i v_i$ where v_i is the net change and ϵ_i is the corresponding price or evaluation coefficient in sector i). The value of each inventory evaluator ϵ_i should depend either on the inventory level, or more exactly, on the inventory-to-sales ratio. If the ratio is higher than is desired, a low ϵ_i tends to substitute inventory depletion for current production; if the ratio is low, the corresponding ϵ_i can be sufficiently high (relative to the c_j) to produce goods for inventory at the expense of final demand.

The desired inventory-to-sales ratio maximizes profits (see Footnote 7); if data are available an auxiliary model can be created for each sector relating ϵ_i to the ratio as illustrated by the dashed line in Figure 4.3.

Summarizing this section, the value of net output is given by the objective function

$$\phi = \Sigma_j c_j e_j - \Sigma_j \beta_j f_j + \Sigma_i \epsilon_i v_i \qquad \begin{array}{l} i = 1, 2, \ldots, \ 8 \\ j = 1, 2, \ldots, 11 \end{array} \qquad (4.26)$$

where c_j = relative value (or price) of domestic sales for the jth category of final demand, e_j = domestic sales for the jth category, β_j = disutility of imports for the jth category, f_j = net imports for the jth category, ϵ_i = relative value of the net change in inventory in sector i, and v_i = net inventory change in sector i.

The units for e_j, f_j, and v_i are constant dollars; the value coefficients, c_j, β_j, and ϵ_i are pure numbers representing relative prices.

The first summation represents the value of final sales to consumers, to government, and for investment (exclusive of inventory investment of goods) produced domestically; the second represents the disutility of imports; the third represents the value of the net inventory change.[11]

---

[11] Expenditure categories 1–11 do not include production resulting in net inventory change; thus this category 12 is not counted twice.

Each β_j is an evaluation of the disutility, or penalty, of importing a particular category of good (or equivalently it is the bonus for the marginal unit produced domestically until the target demand is met). If the only consideration is the balance of payments, it might be reasonable to set $\beta_1 = \beta_2 = \beta$; in this case, the restriction is on total imports, and β can be a function (in an auxiliary model) of total dollar value of all imports. Otherwise, β_j for a strategic good might be set higher; in the numerical example of the next section, $\beta = \beta_1 = \beta_2 = \cdots = \beta_{11}$.

If f_j is considered as final demand denied rather than goods imported, β_j might be an evaluation of inflationary gaps or price pressures. In either case, f_j is the difference between the policy maker's target final demand level and the quantity produced domestically; β_j is the penalty assigned to the unit difference.

4.3.3

The Information System

At each stage in the adaptive modeling procedure, the linear programming algorithm finds a solution that maximizes the objective function as stated for that stage. The solution, which includes the optimum production program x and the resulting supply e, is provided to the policy maker, who revises the stipulation functions before the algorithm is applied in the next stage. The cycle continues until the policy maker obtains a satisfactory solution.

In initial stages, some final demand targets are likely to be met exactly, some exceeded, and others partially denied. If the denial quantity f_j is large, the value initially assigned to β_j may be too low; if the excess e^* is large, the value assigned to c_j may be too high. Thus, after examining the vector e, the policy maker may reconsider the weights (prices) he placed on each category of final demand. To illustrate, the stipulation function in Figure 4.4 approximates the demand function D near points a and b; if e_j is far to the left of point a, say at e'_j, then $c_j + \beta_j$ is too low; if e_j is far to the right of b, say at e''_j, then c_j is too high.

Another way to view the policy maker's setting of the $\bar{e}_j$, c_j, and β_j values is graphically illustrated in Figure 4.4. Specification of a stipulation function implies that a final demand curve D intersects a supply curve S_1 (both are functions of all resources and demands) at point b; that is, the solution to the linear program is an equilibrium solution, thus supply must be equal to demand in all markets. If $e_j < \bar{e}_j$, the supply curve is higher than originally thought; assume it is shown by S_2. Then, with all

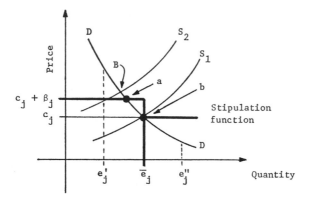

Figure 4.4. Output and price coefficients.

other conditions constant, $\bar{e}_j$ should be reset at point B for the next stage, and the price coefficient c_j should be increased close to the level of point B. The actual slope of S_2 is not known; therefore B is only an approximation of the intersection of D and S_2. Furthermore, since all sectors and demands are interdependent, changing any price coefficient will generally cause a shift in S_2 (and in D).

The information system, in addition to providing the optimum values for the solution variables, provides the shadow price for each constraining resource. The shadow price indicates the marginal contribution to the objective function for each resource fully consumed in the optimum program. Shadow prices evaluate each unit of final demand in terms of the resources consumed to produce the unit and thus guide the policy maker in adjusting price coefficients. The example described in Section 4.4 of this chapter illustrates the adjustment procedure.

4.3.4
Summary of the Linear Programming Problem

The constraints for the static problem are

$$\bar{\mathbf{v}} + (I - A)\mathbf{x} + \mathbf{f} = P\mathbf{e} + \mathbf{v}, \tag{4.27}$$

$$x_i \leq k_i, \tag{4.28}$$

$$m_i = g_i x_i \leq (1 + \delta_i)\bar{m}_i, \tag{4.29}$$

$$\sum m_i \leq m_s, \tag{4.30}$$

$$v_i \leq v_i^{\max}. \tag{4.31}$$

The first constraint states that initial inventories $\bar{\mathbf{v}}$ plus current production $(I - A)\mathbf{x}$ plus net imports $\mathbf{f}$ are identical to current consumption $P\mathbf{e}$ plus final inventories $\mathbf{v}$. The second states that output x_i cannot exceed the physical capacity k_i for each sector. The third states that for the ith sector the output is limited by the manpower available m_i (g_i is the unit manpower requirement) and that the average manpower cannot increase by more than some fraction δ_i available at the beginning of the period $\bar{m}_i$. The fourth states that total employment $\Sigma_i m_i$ cannot exceed the labor force m_s. The fifth states that each industry's inventory position v_i cannot exceed the specified maximum. The minimum restriction on inventory levels is implemented by setting initial inventories equal to actual inventories less the minimum (that is, $\bar{\mathbf{v}} = \mathbf{v}^{\text{actual}} - \mathbf{v}^{\text{min}}$) and by forcing final inventories to be nonnegative.

Relationships 4.26 and 4.31 can be rearranged into a linear programming format:

$$\text{maximize } \phi = \sum_{j=1}^{m} (c_j e_j - \beta_j f_j) + \sum_{i=1}^{n} \epsilon_i v_i \tag{4.32}$$

subject to the constraints:

$$\mathbf{v} + P\mathbf{e} - (I - A) - \mathbf{f} = \bar{\mathbf{v}},$$

$$\mathbf{x} + \mathbf{s} = \bar{\mathbf{k}},$$

$$D_g \mathbf{x} + \mathbf{u} = \bar{\mathbf{m}},$$

$$\sum_{i=1}^{n} g_i x_i + u_s = \bar{m}_s,$$

$$\mathbf{v} + \boldsymbol{\gamma} = \bar{\mathbf{v}}^{\text{max}},$$

$$\mathbf{e} - \mathbf{e}^* + \mathbf{f} = \bar{\mathbf{e}}.$$

The solution variables are the vectors $\mathbf{e}$, $\mathbf{f}$, and $\mathbf{v}$. These directly determine $\mathbf{e}^*$ (that is, $\mathbf{e}^* = \mathbf{e} + \mathbf{f} - \bar{\mathbf{e}}$) and $\mathbf{x}$ (see Equation 4.27), where $\mathbf{s}$, $\mathbf{u}$, u_s, and $\boldsymbol{\gamma}$ are the vectors of slack variables on physical capacity, sector manpower, total manpower, and inventories, respectively, and D_g is a diagonal matrix with the unit manpower requirements g_i on the diagonal; the bars indicate values at the beginning of the period (except $\bar{\mathbf{e}}$).

Figure 4.5 and Table 4.3 are, respectively, the flow chart and the symbols used for the static primary model.

The linear programming algorithm maximizes the output of the economy subject to supply constraints of labor, capital, and inventories; it

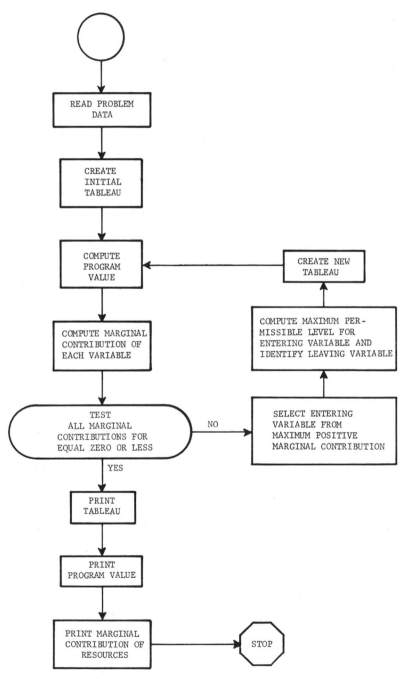

Figure 4.5   Primary model for the static case.

Table 4.3 Symbols for Static Primary Model

Typical Element	Matrix or Vector	
a_{ij}	A	Interindustry technology coefficients.
b_{ij}	B	Final demand expenditures.
g_i	D_g	Unit labor requirement (D_g is a diagonal matrix of the g_i).
p_{ij}	P	Expenditure pattern coefficients.
—	I	Identity matrix of appropriate size.
c_j	$\mathbf{c}$	Value coefficients on final demand.
e_j	$\mathbf{e}$	Current expenditures on final demand.
$\bar{e}_j$	$\bar{\mathbf{e}}$	Minimum expenditures (targets) on final demand.
e_j^*	$\mathbf{e}^*$	Net expenditures in excess of targets on final demand.
f_j	$\mathbf{f}$	Imports or deficiency relative to the targets.
k_i	$\mathbf{k}$	Physical capacity.
m_i	$\mathbf{m}$	Sector labor force.
m_s	—	Total available labor force.
s_i	$\mathbf{s}$	Slack on physical capacity.
u_i	$\mathbf{u}$	Slack or unemployed labor force available to individual sectors $= m - (1 + \delta)\bar{m}$.
u_s	—	Total unemployed labor force (slack).
v_i	$\mathbf{v}$	Ending inventory.
$\bar{v}_i$	$\bar{\mathbf{v}}$	Current inventory in excess of minimum (beginning).
x_i	$\mathbf{x}$	Gross output.
β_j	$\boldsymbol{\beta}$	Value coefficient (penalty) on imports.
γ_i	$\boldsymbol{\gamma}$	Slack variable on inventory.
δ_i	$\boldsymbol{\delta}$	Maximum labor force increase without retraining.
ϵ_i	$\boldsymbol{\epsilon}$	Value coefficient on inventories.

evaluates the output according to price coefficients of the objective function specified by the policy maker.

At each stage the policy maker examines the optimum feasible final demand vector computed by the linear programming algorithm and modifies the stipulations function to obtain an "improved" solution. Section 4.4 demonstrates these steps with a numerical example.

4.4
A Numerical Example of the Static Case
4.4.1
The Coefficients

In the illustrative example described in this section, the United States economy is represented by eight industrial sectors and final demand is divided into eleven categories of consumption, investment, and government expenditure. This section notes the data sources; some data (for example, the A and P matrices) were based on reliable statistics, and others (for example, industry capacities) were based on convenient assumptions.

Coefficients for the A matrix, representing interindustrial flows, were taken from a paper by Michael D. McCarthy of the Brookings Institution;[12] Table 4.4 lists the elements of the A matrix. Data required to calculate the unit manpower requirements g_i were obtained from a Department of Labor publication;[13] Table 4.5 shows the factors that were computed for each sector. Unit manpower requirements g_i were calculated

Table 4.4 1958 $(I - A)$ Matrix (dollars/dollar)

Industrial Sector	1	2	2	3	4	5	7	8
1	0.71006	−0.00348	−0.00189	−0.00066	−0.01277	−0.00647	−0.13798	−0.06970
2	−0.01198	0.99988	−0.00814	−0.03261	−0.03886	−0.00206	−0.00239	−0.13664
3	−0.03776	−0.09173	0.98245	−0.02060	−0.02127	−0.03861	−0.03162	−0.01200
4	−0.02388	−0.03626	−0.04162	0.89549	−0.03709	−0.04237	−0.04475	−0.14661
5	−0.07768	−0.06495	−0.13548	−0.09600	0.86204	−0.05488	−0.10647	−0.05538
6	−0.01128	−0.33001	−0.01705	−0.02528	−0.05607	0.63616	−0.03802	−0.00836
7	−0.10837	−0.05450	−0.03836	−0.04290	−0.06548	−0.05696	0.70991	−0.05489
8	−0.00020	−0.00022	−0.01405	−0.05873	−0.01024	−0.00164	−0.00212	0.99868

Source: Michael D. McCarthy, *On the Aggregation of the 1958 Direct Requirements Input-Output Table* (Washington, D.C.: The Brookings Institution, June 1965).

[12] Michael D. McCarthy, *On the Aggregation of the 1958 Direct Requirements Input/Output Table* (Washington, D.C.: The Brookings Institution, June 1965).
[13] U.S. Department of Labor, *Projections 1970* (Washington, D.C.: U.S. Government Printing Office, December 1966), Table A-4, p. 152.

Table 4.5   Sector-Labor Coefficients (workers/$1,000 output)

Industrial Sector	1	2	3	4	5	6	7	8
g	0.08370	0.03713	0.29967	0.06138	0.05300	0.04848	0.02908	0.16556

Source: U.S. Dept. of Labor *Projection 1970* (Washington, D.C.: U.S. Government Printing Office, December 1966), Table A-4, p. 152.

by dividing the number of workers employed in 1958 by the gross production x_i; physical capacity k_i was estimated as 1958 gross production plus 10 percent; the permissible labor force increase δ_i was assumed to be 10 percent of the 1958 employment level; the total available labor force $\bar{m}_s$ was approximately the actual number of persons employed in 1958 (a tight restriction in the illustrative example).

Distribution pattern data for final demand were obtained from a study by Nancy Simon[14] and from the 1958 OBE Input-Output Study[15] and used to compile a B matrix of final demand. From the B matrix, the P matrix of final demand expenditure patterns was computed; data are given in Tables 4.6 and 4.7.

4.4.2

The Constraints and Stipulation Functions

Table 4.8 provides the linear programming tableau (each variable, except u_s, in the top column is a vector), and Table 4.9 gives the input values for the constraints of the sample problem.

Three simulations (Run 1, Run 2, Run 3) were made. Run 1 is typical of conditions where resources and final demand are near equilibrium and all targets can be met. However, an unbalanced situation was needed to illustrate the usefulness of the model; such a situation can be obtained either by decreasing the capacity or by increasing the target levels; the latter method was chosen. For Run 2, multiples of $5 billion were randomly added to the targets except for category 11, which was arbitrarily reduced. Run 3, the policy maker's response to the imbalance of Run 2, used the procedure outlined below. Table 4.10 lists the targets for Runs 1, 2, and 3; Table 4.11 gives the solutions or instrument values.

The target stipulations for Run 1 were set at levels that approximate

[14] Nancy W. Simon, "Personal Consumption Expenditures in the 1958 Input-Output Study," *Survey of Current Business.* October 1965, Table I, pp. 8–10.
[15] Office of Business Economics, "The Transactions Table of the 1958 Input-Output Study and Revised Direct and Total Requirements Data," *Survey of Current Business,* September 1965, Table I, pp. 8–10.

Table 4.6 1958 *B* Matrix of Final Demand Expenditures

Final Demand Expenditures by Category (Millions of Dollars at Purchaser's Price)

Industrial Sector	1 Food and Tobacco	2 Apparel	3 Housing	4 Medical	5 Personal Business	6 Transportation	7 Education and Religion	8 Fixed Capital	9 Residential Construction	10 Federal Government	11 State and Local Government	Total
1. Agriculture	$7,411	$650	0	0	0	0	0	0	0	$978	−$30	$9,009
2. Construction	0	0	0	0	0	0	0	$36,957	$18,000	4,469	15,408	74,834
3. Trade	377	0	0	0	0	0	0	3,747	0	645	183	4,952
4. Regulated	120	42	$12,238	0	$17	$3,068	0	869	0	1,956	1,078	19,388
5. Residual	0	10,651	42,636	$12,614	12,596	5,993	$7,318	1,209	0	6,504	1,477	100,998
6. Durables	0	8,303	12,330	827	60	12,413	0	20,313	0	14,155	1,385	69,786
7. Nondurables	72,358	29,726	11,485	3,031	0	12,512	0	102	0	2,167	1,433	132,814
8. Government	0	0	638	0	62	244	0	0	0	20,120	19,151	40,215
Total	$80,266	$49,372	$79,327	$16,472	$12,735	$34,230	$7,318	$63,197	$18,000	$50,994	$40,085	$451,996 = GNP

Source: Nancy W. Simon, "Personal Consumption Expenditures in the 1958 Input-Output Study," *Survey of Current Business*, October 1965; columns 1–7 compiled from Table 1, pp. 8–10. Office of Business Economics, "The Transactions Table of the 1958 Input-Output Study and Revised Direct and Total Requirements Data," *Survey of Current Business*, September 1965; columns 8–11 compiled from Table 1, pp. 34–39.

Table 4.7 1958 P Matrix of Final Demand Pattern Coefficients

Final Demand Expenditures by Category (dollars/dollar)

Industrial Sector	1 Food and Tobacco	2 Apparel	3 Housing	4 Medical	5 Personal Business	6 Transportation	7 Education and Religion	8 Fixed Capital	9 Residential Construction	10 Federal Government	11 State and Local Government
1. Agriculture	0.09233	0.01317	0	0	0	0	0	0	0	0.01918	−0.00075
2. Construction	0	0	0	0	0	0	0	0.58479	1	0.08764	0.38438
3. Trade	0.00470	0	0	0	0	0	0	0.05929	0	0.01265	0.00457
4. Regulated	0.00150	0.00085	0.15427	0	0.00133	0.08963	0	0.01375	0	0.03836	0.02689
5. Residual	0	0.21573	0.53747	0.76578	0.98908	0.17508	1	0.01913	0	0.12754	0.03685
6. Durables	0	0.16817	0.15543	0.05021	0.00471	0.36263	0	0.32142	0	0.27758	0.03455
7. Nondurables	0.90148	0.60208	0.14478	0.18401	0	0.36553	0	0.00161	0	0.04250	0.03575
8. Government	0	0	0.00804	0	0.00487	0.00713	0	0	0	0.39456	0.47776

Source: Computed from Table 4.6: $\dfrac{\text{Category } j \text{ dollars spent in sector } i}{\text{Total dollars spent for category } j}$.

Table 4.8 Tableau for Sample Linear Programming Problem

	s	f	n	u	u_s	γ	e	e*	x	v
c_j										
p_i	0	−0.10	0	0	0	0	1.00	0	0	0.99
$\bar{k}$	I								I	
$\bar{e}$		I					I	$-I$		
$\bar{v}$			I				P		$-(I-A)$	I
$\bar{m}$				I					D_q	
m_s					I				g	
$v^{\max}$						I				I

Table 4.9 Constraints of the Sample Problem (in $ millions or 1,000 workers)

Sector	Capacity k	Beginning Inventory $\bar{v}$	Labor $\bar{m}$
1 Agriculture	$ 79,152	$ 17,989	6,625
2 Construction	82,280	18,700	3,055
3 Trade	39,461	8,968	11,825
4 Regulated	71,252	16,194	4,374
5 Residual	205,577	46,722	10,896
6 Durables	200,171	45,493	9,704
7 Nondurables	269,315	61,208	7,832
8 Government enterprises	52,082	11,837	8,623
s Total	—	227,111	57,212*

* Exceeds the sum of the sector's labor force.

actual final demand for 1958. All price coefficients c_j and β_j for the objective function were assigned values of 1.00 and 0.10, respectively. In other words, at output levels less than the target, a bonus of $0.10 was assigned so that the relative price of the marginal unit produced was $1.10 until the target was achieved and $1.00 thereafter. Ending inventory v_i was assigned a price of $0.9999; this gave a small measure of priority to

Table 4.10   Target Expenditures Stipulated for Sample Problem

	Targets (in $ millions)		
Category	Run 1	Run 2	Run 3
1 Food and tobacco	80,000	110,000	110,000
2 Apparel, personal care, and recreation	40,000	90,000	90,000
3 Housing and household operations	35,000	65,000	65,000
4 Medical services	10,000	20,000	20,000
5 Personal business	10,000	20,000	20,000
6 Transportation	20,000	30,000	30,000
7 Education and religion	5,000	10,000	10,000
8 Plant and equipment	50,000	60,000	60,000
9 Residential construction	20,000	50,000	35,000
10 Federal government purchases	50,000	60,000	60,000
11 State and local government purchases	40,000	30,000	30,000

production for final demand over production for inventory. Thus, the objective function used for Run 1 is

$$\phi = \sum_{j=1}^{11} (e_j - 0.1f_j) + \sum_{i=1}^{8} 0.9999 v_i.$$

4.4.3
The Solutions

Note that the minimum stipulation for category 9, residential construction, was increased from $20 billion in Run 1 to $50 billion in Run 2. In the solution to Run 2, only one target was not met; that was $\bar{e}_9$ where f_9 was in the solution at $18,307 million.

After Run 2 was completed, two changes were made to correct the deficit for category 9 and the problem was rerun as Run 3. The first change was to reduce $\bar{e}_9$ from $50 billion to $35 billion; if a higher price had to be paid for residential construction, the overt demand for it was simply

Table 4.11 Instrument Values of the Sample Problem ($ millions or 1,000 workers)

Industrial Sector	Gross Output (x) ($ millions)			Slack Physical Capacity (s) ($ millions)			Ending Inventory (v) ($ millions)			Slack Labor Force (u) (1,000 workers)		
	Run 1	Run 2	Run 3	Run 1	Run 2	Run 3	Run 1	Run 2	Run 3	Run 1	Run 2	Run 3
1. Agriculture	79,151	79,151	79,151	0	—	—	20,552	17,782	17,739	—	—	—
2. Construction	82,276	82,278	82,277	1	1	1	—	—	—	—	—	—
3. Trade	28,751	29,563	29,225	10,710	9,897	10,236	—	—	—	3,208	2,965	3,067
4. Regulated	71,252	71,252	71,251	—	—	—	14,566	11,325	8,721	1	1	1
5. Residual	205,572	205,569	205,573	—	—	—	—	—	—	1	1	—
6. Durables	200,155	200,164	200,164	11	6	6	—	—	20,287	—	—	—
7. Nondurables	269,310	269,311	269,310	—	—	—	—	—	—	—	—	—
8. Government enterprises	36,907	35,446	36,056	15,173	16,635	16,025	316	—	481	—	—	—
Total	973,374	972,734	973,007	25,895	26,539	26,268	35,434	29,107	47,228	3,210	2,967	3,068

Table 4.11 (cont.)

Final Demand Category	Output (e) ($ millions)			Excess e* ($ millions)			Imports or Deficit ($ millions)		
	Run 1	Run 2	Run 3	Run 1	Run 2	Run 3	Run 1	Run 2	Run 3
1. Food and tobacco	80,000	110,000	110,000	—	—	—	—	—	—
2. Apparel, personal care, and recreation	97,418	90,000	90,000	57,418	—	—	—	—	—
3. Housing and household operations	35,000	116,876	134,352	—	51,876	69,352	—	—	—
4. Medical services	10,000	31,878	20,000	—	11,878	—	—	—	—
5. Personal business	67,372	20,000	20,000	57,372	—	—	—	—	—
6. Transportation	183,221	77,916	76,935	163,221	47,917	46,935	—	—	—
7. Education and religion	5,000	10,000	10,000	—	—	—	—	—	—
8. Plant and equipment	50,000	60,000	54,205	—	—	—	—	—	5,795
9. Residential construction	34,378	31,691	35,000	14,378	—	—	—	18,309	—
10. Federal government purchases	50,000	60,000	60,000	—	—	—	—	—	—
11. State and local government purch.	40,000	30,000	30,000	—	—	—	—	—	—
Total	652,389	638,361	640,492	292,389	111,671	116,287	—	18,309	5,795

reduced. The second change was to increase the price coefficient for e_9 to $2.00. Examination of the shadow prices of Run 2 (see Table 4.12) indicated that in Run 3 a price as high as $2.00 was more than sufficient to drive f_9 to zero because other f_j have shadow prices of $0.1 or less. One of the other f_j may be forced into the solution when f_9 is forced out; hence, an increase in the price coefficient of e_9 for Run 3 in the neighborhood of $1.10 might be more appropriate.

As expected, when Run 3 was completed, it was found that f_9 was forced to the zero level and $e_9 = \bar{e}_9 = $35 billion in the solution. Gross investment in plant and equipment e_8 dropped from $60 billion in Run 2 to $54,205 million in Run 3 where it is $5,795 million less than its target stipulation; thus, f_8 is $5,795 million. One can understand, by reviewing the results of Run 2, that f_8 would be the first denial variable to enter the solution of Run 3; its shadow price of $0.0301 is the lowest (see Table 4.12).

Figure 4.6 illustrates what took place as a result of increasing the price coefficient on output for category 9 while holding that for category 8 constant. This insures that e_9, output for final demand category 9, is given priority over e_8. If we ignore what happens to other e_j, the programming algorithm forced e_9 to enter the solution up to the level of its target stipulation $\bar{e}_9$ because its marginal contribution to program value was greater than that of e_8. Next, e_8 would enter until its target value e_8 is met. Then if

Table 4.12   Shadow Prices on the Deficits (Runs 2 and 3)

Deficit	Run 2	Run 3
f_1	0.0991	0.0991
f_2	0.1000	0.0999
f_3	0.1000	0.1000
f_4	0.1000	0.1000
f_5	0.1000	0.1000
f_6	0.1000	0.1000
f_7	0.0999	0.1000
*f_8	0.0301	—
f_9	—	0.8400
†f_{10}	0.0866	0.0844
§f_{11}	0.0576	0.0401

* Lowest—Run 2
† Second lowest—Run 3
§ Second lowest—Run 2; lowest—Run 3

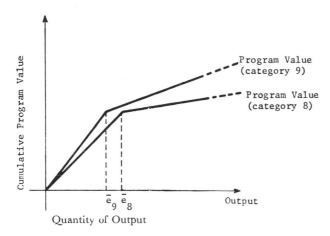

Figure 4.6.   Output and program value for two categories of goods.

resources permit, e_9 would rise above $\bar{e}_9$ to a point where some restriction would bind it. Finally, e_8 would be increased above $\bar{e}_8$ if more resources were available.

Solution of the linear programming algorithm required less than two minutes on a relatively slow-speed computer.[16] It is simple to change the minimum requirements, the target vectors, or the value coefficients and to obtain a new optimum under a new set of values.

The shadow prices on imports (that is, on $f_1, \ldots, f_{11}$) guide the improvement of the static case. The shadow prices on the constraints of physical and human resources may be used to guide the investment process for the dynamic case; this adaptive procedure is described in Chapter 5.

[16] A Bunker-Ramo 340, approximately equivalent to an IBM-1640.

5
Allocating Resources:
The Dynamic Case

5.1
Growth Models and Production Functions

Planning economic growth is a problem of allocating resources in the dynamic case. The first part of this chapter describes well-known growth models and production functions, thus helping to define certain theoretical concepts common to all growth models. Next, the additions required to obtain an adaptive modeling procedure suitable for analyzing economic growth are discussed. Equations are added to the static primary model to tie the sequence of static cases together, thereby creating a new primary model. Ranking and parametric programming algorithms are then used to make the microlevel investment decisions.

5.1.1
A Review of Growth Models

The study of growth is the study of a process; therefore, most of the work on growth theory has been done within the framework of a dynamic model. A growth model usually specifies: (1) a production function that relates output to labor and capital—in some cases, to natural resources and land, (2) an investment function that determines the rate of capital accumulation, (3) a function, usually of an exogenous variable such as time, that determines the rate of the population or labor force increase, and (4) the resultant rate of change in capacity and output (frequently assumed equal and thus providing full employment equilibrium).

Most growth models are normative; they prescribe an "optimum" growth path. Some are predictive, as well; they indicate the consequences of deviating from the optimum path.

AGGREGATED MODELS

Many highly aggregated growth models have only two recognizable inputs (a homogenous capital stock and labor force) and one homogenous output commodity equally useful for consumption or investment. The Harrod-Domar type, which assumes that the ratio of each input to output is fixed, gives rise to single *knife-edge* paths of growth; that is, labor, capital, and output experience the same geometric rate of growth.

The Harrod model is both normative and predictive; it uses a highly simplified accelerator function to explain investment; the model assumes that output in any period is a function of producers' expected sales and that producers expect last period's growth rate to continue.[1] Equilibrium

---

[1] Roy F. Harrod, "An Essay in Dynamic Theory," *Economic Journal*, March 1939, pp. 13–14.

at this "warranted" rate of growth occurs if

$$GW = \frac{s}{C} \qquad (5.1)$$

where GW is the warranted growth rate, C is the additional unit of capital required per unit of additional output (or marginal capital/output ratio), and s is the propensity to save. If the actual growth rate deviates from the warranted rate, the Harrod model will explode into either depression (producers' planned output is less than the warranted rate) or inflation (output exceeds the warranted rate). Thus, long-term equilibrium demands that the warranted rate be just sufficient to absorb the labor force increase (or "natural" growth rate).

Domar's model is normative but not predictive. It seeks to find the growth rate of investment required to use the capacity added in each period.[2] Domar's required rate is identical to Harrod's warranted rate; it equates potential output with actual income.

Solow's model is a two-input, single-commodity-output model that assumes savings equal desired investment; therefore a full employment equilibrium is maintained.[3] This model relaxes the fixed coefficient assumption and permits the capital-to-labor ratio to vary; to each ratio there corresponds a saving-investment rate that will insure equilibrium. The knife's edge becomes one of an infinite number of paths that absorb the increasing labor force.

Phelps' model leads to a "golden" capital accumulation rule;[4] like Solow's model, it uses a Cobb-Douglas production function and disembodied technological change. Solow assumes neutral technological change while Phelps supplies a coefficient for each factor.

The four models are highly abstract and highly aggregated. From a policy viewpoint, the models indicate what is required to maintain full employment equilibrium: Harrod and Domar specify the required growth rate, Solow specifies the required capital/labor ratio as a function of the propensity to save, and Phelps specifies the required payment to capital.

Ackley, in discussing capital-poor economies, expresses the belief that such macroeconomic approaches are inappropriate because total output,

---

[2] Evsey D. Domar, "Capital Expansion, Rate of Growth and Employment," *Econometrica* 1946, pp. 137–147.

[3] Robert M. Solow, "A Contribution to the Theory of Economic Growth," *Quarterly Journal of Economics*, February 1956, pp. 65–94.

[4] Edmund S. Phelps, "The Golden Rule of Capital Accumulation," *American Economic Review*, 1961, pp. 638–643.

in these countries, is not limited by a general shortage of capital but rather by specific shortages of plant and equipment. Therefore, any generalized inducement to invest may inappropriately stimulate investment in all lines, not merely in the bottleneck areas; "what is needed is the provision, by appropriate investment, of more plant capacity in just the right places, and in just the proper sequence . . . ."[5] He further states[6] that this situation is true of even capital-rich economies during periods of inflation; "in a growth context, no economy is more than temporarily capital-rich."

Thus, according to Ackley, these four macroeconomic growth models must be supplemented by a sectorial analysis.

DISAGGREGATED MODELS

Disaggregated growth models[7] recognize more than one producing sector and frequently permit the relative growth rates of individual sectors to vary. The von Neumann model is the most general of all disaggregated growth models; it is a complex input-output model that examines alternative production processes and treats consumed capital as intermediate goods. Equilibrium is a state of steady, balanced, growth along a von Neumann path; all process intensities increase by a constant proportion equal to the interest rate. The model is highly abstract; it has no consumer demand side and no primary factors.[8]

Balanced growth (all capital stocks of a multisector economy increase at the same rate) can be shown to be optimal if initial stocks are in the proper ratio. Optimally balanced growth occurs along a von Neumann path; the turnpike theorem states that in the long run such a path is optimal even if the initial *and* the desired final capital stock mix is different from the mix on the von Neumann path.[9] By assumption, highly aggregative models that use a single homogenous capital stock are special cases of balanced growth models.

Leontief postulates a model with balanced growth on "Leontief trajectories"; this dynamic model (like his static model) is "locked," or determinate—it does not allow for choice. However, the feasibility of Leontief

[5] Gardner Ackley, *Macroeconomic Theory* (New York: The Macmillan Co., 1961), pp. 588–589.

[6] *Ibid.*, pp. 589–591.

[7] A useful (but theoretical) disaggregated approach to growth models is discussed in R. Dorfman, Paul Samuelson, and Robert Solow, *Linear Programming and Economic Analysis*. (New York: McGraw-Hill Book Co., 1958), pp. 265–345. This outstanding text is the basis for the approach used in this chapter.

[8] Ackley, *Macroeconomic Theory*, pp. 381–388.

[9] R. Dorfman, Paul Samuelson, and Robert Solow, *Linear Programming*, pp. 326–334.

trajectories depends on the initial composition of capital stock; in fact, only one initial stock mix can have a Leontief trajectory that is an efficient path.[10] Also, the introduction of a time dimension and stocks of capital can be shown to "unlock" the model. Thus, no matter how rigid the assumptions of fixed production coefficients or fixed capital/output ratios, explicit choice is necessary and thus, optimization is meaningful.[11]

5.1.2
Aspects of Production Functions
The production function is a basic part of any growth model. The static Leontief model, which defines the production functions at any point in time for the static model described in Chapter 4, is highly restrictive; it assumes constant proportions of inputs to outputs, constant returns to scale, and a constant technology. The primary model described in this chapter for the dynamic case maintains these restrictions within a single time period but relaxes them if a longer period is considered; the following paragraphs define the restrictions more explicitly and indicate how they can be relaxed.

The production function, a keystone of classical economic theory, is frequently represented as shown in Figure 5.1. The curves are isoquants that indicate the constant input quantities x and x' required to produce a specified output y.

CHANGES TO SCALE
Parallel isoquants that represent constant technology and neutral scale requirements (Figure 5.2) indicate the proportional increase required in

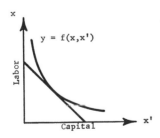

Figure 5.1. Classical production function.

[10] *Ibid.*, p. 344.
[11] *Ibid.*, p. 267. See also S. Chakravarty, "Optimal Programme of Capital Accumulation in a Multi-Sector Economy," *Econometrica*, vol. 33, no. 3 (July 1965), pp. 557–570.

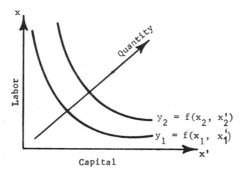

Figure 5.2.   Production functions (constant technology; changing scale).

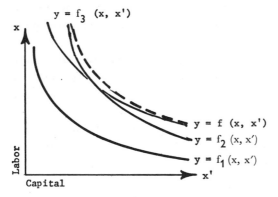

Figure 5.3.   Production functions (changing technology; constant scale).

both inputs to increase output from y_1 to y_2. If $y_2/y_1 = x_2/x_1 = x_2'/x_1'$, the returns to the scale are constant.

CHANGES IN TECHNOLOGY

The curves in Figure 5.3 represent technological change; the curves represent the same output quantities produced by alternative technologies. The dashed line f represents the original production function; any technological improvement means that less input is required to obtain the same output. The function f_1 represents equal savings of capital and labor—a neutral technological improvement over the original function f; the function f_2 indicates a more efficient labor force; and f_3 indicates more efficient capital.

As mentioned in the review of growth models, Solow[12] gives an expression for neutral technological changes that can be represented by a shift

[12] Solow, "Theory of Economic Growth."

from f to f_1, and Phelps[13] provides an expression for changes that are not necessarily neutral but that can be represented by shifts from f to f_1, f_2, f_3 or any mixed case.

5.1.3

Changes Along the Production Functions

Figures 5.1 to 5.3 can be thought of as production functions of a firm, an industry, or on aggregate economy. At any single point in time, only a single point on the line is realized; all other points on the line can be attained if certain conditions are met. If a profit-maximizing firm operates in a competitive market, it attempts to attain a point on the curve at which the marginal rate of substitution between the two input factors is equal to the ratio of the costs of the factors. At equilibrium, each firm, and thus the industry, will have chosen the production function indicated by the point at which the factor-cost-ratio line is tangent to the isoquant.

Exogenous events may affect the supply prices of the input, the demand schedule for the output, and the production function itself. As a result of such events, the point representing current operation on the production function is no longer the optimum point; equilibrium is destroyed. If changes continue, the optimum and actual points never do coincide; the economic unit (firm, industry, or economy) tries to attain an optimum production function by changing the output mix, the production process, or both.

The smoothness of the classical curve indicates that an infinite number of possibilities are available, but because actual changes must be made in discrete moves, a series of points (Figure 5.4) may be more representative of the possibilities in a fixed time period. Thus, the smooth curve may be considered the *ex ante* possibilities; the series of points on that curve, the *ex post* trace of realized conditions.[14]

If it can be assumed that the input proportions are fixed in the shortrun for relatively small changes in output, the production function becomes a set of nested corners as shown in Figure 5.5. This is one assumption of a Leontief input-output system; the ratio of each input to the output remains constant. A second assumption, no joint production, specifies that only one

---

[13] Phelps, "The Golden Rule."
[14] See the discussion of embodied and disembodied technological change by Robert Solow, "Substitution and Fixed Proportions in the Theory of Capital," *Review of Economic Studies*, vol. 29 (June 1962), pp. 207–218.

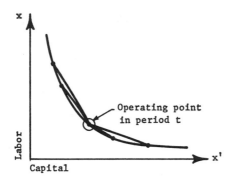

Figure 5.4.   Possible production functions in period $t + 1$.

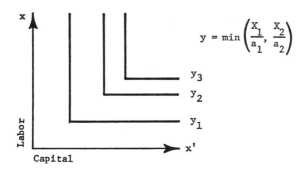

Figure 5.5.   Fixed-proportion production functions.

output can be produced by a single firm or industry.[15] However, profit-maximizing firms and industries do make changes in the output mix and changes in production processes as they adjust to their changing environments; an adaptive process for the dynamic case takes cognizance of these facts.

The Leontief assumptions of Chapter 4 are modified in this chapter so that they only need hold for one time period. Section 5.2 describes how, at the period's end, a series of changes can be defined and a new Leontief system can be specified to operate in the next period. The sequential series of such systems that exist over a time horizon is the *ex post* trace of the changing production function as shown in Figure 5.4.

---

[15] For a fuller discussion of substitutability in Leontief systems, see R. Dorfman, Paul Samuelson, and Robert Solow, *Linear Programming.* pp. 249–254.

The primary mechanism for increases in output is investment in physical capacity or in human resources. The investment can be neutral; but for the aggregate economy, it is likely to change the capital/labor ratio. Section 5.3 describes two algorithms for programming investment, a ranking algorithm, which uses the shadow prices obtained from the static case, and a parametric programming algorithm, which relaxes the static constraints.

5.2
The Extended Primary Model for the Dynamic Case

The adaptive modeling procedure for the dynamic case requires a primary model that contains the relationships required to connect the sequential static world states, that is, to relate X_{t+1} to X_t.

5.2.1
Required Linkages

The primary model for the dynamic case is an extension of the primary model discussed in Chapter 4. The extension, in the typical adaptive model format, is

$$X_{t+1} - F(X_t, Y_t, u_t) \tag{5.2}$$

where u_t is 0 in the case under certainty and X is explicitly defined in terms of constraints that vary from period to period. Thus,

$$(A, P, \mathbf{k}, \mathbf{m}, \mathbf{v})_{t+1} = F(A, P, \mathbf{k}, \mathbf{m}, \mathbf{Y})_t \tag{5.3}$$

where the plan $\mathbf{Y}$ not only includes the static decisions $\mathbf{e}$, $\mathbf{f}$, $\mathbf{e}^*$, and $\mathbf{v}$, but also the investments in $\mathbf{k}$ and $\mathbf{m}$. (See Table 4.3 for notation.)

The required addition to the static primary model is the interperiod linkages for inventory, physical capacity, manpower, and production and distribution coefficients. Final inventories for each sector at the end of the $t - 1$st period are identical to the initial inventories of the tth period; that is, $\bar{\mathbf{v}}^t = \mathbf{v}^{t-1} = \bar{\mathbf{v}}^{t-1} + \Delta \mathbf{v}^{t-1}$.

The interperiod linkage for the physical capacity of each sector is related to depreciation in the previous period, to investment in one or more previous periods, and to the marginal capital/output ratio of relevant investments. Basic data on the marginal capital/output ratios, the lag structure between investment and output, and the real (as opposed to bookkeeping) depreciation are generally inadequate, especially for non-manufacturing sectors. Thus, for each sector, the following assumptions are built into the primary model:

1.

Depreciation is directly proportional to capital stock (capacity) in place at the beginning of the period.[16]

2.

Investment can be divided into that made to expand capacity and that made for replacement purposes.

3.

Investment for replacement purposes equals the depreciation charges in every period. (Since this investment is just sufficient to maintain the capital stock, net investment is always nonnegative.)

4.

The capital/output ratio of net (that is, growth) investment is constant and the additional output is available in the period immediately following investment. (All net investments provide capacity with a one-period lag.)

5.

The varied durability of alternative investments can be represented by varying the replacement factor which determines the depreciation rate. (Alternatively, auxiliary models can be developed.)

5.2.2

The Linkage Equations for Capital and Labor

The relationships between investment and physical capacity can be expressed as

$$e_{10}^t = \Sigma_i (r_i + G_{i,k})^t, \tag{5.4}$$

$$r_i^t = \rho_i k_i^t, \tag{5.5}$$

$$k_i^{t+1} = k_i^t + \frac{G_{i,k}^t}{q_i}, \tag{5.6}$$

where, for all sectors combined, e_{10} is gross private investment for plant equipment;[17] and for each sector, r_i is the investment for replacement purposes, $G_{i,k}$ is the investment in plant and equipment for growth purposes, ρ_i is the replacement factor, k_i is the capital stock, q_i is the capital/output ratio, and t, $t+1$ are the superscripts referring to current and subsequent time periods.

---

[16] This follows if we assume an infinite stream of initial and replacement investments (the replacement made geometrically) beginning with the period following the initial investment. See Dale Jorgenson, "Anticipations and Investment Behavior," *The Brookings Quarterly Econometric Model of the United States* (Chicago: Rand McNally & Co., 1965), pp. 50–51.

[17] From the procedure used to disaggregate final demand in Chapter 4.

The distribution of investment expenditures among the eight sectors is assumed to be unaffected by interindustry composition or purpose (replacement or growth) of investment.[18]

The manpower $\bar{m}_i^t$ available to each sector at the beginning of the tth period equals $g_i x_i^{t-1}$, the product of the unit labor requirement and the previous period's output. Part of Δm_i^{t-1}, the manpower change in the previous period, is assumed to be accomplished without cost; this part is $\delta_i \bar{m}_i^{t-1}$. Total Δm_i is assumed to have occurred at the beginning of the period. A sector that could use more labor (labor-bound) satisfies the equality $g_i x_i = (1 + \delta_i) \bar{m}_i$, or $m_i = m_i^{\max}$; that is, for the optimum program this sector uses all the manpower that it can absorb without the training of additional workers. For this sector, the shadow price on labor is nonnegative; thus investment in training –to provide individuals with skills for employment in the sector—may be economically justified.

If n_i is the cost to train an individual in the labor force for employment in sector i and n_e is the cost to bring an additional worker into the labor force, the investment for training increases the labor available according to

$$\Delta m_i^{\max} = \frac{G_{i,m}^{t-1}}{n_i} \qquad i = 1, 2, \ldots, 8, s. \tag{5.7}$$

If we substitute $\Delta m_i^{\max} = \Delta \delta_i m_i^{t-1}$, the effect of investment on the labor expansion factor is

$$\Delta \delta_i = \frac{G_{i,m}^{t-1}}{m_i^{t-1} n_i} \qquad i = 1, 2, \ldots, 8, s \tag{5.8}$$

where for sector i, the $\Delta m_i^{\max}$ is the change in the maximum labor available, $\Delta \delta_i$ is the change in one-period manpower expansion, $G_{i,m}$ is the training investment, m_i is the manpower employed, and n_i is the unit training cost.

In Equations 5.7 and 5.8, the subscript s refers to the addition of one worker to the labor force. If he goes to a sector that is saturated, the sum of the training costs ($n_i + n_s$) implies that this new worker was recruited from another sector and replaced, in turn, by an individual who was not

---

[18] It is possible to obtain and use capital flow matrices similar to the A matrix to distribute these expenditures among the producing sectors. However, the errors even in the conceptually best capital/output ratios would seem to be greater than those introduced by using the single distribution vector ($\mathbf{p}_{10}$ in the P matrix of Chapter 4) to allocate total investment expenditures among the producing sectors.

originally in the labor force. To summarize, it is assumed that a sector can add δ_i new workers at zero cost but that n_i dollars must be invested for each additional worker.

The distribution patterns of matrix A or P may also change over time (that is, technology or demand patterns may change). The primary model does not forecast these changes; however, the adaptive procedure allows the policy maker to change to new A and/or P matrices, if he has adequate knowledge to do so.

5.3
The Decision-Making Algorithms for Investment

The decision maker—in the static case of Chapter 4—allocated sector-specific capital and labor resources. The decision rules could be explicitly specified; thus the linear programming algorithm filled the decision-making role. The decision maker in the dynamic case of this chapter also allocates investment funds to maintain or supplement resources. A ranking algorithm—based on shadow prices divided by retraining costs or capital/output ratios—and a parametric programming algorithm act as the decision maker to allocate investments in plant and equipment and for human resource development in order to relax constraints on labor and capital. Other methods are used to allocate investments in inventories and residential housing and to allocate depreciation funds for maintenance and replacement of capital stock.

5.3.1
The Ranking Algorithm

The ranking algorithm orders the alternative investments in physical and human resources on the basis of their marginal efficiencies.

DETERMINING THE SHADOW PRICES

Some of the most significant results obtained from the linear programming solution to the static case are the various shadow prices.

The simple model (Section 4.2.1) had only one scarce resource—the homogenous labor supply. The static case described in Chapter 4 has 25 scarce resources: total labor supply and, for each of eight sectors, capital, labor, and beginning inventory; of these, 16 (capital and labor for each of eight sectors) are the same variables discussed for the production function (Figures 5.1 to 5.5). If an economic system is in long-run equilibrium, the actual production function for each sector is at a corner formed by the intersection of the two constraints; in this case, labor and capital are equally limiting in all sectors, and all shadow prices are equal and close to zero; but in any real situation, with change always present and adjustment made imperfectly and in discrete steps, this case would be highly improbable.

Positive slack, and thus a zero shadow price, is associated with any constraint that is not limiting. Alternatively, a zero slack and thus a positive shadow price indicates that the program value would be improved if one more unit of the constraining resource could be made available. The shadow prices are the marginal productivities of each unit of manpower or capital added to each sector.

In Chapter 4, the optimum program completely exhausted the labor supply; thus, labor-bound sectors can be constrained because either the sector's manpower or the total labor force cannot be increased further (without investing in training). Labor-bound sectors with a nonzero shadow price for sector-specific manpower have reached the δ_i (say 10 percent) limit on manpower growth; those with a nonzero price on total manpower have reached the limit imposed by the total manpower restriction.[10]

Since the optimum program in the example of Chapter 4 fully employs the labor force, it must have reassigned all "excess" labor from capital-bound to labor-bound sectors; thus capital-bound sectors are near the corner of the production function, and if any additional capital stock is to be used, the labor force must increase correspondingly. If the optimum program does not fully employ the labor force (for example, in a case of structural unemployment), an increase in capital stock increases output and employment.

The following are observations based on the shadow prices in Table 5.1. Addition of one worker to sector 2 (construction) increases the value of the objective function (or GNP) by $1,000(7.6736) or $7,674.[20] An increase in physical capacity in sector 5 (residual industry), which allows an industry to produce an additional $1,000/year of goods, increases the value of the objective function by $1,000(0.4518) or $452. If beginning inventories are decreased to their minimum value, their shadow prices are positive; further, it is possible that the inventory of a bottleneck sector is considerably

[19] The numerical value of this latter shadow price really applies only to the sector that would receive the next available worker.
[20] This may be considered as the benefit obtainable from a retraining program that makes such a transfer possible.

Table 5.1 Shadow Prices of the Sample Static Problem (in $/$ except labor, which is $1,000/worker)

Sector	Physical Capacity s	Beginning Inventory v	Sector Labor u	Total Labor u_s
1	0	0	2.0546	—
2	0	0.0001	7.6736	—
3	0	0.2055	0	3.0958
4	0.4243	0	0	—
5	0.4518	0.0001	0	—
6	0	0.0002	5.6766	—
7	0.2500	0.0001	0	—
8	0	0	0	3.0958

more valuable than the price established by ϵ_i because of interindustry relations.

The linear programming algorithm provides the shadow prices, or marginal values of each resource for the optimum program. However, the marginal costs of adding them to each resource are not provided by the primary model; for labor, it is the cost of retraining; for capital, it is the capital/output ratio. These costs can either be informally estimated or be computed by an auxiliary model. Shadow prices divided by relevant training costs or capital/output ratios are a measure of the anticipated increase in GNP per dollar of investment and a measure of aggregate marginal efficiency of investment (MEI).[21] Thus, potential investments in human or physical resources can be ordered; the following numerical example illustrates the computations involved.

Sector	Shadow Price on Capital	Assumed Capital/Output Ratio	Marginal Efficiency of Investment (MEI)	Rank of MEI
5	0.4518	3	0.1506	2
4	0.4243	2	0.2122	1

[21] At this point we ignore the durability of the investment or the length of time for which the additional output will be forthcoming. The primary model for the dynamic case does include the capital replacement rate, but this is not explicitly considered in the investment determination equations unless the capital/output ratios are adjusted (again, informally or by using an auxiliary model) to account for it.

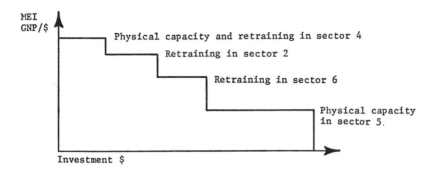

Figure 5.6. Typical flow of investment.

ALLOCATING INVESTMENT AMONG SECTORS

Ordering investment opportunities by their respective marginal efficiencies does not provide an optimum investment program; that is, ranking does not indicate how the total investment should be allocated. An optimum program can be obtained by repeating the following process until investment funds are exhausted. First, determine how much investment must be allocated to the most efficient alternative (resource with the highest MEI) to change its rank; allocate that amount; then recompute the new shadow prices and MEIs and allocate appropriate funds to the new top-ranked alternative.

The argument is that application of a linear programming algorithm assumes that each retraining resource has a constant MEI that falls to zero when the resource is sufficiently increased by investment.[22] (Figure 5.6 illustrates the concept.) Since any resource has a positive MEI if the shadow price is positive, investment should flow to increase the resource with the highest MEI sufficiently or until that constraint is no longer limiting and until the shadow price (and MEI) fall to zero. At this point, under the new conditions, the shadow prices should be recalculated and the investment directed to the most productive resource; the process continues until all investment funds are expended.

Parametric programming methods can be used to vary the resource constraint systematically and to determine the amount of funds that must

---

[22] The shadow price may again become nonzero at a later iteration after other constraints are relaxed; in fact, it is likely that the relaxed constraint will quickly become binding if any other constraint is relaxed. The likely result is that both constraints will then have to be relaxed simultaneously.

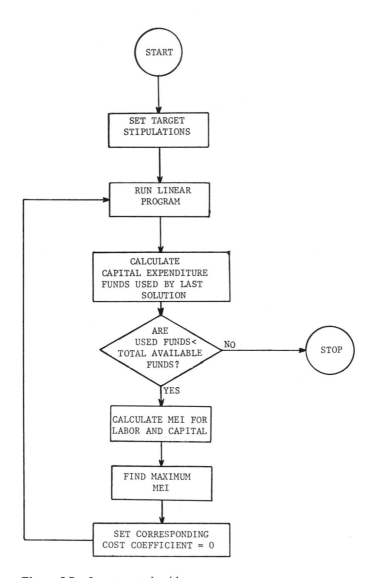

Figure 5.7. Investment algorithms.

be invested before the shadow price falls to zero. In Figure 5.6, the shadow price divided by the capital/output ratio, or MEI, determines the height of the line, and parametric programming determines the length of the line segments. The single line for physical capacity and retraining implies that these two constraints must be jointly relaxed. Section 5.3.2 describes the way in which parametric programming is applied in this procedure.

5.3.2
Applying Parametric Programming to Investment Decisions

Formulation of the parametric programming problem is similar to that of the linear programming problem except for the following additions: Growth variables ($\Delta \mathbf{k}$, $\Delta \mathbf{m}$, and Δm_s) were added to the constraint Equations 5.11, 5.12, and 5.13 and to the objective function; a constraint on total investment was added (Equation 5.16). Figure 5.7 is the flow diagram and Table 5.2 is the tableau for the parametric program.

With these additions, the following parametric programming problem was formulated: Maximize

$$\phi = \sum_{i=1}^{8} \left(c_{v_i} v_i + c_{\Delta k_i} \Delta k_i + c_{\Delta m_i} \Delta m_i \right) - c_{\Delta m_s} \Delta m_s + \sum_{j=1}^{3} \left(c_{e_j} e_j + c_{f_j} f_j \right)$$

$$(5.9)$$

Table 5.2   Tableau for the Sample Parametric Programming Routine

Vectors of Solution and Stock Variables	s	u	u_s	f	n	γ	e	e*	x	v	Δk	Δm	Δm_s
c_j	0	0	0	−0.10	0	0	1.00	0		0	0.999	−999	−999
p_i													
k	I								I		−I		
$\overline{\mathbf{m}}$		I							D_g			−I	
$\overline{m}_s$			I						g				−I
$\overline{\mathbf{e}}$				I		I	−I						
$\overline{\mathbf{v}}$					I	P			−(I − A)	I			
$\overline{\mathbf{v}}^{\mathrm{max}}$						I				I			

subject to

$$v + Pe - (I - A)x - f = \bar{v} \tag{5.10}$$

$$x + s - \Delta k = \bar{k} \tag{5.11}$$

$$D_g x + u - \Delta m = \bar{m} \tag{5.12}$$

$$\sum_{i=1}^{8} g_i x_i + u_s - \Delta m_s = \bar{m}_s \tag{5.13}$$

$$\gamma + v = \bar{v}^{\text{max}} \tag{5.14}$$

$$e - e^* + f = \bar{e} \tag{5.15}$$

$$\text{CEFU} \leq \text{CEF}. \tag{5.16}$$

For each iteration,

$$\text{MEI} = \frac{\text{SP}}{\text{COR}} \tag{5.17}$$

and

$$\sum_{i=1}^{8} (\text{COR}_{\Delta k_i} \, \Delta k_i) + \sum_{i=1}^{8} (\text{COR}_{\Delta m_i} \, \Delta m_i) + \text{COR}_{\Delta m_s} \Delta m_s = \text{CEFU}. \tag{5.18}$$

The additional notations are

Δk = Vector of change in capacity to permit growth by sector.

Δm = Vector of change in labor force by sector.

Δm_s = Change in total labor force.

CEF = Total capital expenditure fund.

CEFU = Capital expenditure fund used.

$\text{COR}_{\Delta k_i}$ = Capital/output ratio by sector = q_i.

$\text{COR}_{\Delta m_i}$ = Retraining cost by sector = n_i.

MEI = Marginal efficiency of investment.

SP = Shadow price by sector.

In order to reduce the size of the P matrix (see Table 5.3) so that the problem would not exceed the computer storage capacity, the seven personal consumption expenditure (PCE) categories were combined into one PCE category; fixed capital formation and residential construction expenditures were combined into one investment category; and federal, state, and local government expenditures were combined into one government category. As a result, the parametric model has only three final

Table 5.3 1958 B Matrix of Final Demand Expenditures (millions of dollars at purchaser's price)

| Industrial Sector | Final Demand Expenditures by Category | | | |
	1 Consumption	2 Investment	3 Government	Total
1. Agriculture	$8,061	0	$948	$9,009
2. Construction	0	$54,957	19,877	74,834
3. Trade	377	3,747	828	4,952
4. Regulated	15,485	869	3,034	19,388
5. Residual	91,808	1,209	7,981	100,998
6. Durables	33,933	20,313	15,540	69,786
7. Nondurables	129,112	102	3,600	132,814
8. Government	944	0	39,271	40,215
Total	$279,720	$81,197	$91,079	$451,996 (GNP)

Source: Computed from Table 4.4. Categories 1–7 were combined as consumption; 8 and 9, as investment; 10 and 11, as government.

demand categories—personal consumption, investment, and government. The aggregated B matrix is given in Table 5.4 for the three categories.

The same eight industrial sectors were retained. Table 5.5 lists initial constraints and capital/output ratios for the sectors.

A parametric programming algorithm, like a linear programming algorithm, is iterative. In the first iteration, high negative values are assigned to the coefficients of the growth variables; the solution obtained is identical to the linear programming solution for the static case. Subsequent iterations proceed as follows: The program identifies the growth variable associated with the highest MEI (highest SP/COR ratio), and the large negative penalty (value coefficient) is removed (set at 0) to release the variable for expansion. The iterations continue, releasing one slack variable at a time (thus, a new solution at each stage) until the limit set by available capital expenditure funds (CEF) is reached.

In the sample problem, CEF was set high—$200 billion—to allow many iterations (or solutions); as a result, each of eight iterations released a growth variable (either a Δk or a Δm). Table 5.6 lists the solutions variables (that is, instrument values) and Table 5.7 lists the shadow prices for the eight iterations.

Table 5.4   1958 P Matrix of Final Demand Pattern Coefficients

Industrial Sector	Final Demand Category (dollars/dollar)		
	1 Consumption	2 Investment	3 Government
1. Agriculture	0.02882	0	0.01040
2. Construction	0	0.67684	0.21824
3. Trade	0.00135	0.04615	0.00909
4. Regulated	0.05536	0.01070	0.03331
5. Residual	0.32821	0.01489	0.08763
6. Durables	0.12131	0.25017	0.17062
7. Nondurables	0.46158	0.00126	0.03953
8. Government	0.00337	0	0.43118

Source: Computed from Table 5.3: $\dfrac{\text{Category } j \text{ dollars spent in sector } i}{\text{Total dollars spent for category } j}$.

Table 5.5   Constraints in the Sample Parametric Programming Problem

Industrial Sector	Labor $\bar{\mathbf{m}}$ (thousands of workers)	Physical Capacity $\bar{\mathbf{k}}$ (millions of dollars)	Beginning Inventory $\bar{\mathbf{v}}$	Maximum Inventory $\bar{\mathbf{v}}^{\max}$	Investment/Output Ratios $\mathrm{COR}^*_{\Delta k}$	$\mathrm{COR}^+_{\Delta m}$
1. Agriculture	8,000	$79,152	$12,000	$24,000	1.8	0.4
2. Construction	4,000	82,280	12,000	24,000	0.8	0.2
3. Trade	14,000	39,461	6,000	12,000	0.9	1.5
4. Regulated	6,000	71,252	11,000	22,000	2.2	0.3
5. Residual	13,000	205,577	30,000	60,000	0.8	0.3
6. Durables	11,000	200,171	30,000	60,000	1.2	0.3
7. Nondurables	9,000	269,315	40,000	80,000	1.3	0.2
8. Government	10,000	52,082	8,000	16,000	0.9	0.8
Total	68,000 §	—	$149,000	—	—	0.5

Source: U.S. Dept. of Commerce, Bureau of the Census, *Long Term Economic Growth, 1860–1965*, October 1966.
* Calculated (1958 plant and equipment expenditures)/(growth in output for 1957–60).
† Calculated training cost (estimated as $5,000/worker) $\times$ $(g_i/1,000)$.
§ Total labor force is less than the sum of those available to individual sectors.

Table 5.6   Solutions to the Sample Parametric Programming Problem

Instrument Values by Industrial Sectors	Iteration 1	2	3	4	5	6	7	8
Gross output (x)								
1	79,151	79,151	79,151	79,151	79,151	79,151	79,151	44,775
2	82,278	82,278	107,727	144,771	144,732	144,636	168,868	565,434
3	39,461	45,119	46,718	46,718	48,632	53,441	58,429	132,816
4	71,251	71,251	71,251	71,251	71,251	71,251	71,251	71,251
5	205,574	205,574	205,574	205,574	205,574	205,574	205,574	177,190
6	200,168	200,168	200,168	200,168	200,168	200,168	226,895	682,170
7	269,312	269,312	269,312	269,312	269,312	269,312	269,312	77,986
8	52,081	52,081	52,081	52,081	52,081	52,081	52,081	1,289
Slack capacity (s)								
1	0	0	0	0	0	0	0	34,376
2	0	0	0	0	0	0	0	0
3	0	0	0	0	0	0	0	0
4	0	0	0	0	0	0	0	0
5	0	0	0	0	0	0	0	28,383
6	0	0	0	0	0	0	0	0
7	0	0	0	0	0	0	0	191,326
8	0	0	0	0	0	0	0	50,798
Change in capacity (Δk)								
1	0	0	0	0	0	0	0	0
2	0	0	25,450	62,494	62,455	62,359	86,591	483,160
3	0	5,659	7,257	7,257	9,172	13,981	18,968	93,356
4	0	0	0	0	0	0	0	0
5	0	0	0	0	0	0	0	0
6	0	0	0	0	0	0	26,727	482,005
7	0	0	0	0	0	0	0	0
8	0	0	0	0	0	0	0	0
Unemployed labor (u)								
1	1,375	1,375	1,375	1,375	1,375	1,375	1,375	4,252
2	945	945	0	0	0	0	0	0
3	2,175	479	0	0	0	0	0	0
4	1,627	1,627	1,627	1,627	1,627	1,627	1,627	1,627
5	2,104	2,104	2,104	2,104	2,104	2,104	2,104	3,609
6	1,296	1,296	1,296	1,296	1,296	1,296	0	0
7	1,168	1,168	1,168	1,168	1,168	1,168	1,168	6,732
8	1,377	1,377	1,977	1,377	1,377	1,377	1,377	9,787
s	5,067	3,372	1,948	572	0	0	0	0
Change in labor force (Δm)								
1	0	0	0	0	0	0	0	0
2	0	0	0	1,375	1,374	1,370	2,270	16,994
3	0	0	0	0	574	2,015	3,510	25,801
4	0	0	0	0	0	0	0	0
5	0	0	0	0	0	0	0	0
6	0	0	0	0	0	0	0	22,072
7	0	0	0	0	0	0	0	0
8	0	0	0	0	0	0	0	0
	0	0	0	0	0	1,437	5,128	45,859
Slack on inventory (γ)								
1	13,235	13,232	13,343	10,156	10,159	10,168	10,435	16,000
2	24,000	24,000	24,000	0	0	0	0	0
3	5,563	0	2,331	6,631	4,743	0	0	0
4	15,246	15,454	17,148	12,063	12,140	12,334	14,935	21,999
5	57,693	58,304	59,999	25,003	26,139	26,781	31,028	0
6	38,982	39,004	58,150	59,999	59,999	59,999	59,999	0
7	80,000	80,000	78,389	30,739	30,810	30,989	34,068	79,999
8	4,365	4,443	16,000	4,092	4,119	4,187	4,306	0
Ending inventory (v)								
1	10,765	10,768	10,657	13,844	13,840	13,832	13,565	23,999
2	0	0	0	24,000	24,000	24,000	24,000	24,000
3	6,437	12,000	9,669	5,369	7,257	12,000	12,000	11,999
4	6,754	6,545	4,852	9,937	9,860	9,665	7,065	0
5	2,306	1,695	0	34,116	33,861	33,219	28,971	59,999
6	21,018	20,995	1,849	11,907	0	11,812	0	59,998
7	0	0	1,611	49,261	49,189	49,010	45,931	0
8	11,635	11,557	0	0	11,880	0	11,693	0

Table 5.6 (continued)   Solutions to Sample Parametric Programming Problem

Dependent Variable by Final Demand Category	Iteration 1	2	3	4	5	6	7	8
Final demand (e)								
1	394,572	394,101	385,096	279,709	279,709	279,709	279,709	0
2	80,726	80,658	109,591	137,501	137,421	137,220	172,877	798,974
3	91,078	91,078	117,886	91,077	91,077	91,077	91,077	0
Excess demand (e*)								
1	114,859	114,389	105,386	0	0	0	0	0
2	0	0	28,395	56,306	56,226	56,025	91,683	717,786
3	0	0	26,809	0	0	0	0	0
Imports (f)								
1	0	0	0	0	0	0	0	279,705
2	470	539	0	0	0	0	0	0
3	0	0	0	0	0	0	0	91,073

Table 5.7   Shadow Prices in the Sample Parametric Programming Problem (dollars/dollar except labor, which is $1,000/worker)

Industrial Sector	Iteration 1	2	3	4	5	6	7	8
Capacity ($\bar{k}$)								
1	0.4302	0.4569	0.4320	0.4301	0.2322	0.4556	0.4556	0
2	0.5758	0.6922	0	0	0	0	0	0
3	0.7165	0	0	0	0	0	0	0
4	0.6063	0.6196	0.6086	0.6039	0.4598	0.6150	0.6150	9.7131
5	0.6063	0.9197	0.6396	0.5879	0.4673	0.5944	0.5944	0
6	0.4273	0.4552	0.4271	0.8196	0.6242	0.9521	0	0
7	0.3581	0.3825	0.3398	0.3203	0.2559	0.3368	0.3368	0
8	0.4866	0.4884	0.5162	0.5338	0.1353	0.5427	0.5427	0
Labor force ($\bar{m}$)								
1	0	0	0	0	0	0	0	0
2	0	0	11.4913	0	0	0	0	0
3	0	0	2.3834	2.3689	0	0	0	0
4	0	0	0	0	0	0	0	0
5	0	0	0	0	0	0	0	0
6	0	0	0	0	0	0	19.6391	0
7	0	0	0	0	0	0	0	0
8	0	0	0	0	0	0	0	0
s	0	0	0	0	2.3748	0	0	0
Beginning inventory ($\bar{v}$)								
1	0	0	0	0	0	0	0	0
2	0.1625	0.2122	0.0141	0	0	0	0	0
3	0	0	0	0	0	0	0	0
4	0	0	0	0	0	0	0	10.1833
5	0	0	0.0304	0	0	0	0	0
6	0	0	0	0.6136	0.4876	0.7782	0.7782	0
7	0.0217	0.0238	0	0	0	0	0	0.0417
8	0	0	0.0099	0	0	0	0	0.9307
Maximum inventory ($\bar{v}^{max}$)								
1	0	0	0	0	0	0	0	0.3132
2	0	0	0	0.2121	0.1655	0.2238	0.2238	0.1042
3	0	0.7288	0	0	0	0.7198	0.7198	0.3258
4	0	0	0	0	0	0	0	0
5	0	0	0	0	0	0	0	0.2797
6	0	0	0	0	0	0	0	0.0371
7	0	0	0	0	0	0	0	0
8	0	0	0	0	0	0	0	0
Final Demand by Category								
Target final demand ($\bar{e}$)								
1	0.1000	0.1000	0.1000	0.0356	0.0508	0.0166	0.0166	0
2	0	0	0.1000	0.1000	0.1000	0.1000	0.1000	0.1000
3	0.0737	0.0694	0.1000	0.0516	0.0629	0.0326	0.0326	0

Table 5.8 Additional Output from the Sample Parametric Programming Problem

	1	2	3	4	5	6	7	8
Part A. Summary Figures								
Program Value ($ billions)	624.7	628.7	640.9	655.2	656.6	660.0	685.5	940.1
CEF	200.0	200.0	200.0	200.0	200.0	200.0	200.0	200.0
CEFU ($ billions)	0	5.1	26.9	56.8	59.4	66.5	126.7	1,120.6
Average MEI ($\Delta\phi$/CEFU)		0.796	0.605	0.538	0.538	0.532	0.480	0.281

Part B. Value Coefficient by Industrial Sector

On capital ($c_{\Delta k}$)

	1	2	3	4	5	6	7	8
1	−999	−999	−999	−999	−999	−999	−999	−999
2	−999	−999	0	0	0	0	0	0
3	−999	0	0	0	0	0	0	0
4	999	−999	−999	−999	−999	−999	−999	−999
5	−999	−999	−999	−999	−999	−999	−999	−999
6	−999	−999	−999	−999	−999	−999	0	0
7	−999	−999	−999	−999	−999	−999	−999	−999
8	−999	−999	−999	−999	−999	−999	−999	−999

On labor ($c_{\Delta m}$)

	1	2	3	4	5	6	7	8
1	−999	−999	−999	−999	−999	−999	−999	−999
2	−999	−999	−999	0	0	0	0	0
3	−999	−999	−999	−999	0	0	0	0
4	−999	−999	−999	−999	−999	−999	−999	−999
5	−999	−999	−999	−999	−999	−999	−999	−999
6	−999	−999	−999	−999	−999	−999	−999	0
7	−999	−999	−999	−999	−999	−999	−999	−999
8	−999	−999	−999	−999	−999	−999	−999	−999
s	−999	−999	−999	−999	−999	0	0	0

Part C. Marginal Efficiency of Investment (MEI) by Industrial Sector*

Capital

	1	2	3	4	5	6	7	8
1	0.2390	0.2538	0.2400	0.2390	0.1290	0.2531	0.2531	
2	0.7198	*0.8653*	0	0	0	0	0	
3	*0.7961*	0	0	0	0	0	0	
4	0.2756	0.2816	0.2766	0.2745	0.2090	0.2795	0.2795	
5	0.7579	0.7747	0.7995	0.7348	0.5841	0.7430	0.7430	
6	0.3560	0.3793	0.3559	0.6830	0.5202	*0.7934*	0	
7	0.2755	0.2942	0.2614	0.2463	0.1960	0.2591	0.2591	
8	0.5406	0.5427	0.5736	0.5931	0.1503	0.6029	0.6029	

Labor

	1	2	3	4	5	6	7	8
1	0	0	0	0	0	0	0	
2	0	0	*57.4563*	0	0	0	0	
3	0	0	1.5890	*1.5792*	0	0	0	
4	0	0	0	0	0	0	0	
5	0	0	0	0	0	0	0	
6	0	0	0	0	0	0	*65.4636*	
7	0	0	0	0	0	0	0	
8	0	0	0	0	0	0	0	
s	0	0	0	0	*4.7496*	0	0	

* Maximum MEI for each solution is in italics.

Table 5.8 gives additional information concerning each of the eight iterations. Part A provides summary results. The first row of data shows the increasing "Program Value" as more investment resources are used to relax the constraints. The third row, CEFU, shows how much of the $200 billion available for investment (CEF in the second row) has been used at the end of each iteration (for example, $66.5 million and $126.7 million at the end of the sixth and seventh iterations, respectively). The fourth row is the average MEI (that is, output change/investment) for each level of investment. Note that the number decreases montonically; this behavior is discussed further in Section 5.4.3.

Part B illustrates the procedure of relaxing one constraint per iteration by removing its large negative penalty (replacing −999 by zero). Part C lists the MEI or marginal efficiency of investment (SP/COR) for each constraint at the end of each iteration. These results identify the constraint to be relaxed in the next iteration (that is, its coefficient will be changed from −999 to zero).

5.3.3
Housing, Inventory, and Replacement Investments

The remaining microlevel investment decisions are the allocation of investments to residential construction and inventories and to the replacement (or maintenance) of plant and equipment.

Investment in residential construction may be determined informally by the policy maker or by an auxiliary model; inventory investment is calculated by the linear programming algorithm in the static case; replacement investment is assumed equal to depreciation changes.

Section 5.4 discusses the macrolevel investment decision in an attempt to answer the question: What should the total amount of investment be?

5.4
The Macrolevel Investment Decision

The most important single problem that growth theory attempts to solve concerns the optimum division of output between consumption and investment; that is the subject of this section.

5.4.1
Full Employment Investment Programs

In national accounting terms, the primary model's investment items are residential construction, inventory investment, and net investment for plant and equipment. Only the last of these is an instrument of the adaptive procedure; to it must be added the human resource investment h, which is assumed to be made by state and local governments. Thus, in the procedure, the macrolevel investment decision—the establishment of growth investment G—is expressed symbolically as

$$G = \Sigma_i(G_{i,k} + G_{i,m});$$ (5.19)

where the $G_{i,k}$ and $G_{i,m}$ are the growth investments made to relax the constraints on capital and manpower for sector i.

One approach, similar to that used by Keynesian growth models of the Harrod-Domar type, is to establish minimum investment at a level which insures full employment of new capacity. This approach is taken if the economic concern is that demand is insufficient relative to capacity; such an economic condition is simulated by assigning a zero value coefficient to consumption above the target demand level (that is, to c_i^* where $i = 1, 2, \ldots, 7$) and by restricting inventory growth so that the program will increase the remaining profitable final demand categories (plant and equipment investment e_{10} and state and local government expenditures e_9). Thus, growth investment G is

$$G = (e_{10} - r) + (e_9 - \text{nontraining } e_9)$$

and (5.20)

$$r = \Sigma_i \rho_i k_i$$

where r is depreciation and $(e_9 - \text{nontraining } e_9)$ is state and local expenditures for training programs.[23]

The first step in using the procedure to obtain a full employment investment level is to establish a tentative target for final demand for each category other than 9 and 10. The consumer demand C^t resulting from the investment G^{t-1} is $(G^{t-1})/(1 - b)$ where b is the aggregate propensity to consume and $1/(1 - b)$ is the one-period Keynesian multiplier (which is assumed constant and independent of the composition of G).

To obtain a full employment investment level, assume that the induced demand is distributed uniformly among categories e_j ($j = 1, 2, \ldots, 7$) and that the residential construction investment and government expenditures (except for h) are provided exogenously (perhaps by auxiliary models containing population growth and GNP as explanatory variables). Thus,

---

[23] The following assumes that state and local government expenditures for manpower training is deficit financed. This assumption can be easily relaxed.

all required variables ($\bar{e}_j$ where $j = 1, 2, \ldots, 8, 11$) can be estimated and substituted in the static primary model to solve for e_9 and e_{10}. Depreciation r can be calculated, and state and local funds expended for purposes other than training can be set exogenously or by an auxiliary model; then G can be computed using Equation 5.20.

The next three sections consider the alternative problem that arises when the optimum level of investment exceeds the minimum required to maintain full employment and, thus, a choice must be made between consumption and investment.

5.4.2

The Growth Path

Conceptually, the growth path may be viewed as a trace of the process of production, consumption, and investment. Investments made in each period relax the constraints on production in future periods.

The efficiency of the growth investment G is measured in terms of the policy maker's objective function; the efficiency E is given by

$$E = \frac{\Delta\phi}{G} \,. \tag{5.21}$$

From equation 5.19, $G = \Sigma_i(G_{i,k} + G_{i,m})$, so that total net investment equals the sum of net investments in capital and human resources. For a single period, this equals the sum of individual investment increments $(1, 2, \ldots, z)$ allocated in the parametric programming routine (see Figure 5.6 and Table 5.8); thus, in any period,

$$G = \Sigma_z\Sigma_i(G_{i,k} + G_{i,m})_z. \tag{5.22}$$

If the output of the economy is bound by the capacity of a single sector (say a) and if sector a is bound by capital but not by labor, then the first increment of investment will be allocated to sector a capital to relax this constraint. The efficiency of the investment increment E_1 is the ratio of the shadow price to the capital/output ratio:[24]

$$E_1 = \frac{\text{SP}_a}{q_a} \,. \tag{5.23}$$

[24] The numerical subscripts used in the remainder of this section refer to investment increments $1, 2, \ldots, z$. The time superscripts have been omitted to simplify the notation. The marginal efficiencies (or MEI) previously used refer to an investment for a single constraint (that is, capacity or manpower for a single sector). The efficiency E refers to the investment made in a single time period in all constraints.

The solution to the numerical example for the static case (Chapter 4) fully employed the labor force; thus the algorithm automatically re-assigned "excess" workers from capital-bound sectors to sectors that were labor-bound. Equation 5.23 would not hold for that particular example since the labor force would have to expand hand-in-hand with capital (at a cost of n_s per additional worker); thus Equation 5.23 would become

$$E_1 = \frac{SP_a}{(q_a + n_s)_1} = \frac{SP_a}{G_1}. \tag{5.23a}$$

The efficiency of investment would be given by Equation 5.23a until sector a could no longer increase its labor force without expending training funds; then all three constraints (total labor force, sector a physical capacity, and sector a labor force) must be increased jointly. Thus the efficiency of the next increment of investment would be

$$E_2 = \frac{SP_a}{(q_a + n_a + n_a)_2} = \frac{SP_a}{G_2} \tag{5.24}$$

where $E_2 < E_1$.

Efficiency of the combined investment would be the weighted sum of the two; thus,

$$E_{1,2} = \frac{G_1}{G_2 + G_1} E_1 + \frac{G_2}{G_2 + G_1} E_2. \tag{5.25}$$

If investment continues to increase the capacity of sector a, the point will be reached where it is no longer binding; that is, the shadow price will be zero and a new sector (say sector b) will call for the next investment increment. However, it is unlikely that the capacity of sector b could be increased much without a corresponding increase in sector a; thus the efficiency of the third increment of investment might be

$$E_3 = \frac{SP_{a,b}}{(q_a + n_s + n_a + q_b + n_b)_3} = \frac{SP_{a,b}}{G_3}. \tag{5.26}$$

The process of allocating investment continues until no bottlenecks exist and all resources are equally binding; at this point, the resources of the economy are balanced and the economy is in a state of long-run equilibrium.

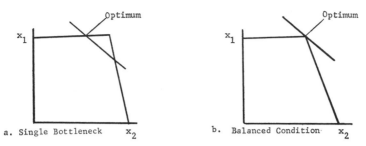

Figure 5.8. Relaxing constraints in a two-good, three-constraint economy.

Figure 5.8 illustrates the concept of relaxing constraints until a balanced condition is attained for a simple two-good, three-constraint economy. The initial investment increment relaxes the bottleneck constraint; next, a balanced condition is reached and, from this point on, all constraints must be simultaneously relaxed.

5.4.3
Equilibrium Growth

The simplest growth path to analyze is an equilibrium path in which technology, demand patterns, tastes, and prices remain constant; that is, this path has successive periods with constant A and P matrices and $\bar{e}$ and c^* vectors. At the beginning of the path, few bottlenecks exist and the amount of investment required to change the rankings at each iteration of the parametric programming routine is large; thus, few increments are required to fully exhaust available investment funds. As a result, the denominator of equations, such as Equation 5.26, is relatively small and the investment efficiency is relatively high. As time proceeds along this path, the economy becomes more nearly balanced; ultimately, a point of complete equilibrium is reached and all the constraints must be simultaneously relaxed for production to expand. From this point of long-run equilibrium, maximal balanced growth occurs along a Leontief trajectory, and therefore, along an efficient von Neumann path.[25]

The marginal efficiency of each increment of investment along the balanced growth path will be less than when fewer bottlenecks were present; accordingly,

$$E_e = \frac{SP}{\sum_{i=1}^{8} q_i + \sum_{i=1}^{8} n_i + n_s} . \tag{5.27}$$

[25] R. Dorfman, Paul Samuelson, and Robert Solow, *Linear Programming*, pp. 326–345.

Thus, while balanced growth may be efficient, the efficiency or return on investment is low—perhaps too low to call forth investment necessary to maintain full employment. This is the stagnation situation described by Keynes and others.

If the economy is truly dynamic so that the technology and demand pattern matrices and the price and demand vectors change, the adaptive procedure easily shows that new bottlenecks arise; in a situation of stochastic growth, complete balance is never achieved and stagnation will never occur.

5.4.4

Stochastic Growth

Real-world growth does not take place along an equilibrium path. Technology, demand patterns, prices, tastes, world conditions, and so forth constantly change; these changes are reflected in the model by changes in the A and P matrices, the c^* vector, and the $\bar{e}$ values (for example, population growth or increased defense spending will change elements of the e vector). Thus, truly balanced growth is never attained and bottlenecks, with corresponding investment opportunities, are always present.

If changes in the real world system are determined probabilistically, the growth is stochastic, and the question of allocating output between consumption and investment becomes a dynamic decision problem under uncertainty; then the programming algorithms of Chapters 4 and 5 can no longer fill the decision-making role. The following chapters describe an adaptive procedure for this class of problem but in the context of stabilization rather than growth policy. However, preliminary remarks about the problem in a growth context are made here.

The major decision is: How much net investment is required for each period or how should current production be divided between current consumption and investment? First, output in each period is assumed to be optimized and the portion set aside for investment optimally allocated to the producing sectors;[26] next, available information is assumed to provide, with certainty, the past performance of the economy and the efficiency of each increment of current investment; and finally, the auxiliary models (based on predicted changes in technology, demands, and so

---

[26] The optimum consumption-investment split is contingent on the other two optima being obtained (from linear and parametric programming routines), but it can be considered as a separate and independent problem.

forth) are assumed to provide uncertain estimates of the investment efficiency for future periods.

For this dynamic problem under uncertainty, the instrument, or decision variable, is the consumption-investment split; the variable that describes the relevant aspect of the state of the world is the MEI for various levels of investment; and the planning horizon is infinite.

If the planning horizon is infinite, it is generally necessary to truncate after a "manageable" number of stages; however, the terminal conditions of the problem must reflect the relevance of the period beyond the truncation point.[27] (This is a realistic planning procedure, because it is impossible for planners to deal with the infinite number of choices that an infinite period of time makes possible.) As a result, the time span between the present and the truncation point is the planning horizon.

The objective function must consider both the path (from the present time, at $t = 0$, to the end of the planning horizon at $t = T$) and the terminal conditions at the end of the planning horizon; thus it should be a function of consumption $\mathbf{C}$ along the path and a function of capital and labor force resources $\mathbf{Z}$ at the terminal point. If the terminal resource structure is evaluated in terms of potential output, the dynamic problem is written as

$$\text{maximize} \sum_{t=0}^{T-1} \mathbf{c}^t \mathbf{C}^t + \mathbf{c}^T \mathbf{Z}^T, \tag{5.28}$$

subject to $G^t \geq G^{\min}$ and $E_n^t \geq E^{\min}$ as well as all constraints of the single-period static case.

The objective function (Equation 5.28) states that the solution to the dynamic problem maximizes the sum of the values of the consumption vectors along the time path plus the value of the terminal stock of capital and manpower resources. Initial values of $\mathbf{c}^t$ may be based on a time-preference interest rate with $\mathbf{c}^T$ derived by extending that interest rate to infinity. The first constraint requires that growth investment G be at least sufficient to maintain full employment; the second, that the last

---

[27] Abraham Charnes, Jacques Dreze, and Merton Miller, "Decision and Horizon Rules for Stochastic Planning Problems; A Linear Example," *Econometrica*, vol. 34, no. 2 (April 1966), p. 307; see also Richard Bellman, *Dynamic Programming* (Princeton, N.J.: Princeton University Press, 1957); and see Henri Theil, *Optimal Decision Rules for Government and Industry* (Chicago, Ill.: Rand McNally Co., 1964).

investment increment in any time period have some minimum rate of return.

The next section, which summarizes Chapters 4 and 5, leaves the macrolevel investment decision to the policy maker's judgement rather than attempting to define algorithmic decision rules.

5.5
The Adaptive Procedure for the Combined Case

This, the final section of Chapter 5, describes an adaptive modeling procedure designed to allocate resources for the combined static-dynamic case.

5.5.1
The Steps in the Procedure

The adaptive procedure for the combined case consists of three sequential steps that are performed for each time period in the planning horizon.

Step 1:

Applies the linear programming algorithm to the primary model for the static case: it solves the single-period problem to give the production program that maximizes net output and the corresponding shadow prices of the resources. The decisions are determined as a function of the policy maker's objective function.

Step 2:

Applies parametric programming and the ranking algorithm, based on the shadow prices from Step 1 divided by the exogenously determined capital/output ratios: it solves the micro part of the dynamic case to optimize investment of total funds available for growth in human and capital resources. These decisions are also determined by the algorithms as a function of the policy maker's objective function.

Step 3:

Applies the linkage equations of the primary model for the dynamic case and the results of Step 2 to tie together the solutions from Step 1: it provides beginning values for physical capacity, inventory, manpower and for allowable manpower expansion factors for each period after the first. The decision that determines the consumption-investment split is made heuristically by the man in the man-machine system.

The three steps of the adaptive procedure are shown in Figure 5.9. Operation is initiated with historical data on the initial capacity, inventory, and manpower as well as data for the A and P matrices. To begin

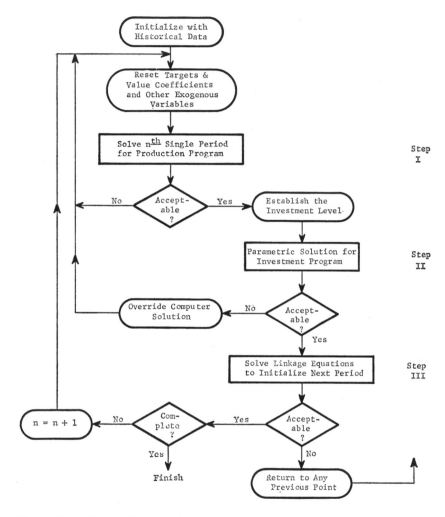

Figure 5.9. The adaptive procedure.

Step 1, the policy maker sets the value coefficients and the target final demand levels for the stipulation function and the computer applies the linear programming algorithm to this data to determine corresponding optimum production levels. Then, the policy maker evaluates the results to determine if the quantities for each of the final demand categories approximate the quantities he assumed when he established the stipulation functions. If necessary he repeats the process—resetting the value coefficients and the final demand target levels—until a satisfactory solution is obtained for the single-period problem. During the process, he can set stipulation functions that force the investment and government expenditure levels of the final solution to reach a predetermined value.

In Step 2, the policy maker establishes the level of investment for capital and human resources; the computer applies the ranking and parametric programming algorithms to allocate investment to various labor and capital bottlenecks for the single time period.

In Step 3, the computer solves the interperiod linkage equations of the primary model to tie together the single-period solutions providing values for each constraint of the next period. If for any reason the results for the next period are unsatisfactory (for example, the investment made in period $t - n$ is found to be unsatisfactory in period t), the policy maker may go back to any previous point and make modifications; if modifications are unnecessary, he can repeat the process (Steps 1, 2, and 3) for the next time period. At the beginning of each period, the policy maker can modify the technological and demand pattern matrices (A and P), the vectors of capital/output ratios ($\mathbf{q}$), the retraining costs ($\mathbf{n}$), and the manpower expansion factors ($\boldsymbol{\delta}$).

The procedure assumes that there are three sets of decisions (corresponding to Steps 1, 2, and 3 of the computer program) and that these can be solved independently although they are ultimately connected. The three decision sets are the static problem of obtaining the optimum production program, the microdynamic problem of allocating the investment funds to the producing sectors, and the macrodynamic problem of allocating net output between consumption and investment. The first two decisions are made mechanically by the algorithms; the third decision, heuristically by the policy maker-decision maker. Figure 5.10 illustrates the correspondence between parts of the primary model and three decision sets: the production program, the investment program, and the consumption-investment split.

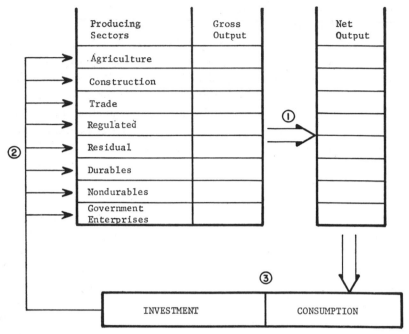

Decision sets: 1) production program, 2) investment program, 3) consumption-investment split.

Figure 5.10.   The primary model and the corresponding decisions.

5.5.2
The Implicit Growth Theory
The adaptive modeling procedure described in Chapters 4 and 5 implicitly assumes a theory of growth; this section tries to make the theory more explicit.

The linear relationships of the input-output model, represented by the A and P matrices, are used to obtain the first decision set: the production program, or the gross output of each of the industrial sectors. In a single period, the simplicity and linearity of a Leontief fixed-production function is advantageous in determining an optimum production program; in the long run, however, the shape is unrestricted. The idea that the *ex post* shape of the production function differs from the *ex ante* shape is closely related to Solow's idea that "permits virtual substitution of labor and capital *before* capital goods take concrete form but not after."[28] Thus, the policy

[28] Robert M. Solow, "Technical Progress, Capital Formation, and Economic Growth," *American Economic Review Papers and Proceedings*, May 1962, p. 68; see also Robert M. Solow, "Substitution and Fixed Proportions," *Review of Economic Studies*, vol. 29, June 1962.

maker may change any input factor such as g_i, the unit labor requirements, between period t and $t + 1$.[29]

Endogenous changes in production functions result from the second set of decisions; those that allocate investment among the capital and labor stocks of individual sectors; growth investment, scheduled by parametric methods, allocates the funds optimally in terms of constraints on the economy's performance (as measured by the objective function) in the previous period. Thus, because the primary model is disaggregated, the procedure estimates not only the investment required to change capital and employment but also (in a simplified way) the investment in human resources required to realize growth.

The third decision allocates output between consumption and investment and thus determines the growth rate of the economy. The decisions resulting from this multistage process are a function of a stochastic variable—investment efficiency—whose value tends to decrease along an equilibrium path. If allocation is formulated as a dynamic decision problem, the investment rate required to maintain full employment is a constraint, and the maximization of the values of consumption summed over the planning horizon plus the potential industrial capacity at the end of that period is the objective.

5.6
Conclusions
The variables of the adaptive procedure should be meaningful to the economic policy maker who must specify target consumption, investment, and government expenditure levels, decide on relative values for various categories of consumption goods, and make judgements on inventory levels and limits for imports. His value judgement (or other data) can be changed, and all (or portions) can be rerun easily and quickly.

Since the model is open ended, the policy maker may enter information about changes in technology, labor force, demand, and so forth, or he may use auxiliary models to generate information about these changes. Thus, the model is designed to give the policy maker (or planner) a feel for what is going on in the real economic system and to provide him with the capability of modifying its results; it is not an analytical black box that gives results he must either accept or discard.

[29] A. P. Carter, "The Economics of Technological Change," *Scientific American*, April 1966, pp. 25–31, describes an attempt to predict change in input-output factors.

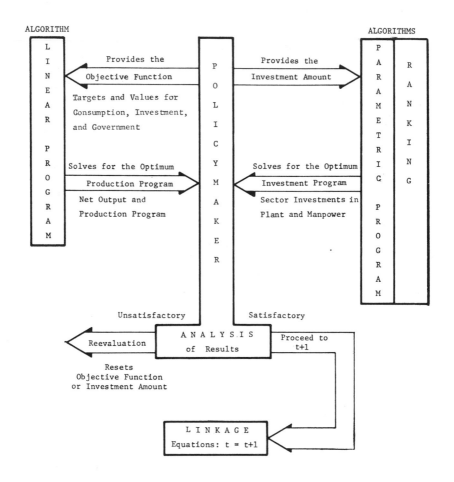

Figure 5.11. The dynamic environment for the resource allocation problem.

The man-machine system must include a policy maker or knowledgeable planner if the loop is to be closed; the dynamic environment created by the man-machine interaction is illustrated in Figure 5.11. The policy maker provides the objective function, and the linear programming portion of the model returns a corresponding optimum production program. The policy maker provides the level of investment and the other algorithms return the optimum investment program. The policy maker may use his knowledge of the system or he may use auxiliary models to make changes in exogenous variables (for example, the A and P matrices, unit labor requirements, and so forth); the primary model linkage equations then establish the conditions for the next time period.

The objective in Chapters 4 and 5 is to develop a model sufficiently disaggregated and realistic to be useful in economic planning. The objective is partially achieved by combining heuristic features with the manipulative power of mathematical programming algorithms. The results (similar to those of economic growth theory) are estimates of the optimum production and investment programs for each period and for the resulting growth path.

However, the attempt is only partially successful. The most serious drawback is that the instruments are not those generally available to planners of free world economies (that is, they do not have control over prices and production quantities). Even though forecasts can be substituted for uncontrolled target values and the remaining (controllable) final demand categories can be used as instruments, the procedure's usefulness for free, developed economies is still limited except for emergency situations when considerable government control exists.

Another disadvantage is that the procedure's immediate applicability is limited. To develop operational plans, the procedure must have available, accurate, current data. The proposed procedure requires estimates of input-output coefficients, capital and manpower capacities, labor mobility, capital/output ratios, training costs, and so forth. Neither the adequacy of the data estimates nor the sensitivity of the results to various data inadequacies has been investigated.

A third limitation is that the model is not predictive. It does not forecast population and labor force growth or taste and technology changes; it does not investigate the determinants of demand or investment for individual aggregate industries, nor does it relate its variables (for example, investment, sales, and so forth) to any instruments typically manipulated by decision makers.

The logical steps for removing the above-mentioned limitations are to add omitted-instrument and exogenous-event auxiliary models. The proposed additional steps will not be attempted in this book; however, other concepts of adaptive procedures (primarily the treatment of uncertainty) are illustrated by the stabilization problem (Chapters 6, 7, and 8). Because of the difference in planning horizons, the stabilization problem's primary model and the objective function are different from that used for the growth problem.

6

A Pilot Procedure for the Stabilization Problem

Chapter 6 describes a pilot adaptive modeling procedure designed for the stabilization problem. This procedure is substantially different from that described in Chapters 4 and 5. First, the decision making roles are played by the men in the man-machine system rather than by computer algorithms; second, uncertainty is treated explicitly. The pilot procedure contains five components: a primary macroeconomic model, decision-making roles (monetary and fiscal), an objective function, an information system, and a dynamic environment. The primary model is a nonestimated Keynesian model chosen for illustrative and experimental purposes only.

The procedure is described in terms of players, a referee, rules, and a scoring function. Two "policy players," acting as economic decision makers, establish fiscal and monetary policies. The referee alters model parameters to reflect the effect of exogenous events on the economic environment. The economy's performance (the result of interactions in the model) is evaluated by GNP growth, by price level changes, and by the unemployment rate. In this cooperative game, the players try to maximize their joint score; they play against nature as represented by the primary model and the referee-generated exogenous events.

6.1
The Primary Model of the Pilot Procedure

The primary model does not simulate an actual economy; twenty-three equations represent a general closed Keynesian economic system containing both a real sector and a monetary sector; aggregate output is measured by the final demands of consumers, investors, and government. Incomes received by wage earners and nonwage income recipients are supplemented by money transfers from the public sector. Changes in money stock influence the price level and interest rate—two variables which in turn influence other endogenous variables in a dynamic fashion.

Definitions of the macroeconomic variables are given in Table 6.1, equations are presented in Table 6.2 in the same order used to solve the model. The dependent variables, listed in Table 6.1, compose—for the pilot procedure—the set X^{**}, or uncontrollable endogenous variables which, with the exogenous variables X^*, define the state of the world; the instruments are the set Y that defines the plan; the referee variables are a subset of the parameters Π.

Table 6.1   Definitions of Pilot Model Variables

Dependent Variables

W = Wage income.*

WN = Nonwage cash flow (profits, wages, rents, and depreciation).*

C = Consumption expenditures.*

I = Gross private domestic investment.*

Y = Real GNP.*

K = Capital stock (including inventories).*

SP = Personal and business savings (private).*

DB = Government deficit.

SG = Government savings (public) = $-DB$.

ST = Total savings (gross).*

SGA = Accumulated government debt.*

IWN = Propensity to invest nonwage income.

MS = Money supply.

R = Interest rate.

GR = Growth rate of Y.

U = Unemployment rate.

P = Price index (1958 = 100).

YN = Nominal GNP (billions of current dollars).

Instruments

B = Net new government securities issued.*

HM = High-powered money.*

G = Government expenditures on goods and services.*

TR = Transfer payments.*

TW = Tax rate on wage income.

TWN = Tax rate on nonwage cash flow.

Referee Variables

CW = Propensity to consume wage income.

CWN = Propensity to consume nonwage income.

D = Rate of depreciation on capital stock.

IK = Propensity to invest capital stock.

WY = Ratio of wage income to national income.

---

* Measured in billions of 1958 dollars.

Table 6.2   Pilot Model Equations*

Equation No.	Equations	Parameter Values
(M.1)	$B_t = -SG_{t-1} - HM_t = DB_t - HM_t.$	—
(M.2)	$\Delta MS_t = B_t + \theta HM_t.$	$\theta = 2.0$
(M.3)	$MS_t = MS_{t-1} + \Delta MS_t.$	—
(M.4)	$\Delta YN_t = YN_t - YN_{t-1}.$	—
(M.5)	$\Delta R_t = (CR1)\,\Delta YN_t + \alpha B_t - \phi\,\Delta MS_t.$	$\begin{cases}\alpha = 0.01 \\ \phi = 0.02\end{cases}$
(M.6)	$R_t = R_{t-1} + \Delta R_t.$	—
(M.7)	$IWN_t = IWN_{t-1} - \sigma\,\Delta R_t.$	$\sigma = 0.15$
(M.8)	$Y_t = C_t + I_t + G_t.$	—
(M.9)	$I_t = IWN_t(1 - TWN)WN_t + IK_t(K_{t-1}).$	—
(M.10)	$C_t = CW(1 - TW)W_t + CWN(1 - TWN)WN_t + TR_t.$	—
(M.11)	$WN_t = Y_t - W_t.$	—
(M.12)	$W_t = WY(Y_t).$	—
(M.13)	$K_t = (1 - D)K_{t-1} + I_t.$	—
(M.14)	$SP_t = (1 - TW)W_t + (1 - TWN)WN_t - C_t + TR_t.$	—
(M.15)	$SG_t = TW(W_t) + TWN(WN_t) - G_t - TR_t - DB_t.$	—
(M.16)	$ST_t = SP_t + SG_t.$	—
(M.17)	$SGA_t = SGA_{t-1} + SG_t.$	—
(M.18)	$GR_t = [(Y_t - Y_{t-1})/Y_{t-1}] \cdot 100.$	—
(M.19)	$\Delta U_t = \Gamma - (CR2)GR_t.$	$\Gamma = 1.8$
(M.20)	$U_t = \sqrt{(U_{t-1} + \Delta U_t)^2}.$	—
(M.21a)	$\Delta P_t = [-\lambda + \Psi GR_t - \omega\Delta R_t] + (CR3)/U_t, \quad \text{if}\quad U_t \geq \kappa.$	$\begin{cases}\lambda = -3.0 \\ \Psi = 0.5 \\ \omega = 0.5\end{cases}$
(M.21b)	$\Delta P_t = [-\Omega + \gamma GR_t - \omega\Delta R_t] + (CR3)/U_t, \quad \text{if}\quad U_t < \kappa.$	$\begin{cases}\Omega = -5.0 \\ \gamma = 1.0 \\ \kappa = 4.0\end{cases}$
(M.22)	$P_t = P_{t-1} + \Delta P_t.$	—
(M.23)	$YN_t = Y_t(P_t)/100.$	—

* The t designates the annual time period; definitions of the variables are in Table 6.1; recommended values for the parameters that may be changed from the console are listed in Table 6.7.

6.1.1
Explanation of the Model Equations
This section explains briefly the equations listed in Table 6.2. The explanations follow the same order as the table; however, some closely related equations are grouped together. In the text, the equation numbers appear in parentheses to the right of the section headings.

NET ISSUES OF NEW GOVERNMENT SECURITIES (EQUATION M.1)

Any government deficit (DB) or surplus (SG) developed in period $t-1$ must be offset in period t. The monetary policy alternatives are either to issue new securities (bonds sold directly to the public), or to increase the stock of high-powered money (through central bank operations), or to use some combination of the two.[1] Both the new securities B_t and the new high-powered money HM_t are policy variables; however, since $B_t + HM_t$ must equal SG_{t-1}, there is only one degree of freedom; compensating changes in the two variables may be effected even if the government budget is balanced $(SG_{t-1} = 0)$.

CHANGE IN MONEY STOCK (EQUATIONS M.2 AND M.3)

Changes in the stock of money (ΔMS) result from the sum of the changes in B and HM; the latter is characterized by a money-multiplier greater than that of B $(\theta > 1)$. Thus, the new money supply is the previous money stock plus the results of the monetary alternative chosen for B and HM.

THE RATE OF INTEREST (EQUATIONS M.4, M.5, AND M.6)

Money stocks (MS) are demanded for transactions and precautionary purposes and for speculation. Transactions demand is a fraction, CR1 of last period's nominal GNP (YN_{t-1}); speculative demand is a fraction α of new government issues (B_t). If changes in the money stock do not equal the change in demand, the money market must be equilibrated by a change in the interest rate (ΔR). Thus, ΔR is positive when $\phi \Delta MS_t$ is less than the sum of (CR1) ΔYN_t and αB_t, and conversely.

THE PROPENSITY TO INVEST (EQUATION M.7)

The change in the propensity to invest out of nonwage cash flow for growth purposes $(IWN_t - IWN_{t-1})$ is negatively related to changes in the interest rate. (See discussion of equation M.9.)

---

[1] A similar model of meeting the budget constraint with new securities and high-powered money is described by Carl Christ in "A Short-Run Aggregate-Demand Model of the Interdependence and Effects of Monetary and Fiscal Policy with Keynesian and Classical Interest Elasticities," *American Economic Review*, vol. 57 (May 1967) pp. 434–443.

GROSS NATIONAL PRODUCT (EQUATION M.8)

The basic identity for gross national product (GNP) states that the value of aggregate final gross output (Y_t) is the sum of consumption expenditures (C_t), gross private domestic investment (I_t), and government expenditures for goods and services (G_t). Gross output Y_t also equals wage and nonwage income plus depreciation (nonwage income plus depreciation is referred to as nonwage cash flow).

THE INVESTMENT FUNCTION (EQUATION M.9)

Gross private domestic investment is the sum of investment for growth and for replacement.[2] Growth investment is a function of nonwage, disposable (after tax) cash flow; replacement investment is a proportion IK of the capital stock. The propensity to invest out of nonwage cash flow IWN is influenced by changes in the rate of interest (see Equation M.7); the game referee specifies IK the propensity to replace capital stock.

THE CONSUMPTION FUNCTION (EQUATION M.10)

Consumption of current output is a variable proportion of disposable (after tax) incomes from wage and nonwage sources plus transfer payments from the government to individuals (variable propensities are CW and CWN and the propensity to consume transfer payments is fixed at unity). The referee may change the propensities to consume (CW and CWN) to reflect changes in employment levels, in imports, or in other exogenous demand factors. Policy players can directly influence the level of consumption by altering either or both of the tax rates (TW and TWN) on the two types of income (W_t and WN_t) and/or by changing the magnitude of transfer payments TR_t. Players indirectly affect consumption by altering either the level of G_t or the monetary instruments HM and B.

NATIONAL INCOME (EQUATIONS M.11 AND M.12)

The GNP (Y_t) is distributed as factor payments in the form of wage income and nonwage cash flow. The referee may change the pattern of income distribution WY to reflect changes in the distribution of income that occur as the economy moves through a business cycle.

CAPITAL STOCK (EQUATION M.13)

The stock of capital K_t measures the size of the productive economic base (plant and equipment) plus inventories of raw materials, in-process stocks

---

[2] This definition follows the model described by Dale Jorgenson, "Anticipations and Investment Behavior," *The Brookings Quarterly Econometric Model* (Chicago, Ill.: Rand McNally & Company, 1965), pp. 41–43.

and finished goods, and the stock of houses. Capital stock depreciates each period of play at a rate D specified at the beginning of the game; the rate D is a referee variable, which may be changed periodically.

SAVINGS OR DEFICITS (EQUATIONS M.14, M.15, M.16, AND M.17)

Personal and business (private) savings SP_t equal the total disposable (after tax) cash flows (including transfer payments) less consumption expenditures. Government savings SG_t or government deficit DB_t are the differences between total tax receipts and total government outlays for goods and services and for transfer payments. Unbalanced budgets must be financed in the next period (see equation M.1).

The sum of private and public savings equals gross savings ST_t and also equals gross investment. Cumulative government savings SGA_t (net surplus or deficit) is set equal to zero at the beginning of the simulated period to reflect the change in government debt for the simulated period.

RATE OF ECONOMIC GROWTH (EQUATION M.18)

Economic growth GR is the percentage change in real GNP from one time period to another.

CHANGE IN UNEMPLOYMENT RATE (EQUATION M.19)

Normal labor force expansion due to population growth is assumed to be Γ/CR percent per year. In an economy characterized by increasing productivity the growth rate of output must exceed that of the labor force if the employment rate is to increase. The labor market is in equilibrium if the GNP growth rate GR is equal to the ratio of the parameters $\Gamma/CR2$. Growth less than $\Gamma/CR2$ tends to increase the unemployment rate, and conversely.

LEVEL OF UNEMPLOYMENT (EQUATION M.20)

The labor force participation rate responds to the level of unemployment U_t, which is determined by changes in the unemployment rate and last year's unemployment level (stated as a percent). If ΔU is larger than U_{t-1}, the computed U_t is still positive; it represents an unusual number of entries into the labor force. In other words, the labor force growth rate will exceed 2 percent to prevent the employment rate from exceeding 100 percent (a peculiar representation of the discouraged-worker hypothesis).

THE PRICE INDEX (EQUATIONS M.21 AND M.22)

Prices are affected by labor costs that depend on growth and unemployment rates and by demand for money (disequilibrium in the commodity market is indicated by disequilibrium in the monetary market).[3] Thus, the

---

[3] The relationship between the money and commodity market equilibriums is described in Don Patinkin, *Money, Interest and Prices* (New York: Harper & Row, 1967), pp. 230–236.

price index P_t is positively related to the growth rate of real output and is negatively related to changes in the interest rate. (Falling interest rates indicate excess money supply and, thus, excess commodity demand.) Inflation, reflecting the Phillips relation, is inversely related to the level of unemployment U_t; further, when U_t is less than some given value (say 4 percent), the impact of an increase in economic activity on prices is greater than when U_t exceeds that value.

NOMINAL GNP (EQUATION M.23)

The value of output is multiplied by the current price level to give a nominal (or money value) GNP (YN_t). In the subsequent period, this value determines the requirements for transactions money balances and thus influences interest rates (refer to equation M.5).

CHARACTERISTICS OF THE PILOT MODEL

The pilot primary model is illustrative; no claims are made for its structure or parameter values. Equations were included so that various theories of economic behavior could be included and the implications of alternative hypotheses observed. For example, if the parameter CR1 is increased, the model can reflect the hypothesis that expectations are the most important determinant of interest rates;[4] or, as another example, decreasing CR2 reflects the hypothesis that employers tend to retrain workers in a downturn if skilled workers are scarce (changing CR3 shifts the Phillips curve). Thus, while the model is not accurate and its parameter values are not empirically estimated, it does provide a means of creating various plausible economic environments.

The public sector is represented by players who, acting as fiscal and monetary decision makers, manipulate the model's instruments TW, TWN, G, TR, HM, and B. The game referee, acting as a malevolent or benevolent nature, can change the propensities to consume out of either wage or nonwage income (CW and CWN); he can also affect exogenous investment by changing the capital replacement coefficient (IK), the depreciation rate (D), or the distribution of income (WY).

Because of the simple structure and linear relationships of the model, it is highly sensitive to changes in parameters or instruments and it behaves in an unstable fashion if changes are not limited; Table 6.3 lists the suggested maximum range and frequency of the changes.

[4] Milton Friedman, "The Role of Monetary Policy," *American Economic Review* (March 1968), pp. 1–17.

Table 6.3   Maximum Range and Frequency of Instrument and Parameter Changes

	Suggested Maximum Change	
	Annual Period	Simulated Period
Instrument Changes		
Government purchases of goods and services (G)	$+15\%$ -5%	$+40\%/4$ years $-20\%/4$ years
Transfer payments (TR)	$+10\%$ -5%	$+40\%/4$ years $-20\%/4$ years
Tax rates on wage income (TW)	$\pm15\%$	$\pm25\%/4$ years
Tax rates on nonwage income (TWN)	$\pm15\%$	$\pm25\%/4$ years
High-powered money (HM)	$+\$30$ billion $-\$10$ billion	$+\$40$ billion/2 years $-\$10$ billion/2 years
Bonds (B)	$+\$25$ billion $-\$15$ billion	$+\$30$ billion/2 years $-\$20$ billion/2 years
Parameter Changes		
Propensity to consume out of wage income (CW)	±0.02	±0.05/simulated period
Propensity to consume out of nonwage income (CWN)	±0.02	±0.10/simulated period
Depreciation rate (D)	±0.005	$\pm0.05/5$ years
Propensity to replace capital (IK)	±0.005	±0.10/simulated period
Distribution of income (WY)	±0.01	±0.05/simulated period
Propensity to invest (IWN)*	±0.01	-0.05 to $+0.10$/simulated period

* The intercept IWN_{-1} may be changed ±0.01 in a single period; IWN may be changed from -0.05 to $+0.10$ in a simulated period.

6.2
The Four Other Components of the Pilot Procedure

This section describes the decision-making roles, objective function, information system, and dynamic environment for the pilot procedure.

6.2.1
The Players' Decision-Making Roles

Two decision-making roles are defined for the pilot procedure: one player directs the fiscal operations of government by setting tax rates (TW and TWN), by purchasing goods and services G, and by distributing transfer payments TR. The other (the monetary decision maker) finances the public debt by selling bonds B or by issuing high-powered money HM. The two players may perform independently or together depending on whether or not their interests are mutual; the scoring function measures joint performance.

The players may change instrument values and enter them via a console. They may be set directly (for example, $G_t = 85$) or be established by a simple function (for example, $G_t = 1.1 \times G_{t-1}$). Unaltered instruments retain their values (for example, $G_t = G_{t-1}$) unless otherwise specified.

The fiscal and monetary decision-making roles are thus defined by their respective instrument sets: $\{y\}^f = \{TWX, TWN, G, TR\}$ and $\{y\}^m = \{HM, B\}$, the restrictions on the use of the instruments (see Table 6.3), the single objective function described in the next section, and the communication and other information made available to them as described in Section 6.2.3.

6.2.2
The Objective Function

The limited use of the objective function in adaptive modeling procedures must be emphasized, especially since a cardinal number is computed. At the most basic level, the primary model provides a vector of endogenous variable values; any of these may be elements of a particular decision maker's objective function. At the next level of abstraction, the formal objective function provides an ordinal ranking of alternative solutions. At the most abstract (and least reliable) level, a calculated cardinal number can be used to compare alternative strategies, to measure the significance of exogenous events reflected in parameter changes, and to evaluate information (in terms of accuracy, availability, or timeliness). The limitations of the objective function and its structure are important for any conclusions about the real world but less significant in a gaming context.

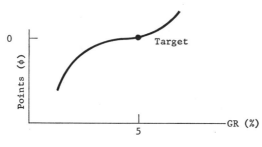

a.   Real growth rate $\phi(GR)$.

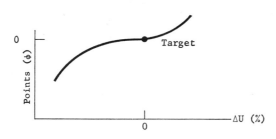

b.   Unemployment change $\phi(\Delta U)$.

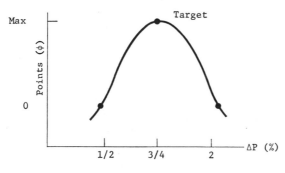

c.   Price change $\phi(\Delta P)$.

Figure 6.1.   General shapes of the scoring functions.

Table 6.4 Scoring Functions for Each Round

Objective Scored	Equation No.	Scoring Function[a]	
Growth rate (GR)	(S.1)	$SGR_t = WGP(GR_t - GR^*)^2$	if $GR_t \geq GR^*$
		$= WGN(GR_t - GR^*)^2$	if $GR_t < GR^*$
Unemployment change (ΔU)	(S.2)	$SDU_t = WUP(\Delta U_t - \Delta U^*)^2$	if $\Delta U_t \geq \Delta U^*$
		$= WUN(\Delta U_t - \Delta U^*)^2$	if $\Delta U_t < \Delta U^*$
Inflation rate ($\Delta P/P$)	(S.3)	$SDP_t = WPM[-\epsilon(\Delta P)^2 + \beta\Delta P + \theta]$	
Round total	(S.4)	$SRT_t = SGR_t + SDU_t + SDP_t$	
Accumulated total	(S.5)	$SAT_t = SAT_{t-1} + SRT_t$	

[a] The single asterisk (*) indicates target values; WGP, WGN, WUP, WUN, and WPM are variable weights; ϵ, β, θ are parameters that determine implicit target values for ΔP. (See Table 6.6 for values.)

Scores are compiled for the rate of growth GR, for the change in the unemployment rate ΔU, and for inflation rates $\Delta P/P$ on a round-for-round basis (see Table 6.4); at the end of the game, additional bonuses and penalties are awarded on the basis of performance during the entire period simulated. Accumulated round scores plus net bonuses (or penalties) equal the game score.

Round scores for the growth rate of GNP (equation S.1) and for changes in the unemployment rate (Equation S.2) are evaluated by asymmetrically weighted quadratic functions of deviations between actual and target values (see a and b in Figure 6.1). The score for the inflation rate (Equation S.3) is evaluated by a parabolic function that assigns a bonus if price changes equal 0.75 ± 1.25 percent or a penalty if prices rise more than 2 percent or fall more than 0.5 percent (see c in Figure 6.1). Table 6.4 lists the scoring functions for each round; changing the parameters in Equations S.1, S.2, or S.3 alters the shape of the corresponding curve in Figure 6.1.

Scoring Equations S.1 to S.4 represent the single-period or static objective function: $\phi_t = \phi(X_t, Y_t)$ described in Chapter 3; in the function shown, Y_t is not present and $\phi_t = \phi(GR_t, \Delta U_t, \Delta P_t)$.

Equation S.5 is one method of evaluating the objective function for the planning horizon: $\Phi = \Phi(\mathbf{\Phi}_t)$ where Φ is a summation of round scores. A more complex function is needed to evaluate long-term performance. The average growth rate of real GNP for a simulated period ($\overline{GR}$) can be

Table 6.5 Scoring Functions for End-of-Game Bonuses and Penalties

Objective Scored	Equation No.	Scoring Function[a]	
Growth rate (GR)	(S.6)	$BGR = AA(\overline{GR} - \overline{GR}^*)^2$	if $\overline{GR} > \overline{GR}^*$
		$\quad\ = AAA(\overline{GR} - \overline{GR}^*)^2$	if $\overline{GR} < \overline{GR}^*$
Unemployment level (U)	(S.7)	$BDU1 = CC(U_T - U_T^*)^2$	if $U_T < U_T^*$
		$\quad\quad\ = 0 \quad$ otherwise.	
Net unemployment change (DU)	(S.8)	$BDU2 = CC(U_T - U_0)^2$	if $U_T < U_0$
		$\quad\quad\ = CCC(U_T - U_0)^2$	if $U_T > U_0$
Price change (DP)	(S.9)	$BDP = DD(\overline{DP} - \overline{DP}^*)^2$	if $\overline{DP} < \overline{DP}^*$
		$\quad\ = 0 \quad$ otherwise.	
Total bonuses	(S.10)	$STB = BGR + BDU1 + BDU2 + BDP$	
Total game score	(S.11)	$STG = STB + SAT_T$	

[a] Notation: The overbar $(-)$ indicates compound growth rate for the simulated period; $AA, AAA, CC, CCC,$ and DD are variable weights. (See Table 6.6 for values.) Subscripts 0 and T indicate first and final rounds.

compared to a target value in a manner similar to that used for the round scores. The total change in unemployment $(U_T - U_0)$ and the level of unemployment at the end of the period (U_T) are arguments in similar functions. Finally, a bonus can be added if the average price level is kept within stated bounds. The equations used to evaluate long-term performance are listed in Table 6.5.

Equations S.1 to S.10 represent the planning-horizon objective function $\Phi = \Phi(\mathbf{X}_t, \mathbf{Y}_t)$ described in Chapter 3; however, the instruments $\mathbf{Y}_t$ do not appear in the pilot procedure objective function and $\Phi = \Phi(\sum_t GR, \sum_t \Delta P, \sum_t \Delta U, U_T) + \sum_t \phi_t$. Equations S.1 to S.9 can be modified by changing the weights and target values via a console. Generally, all parameters indicated by uppercase letters can be changed in this manner.

Table 6.6 lists the suggested target values and weights for the scoring functions.

The pilot procedure illustrates adaptive modeling; however, all five of the components can be improved. For example, the objective function does not reward stability by including interaction terms (for example, the product of two variables in any single period or the ratio of the two values of a single variable in adjacent periods). However, such interaction terms

Table 6.6   Suggested Target Values and Weights for the Scoring Functions

Objective Scored	Annual Changes	
	Target Value	Weight
Growth	$GR^* = 5.0$	$WGP = 3.0$ $WGN = -1.0$
Unemployment	$\Delta U^* = 0$	$WUP = 50.0$ $WUN = -50.0$
Price stability	$\Delta P^* = 0.75\dagger$	$WPM = 8.0$
	Changes per Simulated Period $t = 0$ to $t = T$	
	Target Value	Weight
Growth	$\overline{GR^*} = 5.0$	$AA = 200.0$ $AAA = -20.0$
Unemployment	$U_T^* - U_0 = 0$ $U_T^* = 4.0$	$CC = 100$ $CCC = -100$
Price stability	$\overline{DP^*} = 2.00$	$DD = 200$

† The parameters for the parabolic function are $\epsilon = 0.64$ and $\beta = 0.96$.

can be added by modifying the scoring routine. (Methods of changing various aspects of all five components are described in Section 6.3.)

6.2.3

The Information System

In the pilot procedure, two information systems are available to each of the two players. The first is a computer-assisted system that provides information on past performance and conditional forecasts of future performance. The second is an informal system used to communicate information between the two players or between the players and the referee.

THE COMPUTER-ASSISTED SYSTEM

The computer-assisted system provides information in the following ways: The computer generates values for a standard set of endogenous variables for each period. If a high-speed printer is available it is efficient to print a relatively large set of standard output; thus, the printer can output algebraic symbols and descriptive words (or abbreviations) that identify the variables (Version A). If a teletype or similar typewriter device is used,

TIME PERIOD 3

INDICATORS

GNP	INVEST-MENT	CONSUMP-TION	NON-WAGE INCOME	WAGE INCOME	CAPITAL
(Y)	(1)	(C)	(WN)	(W)	(K)
501.5	97.2	316.3	175.5	326.0	1515.6

PERSONAL SAVINGS	GOVT SAVINGS	GOVT DEBT	MONEY SUPPLY	INTEREST RATE
(SP)	(SG)	(SGA)	(MS)	(R)
108.1	-10.8	10.8	126.7	5.1

GROWTH RATE	CHANGE INT RATE	CHANGE MONEY SUP	PRICE INDEX	NOMINAL GNP
(GR)	(DELTA R)	(DELTA MS)	(P)	(YN)
5.54	.15	9.12	104.51	512.5

CHANGE UNEMPLOY	UNEMPLOY RATE	PRICE CHANGES
(DELTA U)	(U)	(DELTA P)
-.1	5.	2.1

POLICY INSTRUMENTS

WAGE TAX	NON-WAGE TAX	GOVT EXPEND	TRANSFER PAYMENTS	HIGH MONEY	BONDS
(TW)	(TWN)	(G)	(TR)	(HM)	(B)
.150	.400	88.000	42.000	2.000	5.125

MODEL PARAMETERS

WAGE CONSUMP	NON-WAGE CONSUMP	INVEST NON-WAGE	INVEST CAPITAL	DEP	WAGES/GNP
(CW)	(CWN)	(IWN)	(IK)	(D)	(W/Y)
.800	.500	.197	.051	.060	.650

PLAYER'S SCORE FOR THE ROUND

DELTA P SCORE	DELTA U SCORE	GROWTH SCORE	ROUND TOTAL	ACCUM TOTAL
(SDP)	(SDU)	(SGR)	(SRT)	(SAT)
-2.69	.60	.89	-1.20	-1.20

Figure 6.2a.   Typical output from Version A.

```
?TRY
T=1961
REAL SECTOR        1958=100
GNP= 555.5  INVESTMENT= 77.5   CONSUMPTION= 361.8
WAGES= 361=    GOVERNMENT DEBT= 6.99 UNEMPLOYMENT= 3.90
MONETARY
GNP:   CURRENT $ = 612.89 INTEREST= 4.98 PRICES= 110.32
CHANGES IN KEY VARIABLES
REAL GROWTH= 5.86 UNEMPLOYMENT=-.54 PRICES=3.96 INTEREST=-.03
PLAN
TAXES ON WAGES (TW)= .150 TAXES ON NON-WAGES (TWN)= .550
GOVERNMENT PURCHASES (G)= 116.1 TRANSFER PAYMENTS (TR)= 52.0
HIGH-POWERED MONEY (HM)= 9.0 BONDS (B)=-5.091
?TYPE MS
MS = 144.3
?F 2
SP = 75.7
SGA=-3.6
MS = 144.3
DMS=-2.6
?F 3
CW = .810
CWN= .700
IWN= .120
IK = .041
D  = .040
WY = .650
?GO
ROUND SCORE
FOR PRICES=-11.24 FOR UNEMPLOYMENT= 14.85 FOR GROWTH= 2.23
ROUND TOTAL= 5.84 ACCUMULATED TOTAL= 86.79
?END
BONUS SCORE
FOR PRICES= 0.00 FOR UNEMPLOYMENT= 30.12 FOR GROWTH=-.33
TOTAL BONUS= 22.34
TOTAL GAME SCORE= 109.12
```

Figure 6.2b.   Typical output from Version B.

the slow printing speed makes it efficient to restrict the output; then the standard set of output should contain fewer variables (Version B). In both versions players may request additional data via the console. Typical output data from both versions are shown in Figure 6.2a and Figure 6.2b. As illustrated in Figure 6.2b the data requests may be for single items (TYPE MS) or groups of data (F2 and F3).

A five-period data bank maintained in core memory is accessible via the typewriter console; for example, if the player inputs "TYPE Y3," he obtains the value for real GNP for three periods previous. The player may also perform elementary mathematical operations on the data; for example, if he knows the tax rates but not the tax revenues on incomes, he may wish to calculate the tax receipts he would have assuming a new tax setting, or he may wish to compute directly the relative share of G or the growth rate of GNP. To illustrate, the instruction "TYPE G/Y" computes the relative share of government expenditures in GNP. More complex operations can be developed by establishing new variables; for example, "X = G—Gl" followed by "XX = X/GR" computes the ratio of the change in government spending to the change in real GNP.

New variables (for example, "X" and "XX") are automatically maintained in the core memory data bank until a predetermined limit is reached; the data bank is automatically updated as simulated time advances.

The primary model is a source of conditional forecasts; players may establish conditional values for instruments and exogenous variables by typing "TRY" at the console to obtain forecasts for all endogenous variables in the standard output format. Forecasts do not update the data bank nor indicate the round score but otherwise simulate the next period. Though players may forecast only the next time period, the number of forecasts (that is, the number of different plans tried for period $t + 1$) is limited within the game structure only by the mutual consent of the players and the referee.

The computer-assisted information system provides $X_{t-\gamma}$ for all x in X where $\gamma = 0, 1, \ldots, 5$ and (using the forecasting routine TRY) it provides $X_{t+1}^c = F(X_t \mid \hat{\Pi}, \hat{Y})$.

THE INFORMAL INFORMATION SYSTEM

The second information system is the communication between players and between players and the referee. Restricting the communication between players illustrates how the adaptive procedure can be used as an experimental aid to model building; for example, facilitating (or prohibiting) coordination of fiscal and monetary decision making may be evaluated by changing the game rules relative to communication and observing the results.

The treatment of uncertainty in the pilot procedure is limited. The referee introduces uncertainty by creating scenarios and altering the appropriate variables or parameters. Each scenario is a description of an event (escalation of the war, devaluation of the pound, a nationwide rail strike, and so forth) that is to occur or has just occurred. The description of this exogenous change must be realistic in terms of its economic effect (for example, time, magnitude, and direction of change), and it must indicate which variables are affected. Then, the referee determines the nature and magnitude of the parameter changes that result from the exogenous changes and enters them via the console (for example, $CW = CW + 0.01$ increases the marginal propensity to consume by one percentage point).

In terms of the general description of the adaptive modeling procedure in Chapter 2, the informal information system provides reports $R(E)$ describing exogenous events. The referee provides, in an informal manner, the library of exogenous events $\{E\}$ and the auxiliary models $u \equiv \Delta\Pi = f'(E)$.

The descriptions of the first four components of the pilot procedure indicate its dynamic nature; the following paragraphs emphasize this component of the procedure and summarize the description.

6.2.4
The Dynamic Environment

The primary model equations contain lagged relations that require a two-period history before beginning the game; that is, period 3 is $t = 0$ for the simulation. The routine, which generates the required history, is pre-established and stored, but the referee can easily change the initial conditions by changing the file. Files have been created to begin the procedures (that is, at $t = 0$) at a level of economic activity that resembles the existing environment at the beginning of 1969 (see Table 6.7 for the 1969 file).

The game begins with a forecast for period 3 based on instrument values (that were established in the initialization routine) for period 2. The fiscal instruments (tax rates, actual expenditures, and transfer payments) tend to be deflationary if left unaltered and thus demonstrate fiscal drag. In the monetary equations high-powered money (HM) is the explicit instrument; bonds are computed as a residual; thus, if the government runs a continually increasing deficit, a static monetary policy that leaves HM unaltered is also restrictive. Thus a strategy that leaves instruments unaltered logically results in a negative growth rate, increased unemployment, and declining prices.

Generally, players begin to interact with the model by trying to plot a strategy that provides a 5 percent growth rate and reduces unemployment without creating inflation. The fact that a price decline is forecast tells the players that they have some freedom within which they can manipulate instruments without causing inflation. However, they are aware, that if they incur a large deficit in period 3 the monetary decision maker must

Table 6.7   Initialization File to Begin Play in 1969*

110 G = 94	320 CR2 = 0.4
120 TR = 35	330 CR3 = 12
130 TW = 0.15	340 YN1 = Y
140 TWN = 0.5	350 YN2 = Y
150 CW = 0.81	360 GO
160 CWN = 0.6	370 SDP = 0
170 D = 0.03	380 SDU = 0
180 IK = 0.04	390 SGR = 0
190 IWN = 0.15	400 SRT = 0
200 WY = 0.65	410 SAT = 0
210 K1 = 1500	420 G = 95
220 GO	430 TR = 43
230 G = 95	440 HM = 1
235 IK = 0.043	450 CW = 0.81
240 TR = 39	460 CWN = 0.700
250 U = 5.50	470 TWN = 0.550
260 R = 5	480 D = 0.04
270 P = 100	490 IK = 0.043
280 MS = 135	500 TRY
290 YN = Y	510 GO
300 HM = 0.0	520 G = 101
310 CR1 = 0.005	530 TR = 45

* Calling on this file establishes parameter values and generates pregame rounds to establish an environment resembling existing conditions at the beginning of 1969. Numerical final characters (for example, K1, YN1), refer to the data bank.

cover it in period 4. They may gain more information about periods 1 and 2 ($t = -1$ and -2) through the inquiry process and then attempt to set instruments that they feel can achieve their joint or individual objectives. Next they may type "TRY" to forecast the results of their tentative plan (that is, the primary model is solved to obtain $X_{t+1}^e = F(X_t \mid \hat{\Pi}, \hat{Y})$). The decision makers may go through this forecasting process a number of times (up to the limit preestablished by the referee) before obtaining a satisfactory plan. When an acceptable solution is obtained they indicate it to the referee who will type "GO" at the console so the primary model can be solved again to provide $X_{t+1} = F(X_t, Y_t)$ and the round score can be computed to provide: $\phi_t = \phi(X_t, Y_t) = \phi(GR, \Delta U, \Delta P)$.

The standard output for period 3, which is either printed (Version A) or typed (Version B), gives one part of the information set. Next the computer updates the data bank and now $t = t + 1$. The entire process can be repeated for period 4; however, to introduce uncertainty, the referee may announce to the players that one or more of the following situations exist:

1.
Due to a threatened major automobile strike, new cars may not be available, and as a result, the wage earner's and the nonwage earner's propensity to consume (CW and CWN) may be temporarily reduced.

2.
Due to technological advances, the tendency to replace existing capital stock IK may increase.

3.
Due to poor (or excellent) performance of the economy and profits, the distribution of income WY may change in favor of wage earners (or nonwage earners).

4.
Legislation may increase the depreciation rate D and reduce the book value of capital stock K; this may reduce taxes on nonwage cash flow TWN and increase the propensity to replace capital stock IK.

5.
Due to uncertainty about the international situation, the propensity to invest IWN may decrease.

The information provided by the referee to the players in the illustrative situations 1 to 5 (above) are the reports $R(E)$ referred to in Chapter 2.

Policy players may use information from the referee's reports to estimate new parameters and to obtain additional, conditional forecasts $X^c_{t+1} = F(X_t \mid \hat{\Pi}, \hat{Y})$. Parameter changes are provided by the referee's auxiliary models $u = f'(E)$, which in this case, are informal and relate to the error term (or what amounts to the same thing—a draw from the probability distribution of parameter values).

After the policy players obtain a satisfactory plan and type the values for their five instruments into the console, they so indicate to the referee; the referee then types in the new values he determined for the parameters and then types "GO" before the simulation can move to period $t+1$ (that is, to period 5).

The game proceeds in this fashion until the end of the simulation period ($t = T$), which may have been predetermined or mutually agreed on during the course of play. After typing "GO" and receiving the results for period T, the referee types "END".

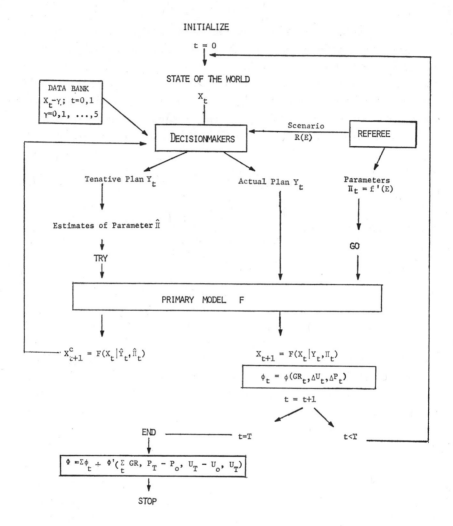

Figure 6.3. The pilot procedure.

The final computations provide the value of the objective function $\Phi = STG$ for the simulated period ($t = 0$ to $t = T$) or for the total game score as described in Section 6.2.2. Thus, the game is over. A new game may be started by typing appropriate code letters and "GAME," which recreates the situation at period 2 ($t = -1$) and a deflationary situation forecast for period 3. (The pilot procedure is illustrated in Figure 6.3.)

The following is a brief description of the computer hardware and operation and various ways of modifying the model—the mechanics of the procedure.

6.3
Mechanics of the Pilot Procedure
6.3.1
Hardware Configurations of the Pilot Procedure

The pilot procedure may employ either of two kinds of computer hardware systems; one option is to use a dedicated small computer with a medium speed printer, typewriter console, and tape drives. The printer would then output standard information for simulated periods X_t and forecasts X_{t+1}^c; the typewriter console would be used for all input and for outputting nonstandard information in response to requests. A central processing unit, which is relatively fast and has access to 9K core storage, would be adequate. A game running for 10 periods of simulated time will require 1 to 2 hours because of the time needed by the players and the referee to make decisions.

A preferable option is a commercial time-sharing system. The time-sharing capacity provides physical flexibility and makes it possible to use multiple consoles—one for each of the two players and one for the referee.

A relatively small portion of the procedure time is spent actually using the computer; most of the time is spent analyzing the output and deciding on new values for the instrument variables. Even when the computer equipment is being used, most of the time is spent in the mechanics of the input-output process; that is, typing input is extremely slow, typing output is somewhat faster, and printing the output is moderately fast. Thus, because of time requirements, a time-sharing computer is the appropriate hardware configuration for real decision-making simulations; the computer can be available for other uses during the extremely slow cognitive decision processes and the relatively slow input-output processes.

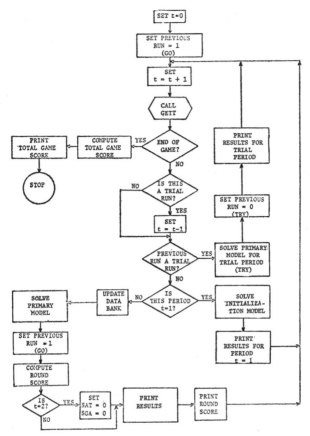

Figure 6.4.   Pilot procedure flow chart.

6.3.2
Initialization of the Game

The game is initialized by assigning starting values to the parameters, the capital stock, the five policy variables, the price index, the unemployment rate, and the constants and coefficients of both the primary model equations and the scoring function (a set of recommended starting values for 1969 is given in Table 6.7). The starting values for the initialization program are standard inputs stored on tapes or on disk files. The referee may change any or all values to create new initial conditions. The model generates required data through successive "pregame" rounds ($t = -2$ and $t = -1$).

After the pregame rounds, play begins with a forecast for period 3 ($t = 0$); then the values for accumulated government debt (or any level of debt may be used as a starting point) and for all the scoring functions are set to zero.

6.3.3
Operation of the Computer Program

The operation of the game requires two computer routines as shown by the flow chart of Figure 6.4. The main routine contains the initialization, the standard printout, and the primary model subroutines. A software routine GETT is necessary to provide a linkage that permits the players and a referee to use the typewriter console for directly entering data, for typing certain programmed instructions, for requesting data from storage, and for computing simple algebraic expressions.

After the information required to establish the data bank is entered into core memory, preestablished input values are entered for time periods 1 and 2 (where $t = -2$ and $t = -1$) to generate the required history.

If a forecast is requested (by entering the instruction TRY) to determine the effects of certain parameter or instrument settings, the model is solved and the solution (under the stated conditions) is printed and labeled, but the time period is not advanced and the data bank is not updated. Trial runs do not contain calculations for accumulated government debt SGA and for players' scores in the round. When the instruction GO is entered, the data bank is updated, the time period advanced, and the round scored.

Instructions allowed by the GETT subroutine are TYPE and END. The instruction TYPE is used to request additional information (for example, TYPE Y3) or calculations (for example, TYPE Y $-$ W*0.54). Finally, END is typed to signal the end of the game; then the program calculates the bonus (or penalty) scores and the total score for the game. After these scores are printed, the game ends.

6.3.4
Rules of Play

The rules of play are simple. The two players may use the computer-assisted information system until they reach a limit established by the referee; two possible limits are: a plan must be decided on within 10 minutes after the referee finishes his description of the economic environment or each player may ask for three forecasts.

After the players decide upon, and enter, the plan for the round, the referee enters the parameter values and types TRY and then GO. The referee tries to create as realistic a situation as possible, but he is constrained (especially by the model's instability) in the range and frequency of parameter changes. (Table 6.3 presents the suggested maximum range and frequency of instrument and parameter changes.)

6.3.5

Modifying the Model

A significant feature of the adaptive modeling procedure is that its components can be modified or adapted as insight is gained from comparing its results to actual conditions.

Four types of changes are

A.

Changes that can be made without altering the computer program or data.

B.

Changes that can be made by altering stored data files.

C.

Minor changes in the program.

D.

Major changes in the program.

The dividing line between Type C and Type D is not definitive; perhaps any change that requires more than a day of programming effort can be defined as a major change.

Type A includes modifying the restrictions on information exchanges among the players or between the players and the referee, changing the number of forecasts permitted prior to reaching a decision, establishing a time limit for arriving at a plan, and revising the constraints on the frequency and range of instrument or parameter changes. Type B includes changing the values of parameters (referee variables), changing the weights and targets in the objective function, extending the data bank, and modifying initial conditions. Type C includes modifying the model or scoring function equations either by changing nondata parameters (for example, see unemployment change; equation M.19) or the form of the equation, or by adding an additional scoring equation or some simple auxiliary equations (for example, balance of payments as a function of interest rates and prices). Type D includes adding new player roles or instruments, significantly changing input or output formats, and making major changes in the primary model.

The operational pilot procedure described in this chapter is used primarily as an illustrative device and as a means of efficiently experimenting with an adaptive modeling procedure. However, to aid in decision making, an adaptive model should include a primary model that incorporates available empirical knowledge about the functioning of the economic system.

The following Chapters 7 and 8 present a design for a prototype procedure that uses the forecasting model developed at the Wharton School's Economic Forecasting Unit (the Wharton-EFU model) as its primary model. Chapter 7 describes the prototype version of the five components developed for the pilot procedure; Chapter 8 describes the two uncertainty components not contained in the pilot procedure: an exogenous-event library and exogenous-event auxiliary models. Thus the prototype is an improvement over the pilot procedure in two important ways: (a) it contains a realistic representation of the economy (the Wharton-EFU model) and (b) it treats uncertainty more systematically and explicitly.

7

The Certainty Components of a Prototype Procedure for the Stabilization Problem

The prototype and the pilot procedures are conceptually similar. The major difference is the use, in the prototype, of a reasonably well-accepted econometric model as the primary model; this requires changes in the other four components of the prototype—the decision-making roles, the objective function, the information system, and the dynamic environment.

The prototype procedure uses the quarterly Wharton-EFU model as the primary model for simulating the economy and links an auxiliary monetary model to it to obtain a composite model that generates (as a function of monetary policy instruments) variables exogenous to the Wharton-EFU.

Generally, the national accounting identities of the primary model are expressed in current dollars, and structural (behavioral) equations are measured in constant dollars. The gross national product (GNP) is defined in both current and constant dollars.

The prototype procedure is designed for four policy players: a monetary authority and three players with fiscal responsibilities; the latter three represent the U.S. Defense Department (DOD), the U.S. Treasury Department, and all other departments combined. The three players, acting as fiscal decision makers, are responsible for seven instruments: two are exogenous expenditure variables, one is military employment N_g^m, three are tax rates, and the seventh is transfer payments.[1]

The two exogenous expenditure variables are total real government purchases of goods and services (G) and real government expenditures for national defense (G_d). The variables N_g^m and G_d are controlled by the DOD player (an auxiliary model is suggested in Chapter 8 to make G_d endogenous) who is heavily influenced by exogenous international shocks generated by the referee. The three tax rates are manipulated by the Treasury Department player to meet fiscal and monetary objectives. The other-department player is responsible for combined purchases for all other government departments (the difference between G and G_d) and the transfer payment rate T_r; he has both fiscal and social program objectives.

Unlike the fiscal players' instruments, which are easily identified in the primary model, the monetary player's instruments can be included only if an auxiliary model is constructed. The only monetary instrument in the Wharton-EFU model is the discount rate; an auxiliary model was

---

[1] Decision makers can, as shown later, vary both the intercept and the slope of tax and transfer payment equations.

developed to provide two other instruments: deposit reserve requirements and open market operations.

The responsibility of the monetary authority, the fourth policy player in the prototype procedure, is to represent both the central bank (Federal Reserve System) and the commercial banking system. The latter accepts only demand deposits, maintains reserves against these deposits, and makes commercial loans; the auxiliary model neglects currency, and reflects all monetary transactions as changes in the level of demand deposits. While this is an overly simplified monetary sector, basic economic principles and relationships are maintained and, at the same time, policy instruments are created for the monetary policy player.

The four policy players are scored on the values of a number of economic indicators at the end of each quarterly period of play. Penalties, representing political and administrative costs of implementing a policy, are assessed whenever certain policy instruments are altered; bonuses (or penalties) are computed, at the end of the simulated period, for the average or absolute change of the indicators. The forms of the prototype scoring equations are similar to those of the pilot procedure; they are asymmetric quadratic functions of deviations from target values for all variables except prices and a parabolic function for prices.

The prototype information system also resembles that of the pilot procedure. Any differences are those required by the two dissimilar primary models; for example, the prototype data bank not only stores values of selected variables for the preceding five years but also contains considerable data for the preceding eight quarters.

The major conceptual change in the prototype process is the treatment of uncertainty through the use of a library of exogenous events and the auxiliary models linking them to the primary model. These include three exogenous-event (or shock) categories: international military, international nonmilitary, and domestic labor disruptions. The auxiliary models can be modifications of existing models if any are available; for example, the defense expenditures model, discussed in Chapter 8, can be used to make G_d endogenous and to provide active and inactive military strength as well as procurement obligations as DOD instruments.

Another example is an auxiliary model for predicting changes in inventories prior, and subsequent, to the expiration of a major labor contract. Inventories would be accumulated in anticipation of a strike, depleted during a strike (if it occurs), and readjusted after a new contract is negotiated.

The referee provides information to the four players on anticipated exogenous events and establishes the probabilities (including 0 and 1) of their occurrence. A random-number generator determines whether an event actually occurs; if it does, the subroutine for that particular auxiliary model is called to determine the value of relevant exogenous variables (for example, the strike variable is not zero if a strike is threatened).

7.1
The Primary Model for the Prototype Procedure

In the prototype procedure, the Wharton-EFU model is the primary model.[2] Other macroeconometric models of the economy were considered but discarded for various reasons. Paul Taubman's seven-equation model[3] and Daniel Suits' annual model[4] have been used extensively, but they lack a monetary sector. The Brookings model[5] is too complex. The Federal Reserve Board–Massachusetts Institute of Technology (FRB-MIT) model is too new; thus its characteristics are insufficiently known.[6] Revisions and operating details of the Office of Business Economics (OBE) model are too frequently kept confidential.[7]

The Wharton-EFU model has the following advantages: it is constantly updated and maintained by an excellent staff at the University of Pennsylvania; it includes a monetary and a foreign sector; it is widely used and understood; and, perhaps most important, its short-term forecasting record is acceptable. The monetary and foreign sectors are somewhat

[2] Michael K. Evans and Lawrence R. Klein, *The Wharton Econometric Forecasting Model* (Philadelphia, Pa.: University of Pennsylvania, 1967). Hereafter referred to as the Wharton-EFU model. Since this book was written a new version of the Wharton-EFU model has become available. The new version, Mark III, has a more completely developed monetary sector.

[3] For an early published version of this model, see I. Friend and Paul Taubman, "A Short-Term Forecasting Model," *The Review of Economics and Statistics*, vol. 46 (August 1964), pp. 229–236.

[4] Daniel B. Suits, "Forecasting and Analysis with an Econometric Model," *American Economic Review*, vol. 52 (March 1962), pp. 104–132.

[5] James S. Duesenberry et al. eds., *The Brookings Quarterly Econometric Model of the United States* (Chicago, Ill.: Rand McNally & Company, 1965).

[6] Frank De Leeuw and Edward Gramlich, "The Federal Reserve-MIT Econometric Model," *Federal Reserve Bulletin*, vol. 54 (January 1968), pp. 11–40.

[7] Maurice Liebenberg, A. Hirsch, and J. Popkin, "A Quarterly Econometric Model of the United States: A Progress Report," *Survey of Current Business*, vol. 46 (May 1966), pp. 13–39; another model reviewed was C. F. Christ, "A Short-Run Aggregate-Demand Model of the Interdependence and Effects of Monetary and Fiscal Policies with Keynesian and Classical Interest Elasticities," *American Economic Review*, vol. 57 (May 1967), pp. 434–473.

inadequate for decision making, but they are adequate as bases for auxiliary models.

The Wharton-EFU model is a synthesis of two models: the Wharton Model developed by L. R. Klein[8] and a Ph.D. dissertation by M. K. Evans.[9] It is described as "genuinely a merger of these two, together with a liberal drawing on recent research results of other econometricians and the authors."[10]

This model, which is a disaggregated version of the general Keynesian model, divides consumption into three categories: autos, other durables, and nondurables, plus services. Investment is divided according to purpose (plant and equipment, housing, and inventories) and according to sector (manufacturing, commercial, and regulated and mining firms). Final demand is converted into factor demand through the use of Cobb-Douglas production functions; the same functions are used to determine industry capacity as a function of the capital stock; price changes, in turn, are a function of capacity utilization. The unemployment level is the difference between the labor demand and labor supply, both endogenously determined. To determine the labor supply, exogenous labor force growth is modified by recent unemployment levels. Wages vary in response to prices and the level of unemployment. The model also determines disaggregated factor shares, depreciation and retained earnings, tax revenues, and implicit deflators. The short-term interest rate, which is a function of the discount rate and free reserves in the banking system, is, in turn, a determinant of the long-term interest rate. The long-term interest rate is a determinant of manufacturing and regulated industry investments in plant and equipment. The spread between long-term and short-term rates influences investments in housing, plant and equipment, and commercial industries.

The 36 identities that complete the primary model are of two types. The first is a series of national accounting identities that measure economic stocks and flows; these include measures of real and nominal GNP, national and personal income, aggregated stocks and expenditures, and returns to economic factors. The second type is a series of ratios and

[8] Lawrence R. Klein, "A Postwar Quarterly Model," *Models of Income Determination*, vol. 58 *Studies in Income and Wealth*. Princeton, N.J.: Princeton University Press, 1964, pp. 11–30.

[9] Michael K. Evans, "A Postwar Quarterly Model of the United States Economy, 1947–1960," unpublished dissertation, Brown University, Providence, R.I., 1963.

[10] Michael K. Evans and Lawrence R. Klein, *The Wharton Model*, p. 3.

indices computed from values estimated by structural equations; these include aggregate price deflators and unemployment rates.

Generally, coefficients for Wharton-EFU equations were estimated by two-stage least squares; however, equations with only one unlagged endogenous variable were estimated by using ordinary least squares regressions; the data are 68 quarterly observations for the period from 1948 to 1964.[11]

7.2
The Monetary Auxiliary Model
Presumably, the FRB-MIT model was developed[12] because models such as the Wharton-EFU did not contain instruments for which monetary decision makers are responsible. The adaptive procedure for this situation was to develop an auxiliary model to link the missing instruments to the primary model; thus, model f'' gives

$$X^* = f''(Y^{**}) \tag{7.1}$$

where X^* are exogenous variables of the Wharton-EFU model and Y^{**} is the set of missing monetary instruments.

The monetary sector equations of the Wharton-EFU model that are most closely related to monetary decisions are

$$i_s = 0.42 + 0.994i_d - 0.0895 \text{ FR} \tag{7.2}$$

and

$$i_L = 0.21 + 0.086i_s + 0.889(i_L)_{-1} \tag{7.3}$$

where i_s is the short-term interest rate (4–6 month commercial paper); i_d is the discount rate; i_L is the Moody's average yield on seasoned Aaa corporate bonds; and FR is net free reserves as a percentage of required reserves.

The discount rate is an explicit monetary instrument; the omitted monetary instruments are the central bank's open market operations and its power to establish reserve requirements. The exogenous variable X^*, in the functional form (Equation 7.1), is the free reserve ratio (FR) in Equation 7.2.

---

[11] For explanations on computational techniques, see Evans and Klein, *The Wharton Model*, pp. 5–7.
[12] Robert Rasch and Harold Shapiro, "The FRB-MIT Econometric Model: Its Special Features," *American Economic Review*, May 1968, p. 123.

The following auxiliary model links the omitted instruments to the primary model.[13]

The interest rate on commercial loans r_{CL} is determined by

$$r_{CL} = 0.762 + 0.448i_L + 0.160i_s + 0.341(r_{CL})_{-1}; \tag{7.4}$$

the effect on commercial and industrial loans is shown by

$$\Delta CL = 0.1167I_i - 0.450\Delta r_{CL} + 0.544\Delta(CL)_{-1} \tag{7.5}$$

where I_i is inventory investment in billions of 1958 dollars and CL are loans in billions of current dollars. The amount of loans CL determines the level of demand deposits in commercial banks DD; that is,

$$DD = DD_{-1} + \Delta CL. \tag{7.6}$$

Open market operations, OMO, change the total reserves of the member banks, that is,

$$RT = RT_{-1} + OMO. \tag{7.7}$$

The following six equations (added to Equations 7.2 to 7.5) complete the auxiliary model.

Net free reserves are defined by

$$NFR = RT - RR(DD) \tag{7.8}$$

where RR is the remaining monetary instrument: reserve requirements. The exogenous variable of the primary model is given in the auxiliary model by

$$FR = \frac{NFR}{RR(DD)} \tag{7.9}$$

where FR is a percentage of total required reserves—that is, the net free reserve ratio.

New securities issued by the government are

$$B_t - (P_gG + T_r + I_g - \text{SocSec} - T_b - T_p - T_c)_{t-1} \tag{7.10}$$

where T_b = indirect business taxes and transfers, T_c = corporate income taxes, T_p = personal tax and nontax payments, SocSec = social security contributions of employers, employees, and self-employed, P_g = implicit price deflator for government purchases, G = government purchases of

[13] Parameter values are from the FRB-MIT model; see Frank de Leeuw and Edward Gramlich, "The FRB-MIT Model."

goods and services, I_g = government interest payments, and T_r = transfer payments. All terms (including P_gG) are in billions of current dollars.

The interest paid by the government is determined by

$$I_g = \Delta i_s(\text{SGA}) + (i_s - 0.025)B + (I_g)_{-1}. \tag{7.11}$$

The remaining identities are

$$I_{gc} = I_g + I_c \tag{7.12}$$

and

$$SGA = SGA_{-1} + B \tag{7.13}$$

where the new variables are I_{gc} = total government and consumer interest payments, I_c = consumer interest payments, and SGA = accumulated government deficit (or surplus), or the public debt.

Variables B, CL, DD, I_g, NFR, OMO, r_{CL}, RR, RT, and SGA do not appear in the Wharton-EFU model; they were added for the auxiliary model. The structural Equations 7.4 and 7.5 were taken from the FRB-MIT model; the other equations are identities except for Equation 7.11, which contains an approximation of the spread between the interest rate on new government securities and the commercial paper rate.

Statistical errors are introduced by linking the auxiliary model to the primary model in this fashion;[14] however, short of reestimating a model with the composite structure or developing a completely new model (the FRB-MIT response to the omitted instruments), this is suggested as an efficient procedure for using the Wharton-EFU model to develop joint fiscal and monetary economic policy.

7.3
The Decision-Making Roles

The single fiscal decision-making role of the pilot model is disaggregated into three for the prototype model. The first represents the Treasury and taxing powers of government; the second represents DOD; the third represents all remaining government spending units combined.

The treasury player controls three pairs of tax parameters: TB and TB', TC and TC', and TP and TP'; these six parameters are not part of the original primary Wharton-EFU model. Therefore, the Wharton-EFU tax equations were modified so that business, corporate, and personal taxes

[14] See discussion in Chapter 2.

T_b, T_c, and T_p are given by:

$$T_b = -(2.90 + TB') + (0.0721 + TB)(NI) + 0.3839(t), \qquad (7.14)$$

$$T_c = -(4.26 + TC') + (0.46 + TC)(P_{cb} - IVA), \qquad (7.15)$$

$$T_p = -(12.8 + TP') + (0.153 + TP)(PI + SCI - T_r), \qquad (7.16)$$

where $NI =$ national income, $t =$ time trend (quarters since 1947.4), $P_{cb} =$ corporate profit before taxes, $IVA =$ inventory valuation adjustment, $PI =$ personal income, and $SCI =$ social security contributions of individuals. The NI, P_{cb}, and SCI are in billions of current dollars; IVA and PI are in billions of 1958 dollars. Using two parameters in Equations 7.14, 7.15, and 7.16 allows the treasury player to manipulate both the slope and intercept of each of the three functions.

The DOD player controls the two instruments—government purchases for national defense G_d in billions of 1958 dollars and military personnel N_g^m. To convert to current dollars, G_b must be multiplied by P_g, the price deflator for government purchases. The next chapter introduces an omitted-instrument auxiliary model and describes the uncertainty components; in that model, $P_g G_d$ is a function of such variables as active and inactive military manpower. The procedure for making G_d, an exogenous variable of the primary model, endogenous to the composite model is identical to that described in Section 7.2 for the monetary variable FR.

The other-department player, the third of the administration's fiscal decision makers, controls two instruments: the remaining government purchases in billions of 1958 dollars and the set TR and TR', which determines the rate of transfer payments T_r in the modified Wharton-EFU equation:

$$T_r = -(2.95 + TR') + (1.565 + TR)\frac{U_n N_L^c}{100} + 0.5069t \qquad (7.17)$$

where U_n is the percentage or rate of unemployment and N_L^c is millions of civilians in the labor force. The set TR and TR' is not present in the original Wharton-EFU primary model.

The remaining decision maker is the monetary authority who represents both the central bank (the Federal Reserve System) and the commercial banking system. The three central bank policy instruments are the discount rate, the deposit reserve requirements, and the open market operations of buying and selling government securities to change member bank reserves; of the three, the primary model has one (discount rate) and the monetary auxiliary model, two decision variables.

The fiscal decisions are determined in part by general economic objectives and in part by program objectives.[15] Economic objectives alter the distribution of income and the composition of output by changing tax rates and transfer payments, and modify aggregate final demand by creating a new expenditure pattern. The decisions lead, in part, to new economic growth and unemployment rates and to new price levels; however, the results are not solely determined by fiscal decisions. The net fiscal balance between government receipts and expenditures is determined by interactions among all policy instruments and by exogenous factors (that is, the tax base, interest paid on the public debt, and social security contributed by individuals and employers) that are not directly controlled by players. Furthermore, the net fiscal balance (if it is not equal to zero) leads to a change in the level of public debt and directly influences decisions made by the monetary decision maker in the next period.

The need for cooperative decisions between the fiscal and monetary players in the gaming environment simulates the administration-FRB relationship in the real environment.

The monetary results of fiscal decisions (see Equation 7.10) are based on the assumption that any government deficit must be financed by issuing new securities to the private sector in the next period. Deficit funding, along with the results of open market operations and the demand for commercial loans, determine demand deposits. Generally, demand deposits will expand by some multiple of the increase in reserves created by open market operations; though the initial expansion equals the positive value of open market operations, the multiple expansion depends on the demand for commercial loans. Required reserves are obtained by setting aside that share of demand deposits that is specified by the required reserve rate RR, the third policy instrument.

The fiscal and monetary instruments described in this section and the objective function described below define the four decision-making roles of the prototype model. In the pilot procedure, constraints are specified for the manipulation of the instruments; in the prototype procedure, penalties are incorporated into the objective function to represent political and administrative costs of implementing decisions. (Constraints are also specified, see Section 7.6.3.)

---

[15] Except for certain parts of the Department of Defense budget, program objectives are not discussed in this study. A useful addition would be to create scenarios that the referee may introduce and auxiliary models so that program objectives could be considered.

7.4
The Objective Function

The discussion of objective functions and welfare criteria in Chapter 3 led to two alternatives for the prototype procedure: to use the goals derived from the Employment Act of 1946 of growth, full employment, and price stability to derive an objective function such as the one used in the pilot procedure, or to attempt to measure welfare by the purchasing power of population subgroups.

Population in the Wharton-EFU model is not sufficiently disaggregated to facilitate the second alternative; thus the first is used in both procedures, but it is modified, to some extent, to illustrate a means of approaching the welfare-theoretic alternative.

The form of the scoring functions used in the prototype resembles those of the pilot procedure—quadratic or parabolic functions of the difference between the actual and target (or nominal) values of various variables. All the variables in the objective function must meet two criteria: they must represent generally held measures of economic performance, and they must be endogenous to the composite of the Wharton-EFU and auxiliary models. If a variable is mentioned in the President's economic report, it is assumed to satisfy the first criterion. The structure of the composite model determines if the second criterion is satisfied; however, it is important to recall that disaggregating auxiliary models can extend the number of variables in the objective function (e.g., unemployment by race).

The objective function uses deviations from target (or nominal) values rather than absolute values for the welfare-measuring variables. Theoretically, either may be used since any datum may be employed for the objective function (that is, the function need only be unique up to a linear transformation) if the value is used only for comparisons. Choosing target (or nominal) values rather than zero for the target makes it possible to focus on relevant values when assigning weights. Since weights which evaluate the relative significance of each element need be correct only in the relevant range, choosing a datum in that range makes it somewhat easier to approximate the "correct" weighting of the arguments in the objective function.

In summary, the abstract concept of an objective function is replaced in the prototype procedure by the sum of a set of scoring functions that evaluate the economy's performance. Arguments in the functions include changes in per capita disposable personal income, in the unemployment

Table 7.1   The Short-Term Scoring Function Equations

Objective Scored	Equation No.	Scoring Functions (SF) Measuring Economic Performance in Each Round[a]
Growth rate of real GNP (GR)	(SF.1)	$SGR_t = \alpha_1(GR_t - GR^*)^2$ if $GR_t > GR^*$ $\quad\ = \alpha_2(GR_t - GR^*)^2$ if $GR_t < GR$
Change in a personal disposal income (Y)	(SF.2)	$SDY_t = \alpha_3(\Delta Y_t - \Delta Y^*)^2$ if $\Delta Y_t > \Delta Y^*$ $\quad\ = \alpha_4(\Delta Y_t - \Delta Y^*)^2$ if $\Delta Y_t < \Delta Y^*$
Change in unemployment rate (U)	(SF.3)	$SDU_t = \alpha_5(\Delta U_t - \Delta U^*)^2$ if $\Delta U_t < \Delta U^*$ $\quad\ = \alpha_6(\Delta U_t - \Delta U^*)^2$ if $\Delta U_t > \Delta U^*$
Change in investment in nonfarm residential construction (housing) (I_h)	(SF.4)	$SDH_t = \alpha_7(\Delta I_{h_t} - \Delta I_h^*)^2$ if $\Delta I_{h_t} > \Delta I_h^*$ $\quad\ = \alpha_8(\Delta I_{h_t} - \Delta I_h^*)^2$ if $\Delta I_{h_t} < \Delta I_h^*$
Change in consumer price index (P_c)	(SF.5)	$SDP_t = \alpha_9[\alpha_{10}(\Delta P_{c_t})^2 + \alpha_{11}(P_{c_t}) + \alpha_{12}]$
Short-term interest rate (i_s)	(SF.6)	$SDI_t = \alpha_{13}(i_{s_t} - i_s^*)^2$ if $i_{s_t} < i_s^*$ $\quad\ = \alpha_{14}(i_{s_t} - i_s^*)^2$ if $i_{s_t} > i_s^*$
Total round score	(SF.7)	$SRT_t = SGR_t + SDY_t + SDU_t$ $\qquad\ + SDH_t + SDP_t + SDI_t$
Accumulated score	(SF.8)	$SAT_t = SAT_{t-1} + SRT_t$

Decision Incurring Penalty	Equation No.	Scoring Functions (PS) Measuring Implementing Changes[b]
Changing tax rate on indirect business taxes and business transfers (T_b)	(PS.1)	$PTB_t = \alpha_{15}(TB_t - TB_{t-1})^2$ $\qquad\ + \alpha_{15'}(TB_t' - TB_{t-1}')^2$
Changing tax rate on corporate income taxes (T_c)	(PS.2)	$PTC_t = \alpha_{16}(TC_t - TC_{t-1})^2$ $\qquad\ + \alpha_{16'}(TC_t' - TC_{t-1}')^2$
Changing tax rate on personal taxes (T_p)	(PS.3)	$PTP_t = \alpha_{17}(TP_t - TP_{t-1})^2$ $\qquad\ + \alpha_{17'}(TP_t' - TP_{t-1}')^2$
Decreasing nondefense government expenditure $(G - G_d)$	(PS.4)	$PGN_t = \alpha_{18}[(G - G_d)_t - (G - G_d)_{t-1}]^2$ $\qquad\ \text{when } [(G - G_d)_t - (G - G_d)_{t-1}] < 0$ $\quad\ = 0$ $\qquad\ \text{when } [(G - G_d)_t - (G - G_d)_{t-1}] \geq 0$
Changing demand deposit reserve requirement (RR)	(PS.5)	$PRR_t = \alpha_{19}(RR_t - RR_{t-1})$
Total penalties	(PS.6)	$PRT = PTB_t + PTC_t + PTP_t$ $\qquad\ + PGN_t + PRR_t$
Accumulated penalties	(PS.7)	$PAT_t = PAT_{t-1} + PRT_t$

[a] The variable weights and implicit target values for SF.5 are $\alpha_1 = 1.0$, $\alpha_2 = -1.0$, $\alpha_3 = 1.0$, $\alpha_4 = -1.0$, $\alpha_5 = 4.0$, $\alpha_6 = -4.0$, $\alpha_7 = 10^2$, $\alpha_8 = -10^2$, $\alpha_9 = 1.0$, $\alpha_{10} = -4.444$, $\alpha_{11} = 44.444$, $\alpha_{12} = 5.555$, $\alpha_{13} = 10.0$, $\alpha_{14} = -10.0$. The explicit target values are $GR^* = 1\%$, $\Delta Y^* = 0$, $\Delta U^* = 0$, $\Delta I_h^* = 0$, $i_s^* = 4\%$.

[b] The variable weights are $\alpha_{15} = -100.0$, $\alpha_{15'} = -10.0$, $\alpha_{16} = -100.0$, $\alpha_{16'} = -10.0$, $\alpha_{17} = -100.0$, $\alpha_{17'} = -10.0$, $\alpha_{18} = -10^{-4}$, $\alpha_{19} = -10$.

rate, in investment, in nonfarm residential housing, and in the consumer price index as well as the economic growth rate and the short-term interest rate. In addition, the functions impose penalties when tax rates are altered, nondefense government purchases of goods and services are diminished, or reserve requirements are changed; the penalties represent political and administrative costs of manipulating these instruments.

Bonuses and penalties are computed from the average growth rate over all time periods, the average change in the price index, the absolute change in per capita disposable income, the final unemployment rate, the absolute change in housing investment, and the change in the short-term interest rate. Scores are accumulated on a round-for-round basis. At the end of the game, bonuses and/or penalties are added to the accumulated round scores.

The form of scoring functions is generally an asymmetric quadratic function,

$$\phi(X_1, X_2, \ldots, X_m) = \sum_{i=1}^{m} c_i(X_i - X_i^*)^2, \tag{7.18}$$

in which the X_i are performance values, the X_i^* are target values, and the c_i are positive or negative weights depending on whether the value of $X_i \lessgtr X_i^*$. However, when a feasible target value is optimal and deviations in either direction are harmful, the parabolic function is used. For example, the parabolic form is used to measure the economy's ability to maintain stable prices.

The short-term scoring functions are listed in Table 7.1 with the suggested targets and weights; Table 7.2 lists the functions, targets, and weights for the long-term functions.

7.5
The Information System
For the prototype procedure, the information system resembles the one used for the pilot model. The changes in the data bank and the computer-assisted system are primarily those required by differences in primary models.
7.5.1
The Computer-Assisted System
The data bank for the prototype must contain data necessary to solve the model and data to use in the gaming procedures. Requirements for gaming

Table 7.2   The Long-Term Scoring Function Equations

Objective Scored	Equation No.[a]	Scoring Functions (BS) Measuring Long-Term Economic Performance
Average rate of growth of real GNP (GR)	(BS.1)	$BGR = \beta_1(\overline{GR} - \overline{GR}^*)^2$ if $\overline{GR} > \overline{GR}^*$ $\quad\;\; = \beta_2(\overline{GR} - \overline{GR}^*)^2$ if $\overline{GR} < \overline{GR}^*$
Net change in per capita disposable income (Y/N)	(BS.2)	$BDY = \beta_3[(Y/N)_t - (Y/N)_0]^2$ $\qquad\qquad\qquad$ if $(Y/N)_t > (Y/N)_0$ $\quad\;\;\; = \beta_4[(Y/N)_t - (Y/N_0)]^2$ $\qquad\qquad\qquad$ if $(Y/N)_t < (Y/N)_0$
Rate of unemployment relative to target value (U)	(BS.3)	$BU = \beta_5(U_T - U^*)^2$ if $U_T < U^*$ $\quad\;\; = \beta_6(U_T - U^*)^2$ if $U_T > U^*$
Net change in the level of investment in housing (I_h)	(BS.4)	$BDH = \beta_7(I_{h_T} - I_{h_0})^2$ if $I_{h_T} > I_{h_0}$ $\quad\;\;\; = 0$ otherwise
Average rate of inflation (DP_c)	(BS.5)	$BDP = \beta_9(\overline{DP}_c - \overline{DP})_c^{*2}$ if $\overline{DP}_c < \overline{DP}_c^*$ $\quad\;\;\; = 0$ otherwise
Net change in the short-term rate of interest (i_s)	(BS.6)	$BDI = \beta_{10}(i_{s_T} - i_{s_0})^2$ if $i_{s_T} < i_{s_0}$ $\quad\;\; = \beta_{11}(i_{s_T} - i_{s_0})^2$ if $i_{s_T} > i_{s_0}$
Total long-term score	(BS.7)	$BST = BGR + BDY + BU + BDH$ $\qquad\qquad + BDP + BDI$
Total game score	(BS.8)	$TGS = BST + SAT_T + PAT_T$

[a] Notation: overbar $(-)$ = compound growth rate, subscripts 0 and T = first and final rounds. The variable weights are: $\beta_1 = 10.0$, $\beta_2 = -10.0$, $\beta_3 = 1.0$, $\beta_4 = -1.0$, $\beta_5 = 10.0$, $\beta_6 = -10.0$, $\beta_7 = 10.0$, $\beta_8 = -10.0$, $\beta_9 = 100.0$, $\beta_{10} = 10.0$, $\beta_{11} = -10.0$. The explicit target values (in addition to those given in Table, 7.1) are: $U^* = 4\%$, $DP_c^* = 0.5$ percent.

include the solution requirements specified by the lag structure of the model's equations; this section describes a system designed to meet both.

The data bank contains the values of all endogenous and exogenous variables for the last 8 quarters and selected annual data for the last 5 years. Each quarter the procedure generates new values for all endogenous variables and requires data inputs for all exogenous variables and policy instruments. Part of the gaming process is to have the player request information; therefore, only a limited amount of data is provided automatically. The quarterly data provided to the players each round should contain the values for a limited number of variables. Table 7.3 lists the standard output items. The first three are GNP, total consumption expenditure, and disposable personal income. The GNP may be used to determine several ratios (for example, relative share of government purchases of goods and services in GNP). Consumption and disposable income may be used to determine average and marginal propensities

Table 7.3   Standard Quarterly Output Data

Output Variable Symbol	Standard Output Variable
X	Gross National Product (GNP).*
C	Personal consumption expenditure.*
Y	Disposable personal income.*
PC	Implicit consumption deflator (1958 = 1.00).
$PG1$	Implicit price deflator for government purchases (1958 = 1.00) lagged one period.
U	Unemployment rate.†
CA	Purchases of autos.*
IPM	Manufacturing investment in plant and equipment.*
IH	Investment in nonfarm residential housing.*
PCB	Corporate profit before taxes (adjusted for IVA).§
FF	Income of unincorporated businesses (farm sector).§
B	New government securities issued.§
SGA	Accumulated public debt.§
NFR	Net free reserves.§
IS	Short-term interest rate.†
GR	Growth rate of GNP.†
EXP	Export balance.*

* Billions of 1958 dollars.
† Percentage.
§ Billions of current dollars.

to consume; per capita disposable income can be readily computed by request (that is, "TYPE Y/N").

The fourth item, the implicit consumption deflator, was selected because it is a close approximation of the consumer price index. The fifth item in Table 7.3, implicit price deflator for government purchases, was considered necessary if the policy players are to manipulate expenditure instruments measured in constant dollars.

A group of items listed for certain key sectors follows the unemployment rate; these indicate consumer auto purchases, manufacturing plant and equipment investment, nonfarm residential housing investment, corporate profits before taxes, and farm income.

The new government security issues, the accumulated public debt, net free reserves, and the short-term interest rate will be of special interest to the monetary decision maker. The final indicators are the growth rate of GNP and the export balance.

The eight-quarter data bank includes values for all endogenous variables of the primary and auxiliary models as well as the policy instruments. To conserve computer storage and processing requirements, a more selective list of annual data was specified for the five-year data bank; these include average or annual values of the instruments as well as the data in Table 7.3. Information in the data bank of the prototype procedure is subject to the recall and computational procedures developed in the pilot procedure.

7.5.2

The Referee and the Informal System

The major functions of the referee are to establish the initial economic environment, to change economic conditions during the course of play and provide the players with information about the changed conditions, and finally, to control the play of the game.

The number of players who perform the referee's duties may vary from one to three, depending on the intensity and speed of play. If the game is played continuously and at multiple locations, two or three referees may prove to be desirable; otherwise, a single referee at a central point is sufficient. The responsibilities of the referee are the same regardless of the number of players assuming the role.

The referee establishes the economic environment by specifying initial values for required input (that is, the exogenous variables and the policy instruments) and by running the model until the "history" generated and stored in the data bank is sufficient to solve the model.

To modify or change the economic conditions as play progresses, the referee specifies values for nonpolicy exogenous variables; in addition, he may change model parameters or introduce exogenous shocks. To issue reports to players on potential or realized shocks, the referee may disseminate information at his own initiative or he may respond to inquiries from the players.

The third function for the referee is to control the game's progress. For example, in the absence of programmed constraints on the changes a player may make, the referee must check to insure that the magnitude, timing, and direction of the changes are consistent with the rules of play.

The responsibilities of the referee can be reduced if the first function of initializing the model is carried out before beginning the game. Then results may be stored on tapes or disks to be read in as initialization data when the game begins. This is done in the pilot procedure.

In summary, the computer-assisted information system in the prototype is similar to that of the pilot procedure. Each player may retrieve information from the data bank and use it as arguments in simple functions; he may make trial forecasts of his decisions and his estimates of new parameter values. The major changes are in the informal system (through which the referee issues reports concerning exogenous shocks); these changes are discussed further in the next chapter.

7.6
The Dynamic Environment

The computer programming required to create the dynamic environment for the prototype procedure was not part of this study. Thus this section represents a design, or set of recommendations, rather than a description of the man-machine system necessary to the prototype operation. The section describes the initialization and operation of the prototype procedure and the rules of play for the game and briefly discusses exogenous shocks and random events.

7.6.1
Initialization

Before beginning the game, the referee must create the desired economic environment by running the composite model through at least eight periods to establish a data bank.

7.6.2
Operation

The number of exogenous variables that must be specified (see Table 7.4) to solve the composite model creates a formidable problem for the gaming procedure, especially because variable values must be reasonable and consistent. An answer to the problem is to create simple, easily modified, auxiliary models for sets of exogenous variables that may be called for by the referee.

Certain exogenous variables can be used to create uncertainty, thus the referee should be able to change their values via the console; others (currently specified as referee variables) may become instruments with minor modification of the procedure. Dummy variables are natural places for the referee to enter uncertainty.

Table 7.4   Noninstrument Exogenous Variables of the Wharton-EFU Model

Model Variable Symbol	Description
C_r	Dummy variable for consumer credit terms.
d_1	Dummy variable for change in depreciation tax laws.
d_{kw}	Dummy variable for military involvement.
d_s	Dummy variable for automobile supply shortages.
d_{uw}	Dummy variable for unfilled orders.
D_f	Depreciation for farm investments.*
FF	Income of unincorporated businesses (farm sector).*
I_c	Interest paid by consumers.*
I_{if}	Farm inventories.†
I_{pf}	Farm investments in plant and equipment.†
N	Total population.§
N_c	Self-employed outside agriculture.§
N_e	Self-employed in agriculture.§
N_f	Number of farm workers.§
N_g^c	Number of civilian government employees.§
N_m^c	Manufacturing labor force.§
p_f	Prices received by farmers (1958 = 1.00).
P_g	Implicit deflator for government purchases (1958 = 1.00).
p_{ic}	Implicit deflator for nonfood, nonmaterial imports (1958 = 1.00).
p_{if}	Implicit deflator for food imports (1958 = 1.00).
p_{im}	Implicit deflator for nonfood, material imports (1958 = 1.00).
p_r	Price index of rent (1958 = 1.00).
p_{wt}	Price of world trade (1958 = 1.00).
prod	Productivity trend.
SCI	Social security contributions of individuals.*
SD	Statistical discrepancy, plus subsidies less current surpluses of government enterprises.*
SocSec	Social security contributions of employers, employees, and self-employed.*
STR	Dummy variable for strikes.
W_f	Wages of farm workers.*
W_g	Wages of government employees.*
X_f	Gross output originating in farm sector.†
X_{wt}	Index of world trade (1958 = 100.0).

* Billions of current dollars.   † Billions of 1958 dollars.   § Millions of persons.

There are a number of dummy variables in the Wharton-EFU model (see Table 7.4): the variables C_r and d_1, which are dummies for consumer credit and depreciation tax laws, are set equal to one (from 1955.1 and 1962.1, respectively); this value should be retained initially but can later be added to the list of instruments. The variables d_{kw}, d_s, d_{uw}, and STR are dummies for the Korean War, for auto supply shortages, for unfilled orders, and for steel strikes; generally set equal to zero, the positive values represent disruptions in supply conditions caused by economic shocks (for example, a military involvement or a strike), and the negative values represent the reactions when conditions return to normal. Another dummy variable is "prod," the productivity trend assigned a value of 3.6; the referee may change it to indicate a change in the rate of technological change. The time trend t is automatic.

Because the farm sector is not explained by the Wharton-EFU model, the referee must specify the following exogenous variables: farm income FF, wages W_f, and output X_f, the number of farm workers N_f, the prices received by farmers p_f, farm investment I_{pf}, depreciation of farm investment D_f, and farm inventories I_{if}.

A simple auxiliary model might extrapolate the ratio of prices received by farmers to the deflator for consumer purchases of nondurables and services, p_f/p_{ns}; the model may also include a new instrument to represent price supports PS. The ratio of farm output to consumption of nondurables and services, X_f/C_{ns}, the number of farm workers N_f, the farm wages W_f, investment I_{pf}, and inventories I_{if}—all may be estimated by simple extrapolation. Finally, farm income FF may be explained by the difference between output X_f and factor costs D_f and W_f. Thus, a simple farm auxiliary model might resemble the following:

$$p_f = b_1 + b_2 p_{ns} + b_3 PS$$

$$X_f = b_4 + b_5 C_{ns}$$

$$N_f = b_6 X_f - b_7 t$$

$$W_f = b_8 N_f + b_9 t$$

$$I_{pf} = b_{10}(X_f)_{t-1}$$

$$I_{if} = b_{11}(X_f)_{t-1}$$

$$D_f = (D_f)_{t-1} + b_{12} I_{pf}$$

$$FF = b_{13} + X_f - (D_f + W_f)$$

where the parameters $b_1, b_2, \ldots, b_{13}$ are estimated by ordinary least squares.

The government sector, like the farm sector, is not explained by the primary model. In addition to the two dummy variables C_r and d_1, the referee must specify the following exogenous variables: gross social security contributions SocSec, individuals' social security contributions SCI, wages of government employees W_g, gross output of the government sector X_g, total number of military personnel N_g^m and civilian government employees N_g^c, and the implicit price deflator for government purchases P_g. A simple auxiliary model would make SocSec and SCI linear functions of total wages W and dummy variables R and R' would indicate planned changes in the rates; thus, the rates R and R' could become another pair of instruments. A simple extrapolation may be adequate for N_g^c and adding a dummy variable d_{ng} would provide another instrument to represent changes in government employment practices. Defining the government wage rate in terms of that for manufacturing, provides a means of obtaining the government wage bill W_g as a function of N_g^c and the endogenous variable W_m of the primary model. Similarly, the government deflator P_g may be related to the implicit price deflator for manufacturing p_m. The resulting auxiliary model for the government sector (other than the instruments described in Section 7.3) would be:

$$SCI = b_1 + (b_2 + R)W$$
$$\text{SocSec} = (2 + R')SCI$$
$$(N_g^c)_t = (N_g^c)_{t-1} + b_3 d_{ng} + b_4$$
$$W_g = b_5 W_m N_g^c + b_6$$
$$P_g = b_7 p_m + b_8$$

where the parameters $b_1, b_2, \ldots, b_8$ for the government auxiliary model would be estimated by ordinary least squares.

The foreign sector of the primary model also contains a number of exogenous variables: the implicit price deflators for food p_{if}, nonfood material p_{im}, and other imports p_{ic}, and for world trade p_{wt}, and the index of world trade X_{wt}. These are treated in some detail in sections of the next chapter devoted to uncertainty and international shocks; in the absence of specific shocks, simple extrapolations may suffice.

Exogenous demographic variables that need to be specified for the primary model are the population N and certain components of the labor force (for example, farm workers N_f, the self-employed outside agriculture N_c, and manufacturing workers N_m^c). Simple extrapolations may be used for N, N_c, and the ratio of N_m^c to N_L^c (the endogenously determined total civilian labor force).

The remaining variables are the statistical discrepancy plus subsidies less surpluses of government enterprises SD, the price of rent p_r, and interest paid by consumers I_c. Simple extrapolations may be used for each one.

The referee must, in addition to establishing the exogenous variable values, provide the players with the informal information that they need to understand the initial state of the economic system. The degree of formality associated with setting the stage for the game depends, to a great extent, on the individual players, their objectives, the manner in which they engage in play, and the amount of resources that can be expended. The informal information must be consistent with the economic environment that the referee has generated with the model and stored in the data bank.

7.6.3

Playing the Game

When initial values for variables have been set, play can commence. This section describes the successive steps for each round of play, the general rules, and the limits suggested for the manipulation of the decision makers' instruments.

EACH ROUND OF PLAY

The following steps are required for each round (quarter) of play.

1.

Players receive data output by the computer that lists current values of variables (Table 7.3).

2.

The referee may announce an exogenous shock to the economy with statistical uncertainty (that is, the probability distribution is specified) or with subjective uncertainty (for example, "In the opinion of the Secretary of Defense, the war will be over within six months"). The announcement content and format are presented in the next chapter.

3.

Players may request (via console input) additional information on any data output by the computer in the last 8 quarters or request selected annual data for the last 5 years; requests may include simple arithmetic manipulations of the data.

4.

Players may request conditional forecasts (for example, to estimate the impact of the announced exogenous shock on the primary model's endogenous variables). The referee may restrict policy players to a limited number (say three) of forecasts.

5.

Players make "moves" for the current period of play by typing code names and values of instruments at the console.

6.

The referee provides appropriate input for shock auxiliary models (see Chapter 8) by typing code names and values of the shock parameters at the remote console; the auxiliary model calculates the values of exogenous variables affected by the shock and then uses the values to solve the primary model.

7.

The referee also specifies values for the remaining exogenous variables (Table 7.4), either individually or by referring to a predetermined set.

8.

The referee initiates operation of the primary model by typing "GO" and the model is solved. The endogenous variables indicate the model's estimate of the economy's reaction to the shock and player's moves. The round score is also computed at this point in the procedure.

9.

Selected data (Table 7.3) and the score are printed; players evaluate these and additional information and prepare their moves for the next time period.

The rules and details for performing each of these steps are discussed below.

RULES OF PLAY

The rules of play are designed to be flexible and readily adaptable to alternative playing environments; at the same time, constraints are expected to assist in maintaining a realistic environment in which the policy players may operate. Each player is provided a table that specifies the variables maintained in the data bank and the identifier for its retrieval. Each player may request historical data or computations of ratios, percentages, growth rates, sums, and so forth; there is generally no need to restrict the number of requests. It may be preferable, however, to limit the requests each player may make in any round or the time for requesting information. Such constraints are to be mutually determined and selected before play commences.

Communications between players, which are limited to oral inquiries and responses, allow one player to evaluate what the other is planning for the next period. In this way, players can revise their individual, as well as joint, strategies for achieving economic objectives.[16]

Policy players are also permitted to ask the referee to clarify exogenous shocks or other changes in the environment. The referee must transmit to the players only the information that is necessary to their decisions and that cannot be determined from the data bank or from another player.

Each player is permitted to make a number of four-quarter forecasts, or conditional estimates of the values of economic indicators expected in the next 12 months. Each forecast is independent of those made by the other policy players although the results are available as standard output to all players. Following each forecast, the player may request forecast values of variables not contained in the standard output. If the players are to be provided with the capability of making forecasts for a year into the future, a four-period *forecasting* data bank is required so that it can be updated without disturbing the *permanent* data bank.

LIMITATIONS FOR CHANGES

The decision maker's role specifies what he can and cannot do; his decisions are values for policy instruments he controls. In addition to the scoring penalties, the following limits the values (or changes in values) of fiscal and monetary policy instruments.

Fiscal policy instruments: The level of government purchases of goods and services may be changed as much as ± 5 percent per quarter by the joint decisions of the Department of Defense (DOD) and other-department player; in certain cases, the limit may be exceeded but only when the need for a greater change is caused by a selected exogenous shock and specified by the referee.

The level of national defense expenditures may be changed by the DOD player; in the absence of specific reasons, the DOD player may change the expenditure as much as 5 percent per quarter. The DOD and other-department players must cooperate to maintain the desired difference between total purchases G, and defense expenditures G_d.

---

[16] A worthwhile experiment might be to vary the amount of cooperation and communication or to reorganize functions and responsibilities of the fiscal and monetary players.

The tax rates and transfer payments may be altered by the treasury as much as ± 15 percent, but the rates may not be changed more than once every four quarters; this limitation applies independently to each instrument (that is, the personal tax rate T_p may be changed in one quarter and the corporate income rate T_c changed in the next); several (or all) rates may be changed simultaneously.

Monetary policy instruments: The fiscal instruments and two of the monetary instruments, the discount rate and the reserve requirement rate, maintain their previous values unless changed by the player; once changed, the discount rate cannot be changed again for two quarters, and the reserve requirement rate can be changed only once every four quarters. The third monetary instrument, open market operations OMO, must be specified for each round of play; it may be given any value between ± 10 percent of last period's total bank reserves RT_{-1}; if no value is specified, OMO is zero and the reserves are unchanged.

INTRODUCING EXOGENOUS SHOCKS AND EVENTS

The referee determines which exogenous changes (those that can be specified are described in the next chapter) should be introduced, provides information to the players, and inputs the shock parameters to the computer. For example, if the referee makes a change in the marginal propensity to consume nondurable goods and services, he must also make a qualitative description explaining the change and indicate which variables in the model are likely to be directly affected. In this way, the uncertainty of the new situation can be assessed by the players in terms of specific variables.

As experience is gained, the players and the referee should become more accustomed to the economic environment in which they are operating. Replaying a time period, the players can try new strategies under familiar conditions and then evaluate the changes in performance.

Chapter 8 discusses uncertainty and the nature of the shock auxiliary models referred to so frequently in this chapter; this treatment of uncertainty is a unique feature of an adaptive modeling procedure.

**The Exogenous-Event Library
and Auxiliary Models**

8.1

The Library

Procedures for specifying external shocks to provide realism and to vary conditions against which players of the game must react are described in this chapter. The shocks simulate the underlying uncertainty that is so prominent in economic reality; this treatment of uncertainty is an integral part of the adaptive modeling procedure. The chapter discusses the shock library and the international shock auxiliary models.

8.1.1

Introduction

All econometric textbooks discuss the presence of uncertainty (usually denoted by the random variable u) in econometric models. John Johnston's three explanations are typical:[1]

1.

Errors of observation or measurement of the data,

2.

Exclusion of relevant factors from the formulation of the model,

3.

Basically unpredictable random events that affect endogenous variables.

Econometricians typically assume that the mean of u is zero and that its variance is finite; frequently they further assume u is a random selection from a known (usually normal) probability distribution.

Using these assumptions, it is possible to make statistical inferences and to make conditional point and interval predictions for the endogenous variables, given the values of the exogenous variables. The point predictions are unaffected by uncertainty that affects only the variances of the parameter estimates and the standard error of estimate for the endogenous variables. In other words, uncertainty affects the confidence in, but not the value of, the point prediction, and it determines the interval size of the interval prediction.

However, actual decision making is concerned with unconditional predictions wherein the uncertainties (especially those caused by Johnson's third explanation, basic and unpredictable random events) affect the estimated values. These uncertainties are frequently related to major shocks that the economy may or may not experience. Whether the shocks

[1] John Johnston, *Econometric Methods* (New York: McGraw-Hill Book Co., 1963), pp. 5–9.

are international (wars and monetary devaluations) or domestic (strikes in major industries), these events usually affect variables that are endogenous to most econometric models. Depending on the model form, shocks may be considered as causing infrequent selections from the distribution of u or as modifying exogenous variables. In either case, decision makers facing actual problems cannot ignore the possibility of major random shocks.

This chapter selects a group of shocks for inclusion in the prototype procedure, categorizes them, and indicates how they may be related to the primary model by the development of auxiliary models. This does not purport to be a complete analysis; only selected types of major shocks are considered, and only general economic models are formulated. Statistical estimation of the parameters for these special cases is difficult because of their infrequent occurrence.

8.1.2
Selection Criteria
To choose specific shocks to be included in the exogenous-event library, three criteria were specified:

1.
The frequency with which types of shocks occurred in recent years.
2.
The directly measurable economic impact of the shock in terms of exogenous variables of the primary model.
3.
The perceptible impact on endogenous variables of the primary model.

The meaning of the first criterion is obvious; the second means that the impact of the shock changes the values of exogenous variables in the econometric model chosen as the primary model. For example, increased demand for gold in foreign exchange markets may provide a major shock to the international monetary system and to the level of the U.S. gold stock; however, since neither the international system nor the amount of gold stock is represented in the Wharton-EFU model, the shock cannot be measured directly. A similar example is a sudden loss in investor confidence that results in a sharp drop in domestic stock market prices. Because the stock market is not represented in the primary model, this type of shock cannot be introduced directly.

The third criterion depends primarily on the degree of aggregation in the model. For example, a natural disaster such as a hurricane is considered a shock if its impact on economic activity is measured at the state level, but it is not a shock to national economic activity. That is, if the impact is below a threshold level, it is not sufficient to alter national economic decisions, and it is considered imperceptible for purposes discussed here.

The first step in developing the exogenous-event library is to select the specific shocks. The numerous shocks or stresses on the U.S. economy in the period since World War II were reviewed and classified by applying the three selection criteria. The sixteen shocks that were defined as acceptable were distributed among three categories: international military (4), international nonmilitary (6), and domestic labor disruptions (6). Table 8.1 lists the sixteen specific examples of shocks.

8.1.3

Shock Reports

During the interval between the receipt of one period's results and the players' specification of their decisions for the next time period, the referee announces the possibility that a shock may occur. As he gains experience his reporting may vary to some extent; however, regardless of the variations, certain information is required for his descriptions of the shocks to be consistent with the real-world occurrences.

Descriptive information may be required for one or more time periods prior to the shock, during the shock, and for several time periods after its cessation. Since the players do not know the effects of the shock on the endogenous and exogenous variables of the primary model (that is, they do not know the structure of the shock auxiliary model), realistic descriptions can assist them in deriving contingent strategies. Table 8.2 presents information required for the announcement of each shock selected for the tentative library; these elements of information must be included to maintain some degree of standardization and consistency over time and with various players.

The first type of information the referee must provide is a brief narrative description to identify the shock to the players. One example of a shock is the announcement of the devaluation of the pound sterling; another is a strike by the United Automobile Workers against the U.S. automobile industry to demand higher wages and fringe benefits.

The second type of information that the referee must provide is the possible value of each shock parameter (that is, the variables listed in Table 8.3) to indicate the probable shock level.

The third type of information the referee must provide concerns the

Table 8.1   Shocks Considered for the Exogenous-Event Library

Descriptive Examples of Shocks

Shock Category	International Shocks	
Military	No direct U.S. intervention but perceptible change in military expenditure or world trade flow	1. Small: Arab-Israeli War (1967, 1956) 2. Large: Formation of NATO (1949)
	Direct U.S. intervention	3. Small: Initial stage of Vietnamese War (1963–1966) 4. Large: Vietnamese War (1966–1971); Korean Conflict (1950–1953)
Nonmilitary	Tariffs and nontariff barriers to trade	5. Unilateral change: abolition of internal tariffs by common market (1968) 6. Bilateral change: Kennedy round of tariff negotiations (1967) 7. Nontariff barrier: French imposition of import-export taxes (1957) 8. Nontariff supply restriction: blockage of Suez Canal (1956–1957); Iranian nationalization of oil industry (1951–1954)
	Monetary revaluation	9. Reserve currency country: Britain (1967, 1949) 10. Nonreserve currency country: France (1957); Russia (1950)
	Domestic Labor Shocks*	
Strike	Steel	11. Long: (1959, 1952, 1949) 12. Short: (1956)
	Automobile	13. Long: (1970, 1967, 1952) 14. Short: (1963, 1961)
	Dockworkers	15. Long: (1965, 1962–1963, 1948) 16. Short: (1961, 1954)

* Years in which the shocks occurred are given for each example; "Long" means more than 30 days and "Short" means less than 30 days.

Table 8.2 Information Required by the Referee to Report Shocks to Players

Shock Category	Timing		
	Prior to Shock	Coincident with Shock	Subsequent to Shock
International Military:	Narrative description of changes in international situation	Geographic area of conflict	
No direct U.S. intervention	Plans for changes in the military posture	Change: in active military strength, in procurement obligation, in all other defense expenditures, and in the economic activity level of the conflict area	All elements listed under Coincident column; nature of adjustment to the new conditions
		Planned future changes in military strength, defense obligations, and/or defense expenditure	
Direct U.S. intervention	Narrative description of impending crises Plans for changes in the military posture	All elements listed above plus change in military strength in conflict area	All elements listed under Coincident column; progress of the conflict
International Nonmilitary:	Narrative description of international situation leading to the change	Geographic area involved	Description of domestic and foreign adjustment process
Tariff barriers to trade		Prices of commodities involved; original and changed tariff levels; time plan for proposed tariff change	
Nontariff barriers to trade		Geographic area involved	
		Commodity involved; type of barrier and volume of trade flow before imposing the barrier	
Supply restriction		Geographic area involved	
		Commodity involved; amount of restriction in supply; trade volume prior to restriction	

Table 8.2 (continued) Information Required by the Referee to Report Shocks to Players

Shock Category	Timing Prior to Shock	Coincident with Shock	Subsequent to Shock
Monetary revaluation		Country	
		Original dollar exchange rate; amount of revaluation	
Domestic: Steel strike	Date of contract expiration Progress of negotiations	Length of strike Percentage of industry capacity affected	Inventory situation
Automobile strike	Date of contract expiration Bargaining pattern Progress of negotiations	Length of strike Producers affected Time patterns of strike	Inventory situation
Dockworkers' strike	Date of contract expiration Progress of negotiations	Length of strike Ports affected	Backlog of goods to be shipped

Table 8.3 Information Required from the Referee for Shock Auxiliary Models

Information for the Models Shock Category	Shock Parameter	Type*	Unit and Range of Values
International Military:	Area of conflict	D	Western and Eastern Europe; Middle East; Continental Asia and Southern Asia; Western Pacific; Latin America; Africa
With or without U.S. intervention	Change in expenditure and in military strength	C C	$5–50 billion 25–200 thousand men
	Time period to continue the increase	D	1–36 months
International Nonmilitary:†	Area of conflict	D	U.S.; Britain; Continental members of European Free Trade Assoc.; European Economic Community; Japan; Latin America Free Trade Assoc.; underdeveloped countries

Table 8.3 (continued) Information Required from the Referee for Shock Auxiliary Models

Information for the Models Shock Category	Shock Parameter	Type*	Unit and Range of Values
Tariff barriers to trade	Goods involved	D	Crude and manufactured food products; nonfood crude materials and semi-manufactured goods; goods and services except food products, raw materials, and semimanufactured goods
Nontariff barriers to trade	Area of conflict	D	Same as for tariff barriers
	Goods involved	D	Oil, wheat, cotton, tobacco
	Type of barrier	D	Quota, import taxes, export taxes
	Change in trade flow or quota	C	10–100 percent
	Taxes imposed	C	10–100 percent
Supply restriction	Area of conflict	D	Same as for tariff barriers
	Goods involved	D	Same as for nontariff barriers
	Change in supply restriction	C	10–100 percent
Monetary revaluation	Country	D	Britain; France; West Germany; Canada; Japan
	Amount of revaluation	C	0–50 percent
Domestic			
Steel strike	Length of strike	D	1–18 months
	Percentage of industry affected	C	20–100 percent
Automobile strike	Length of strike	D	1–12 months
	Producers affected	D	Chrysler; Ford; General Motors—singly or in combination
Dockworkers' strike	Length of strike	D	1–18 months
	Ports affected	D	Atlantic; Pacific; Gulf—singly or in combination

* D = discrete; C = continuous
† Also see Supply Restriction category under International Nonmilitary category

probability distribution associated with future shocks and their parameters. For example, a steel strike of 2 to 5 months duration is likely, or the probability of defense expenditures increasing by $10 billion is 30 percent, of increasing by $20 billion is 20 percent, or of remaining unchanged is 50 percent.

In addition to communicating information to the players, the referee must transmit it to the computer program. After inputing the alphanumeric code to identify the category and type of shock, in most cases, he must assign parameters to further define the shock. In this example of a steel strike, he must call for Domestic Labor—Steel, indicate whether the strike is likely to last more than 30 days, and determine how long it is likely to last and what percentage of steel capacity is likely to be affected. If he uses a random-number generator to determine if the strike occurs, he must specify the determining probability distribution; Table 8.3 lists the shock parameters, their units of measurement, and range of permissible values. (The range may have to be changed when the auxiliary shock models are statistically estimated).

8.2
Auxiliary Models for International Shocks
To obtain an adaptive modeling procedure that can be used by decision makers, it is necessary to employ auxiliary models that predict the effects of specific shocks on the primary model variables.
8.2.1
Introduction
This section describes economic models formulated for the international shocks considered for the prototype procedure. These exogenous-event auxiliary models contain relationships only for variables that are hypothesized to be directly affected by the shock; secondary and indirect relationships are disregarded. The dependent variables of the military shock model are government purchases for national defense and world trade variables that are exogenous to the primary Wharton-EFU model; world trade variables are also dependent variables of the nonmilitary shock models.
8.2.2
Relating Military Shocks to Defense Expenditures
By definition, an international military shock, with or without direct U.S. intervention, directly affects the level of government purchases for national

defense. Defense expenditures may be disaggregated as follows:[2]

$$G_d = MP + OM + \sum_j PRO^j + RDTE + CH + CD + RMA + MA$$

$$(8.1)$$

where G_d = government purchases for national defense, MP = military pay, OM = operation and maintenance expenditures, PRO^j = procurement expenditures in category j, $RDTE$ = research, development, test, and engineering expenditures, CH = construction and family housing expenditures, CD = civil defense expenditures, RMA = revolving and management accounts, and MA = military assistance.

Total military pay can be further disaggregated into pay for active, reserve, and retired personnel; the active and reserve components are affected directly if the referee announces that reserve military forces have been activated to meet a threat. It is hypothesized that military pay for active personnel is a function of the level and rate of change of active military manpower, and it rises over time; thus,

$$MPA_t = F(S_t, \Delta S_t, t) \tag{8.2}$$

and

$$MPR_t = F(SR_t, t) \tag{8.3}$$

where MPA = military pay for active duty personnel, S = active military strength, MPR = military pay for reserve duty personnel, SR = active reserve military strength, and t = time.

The proposed model for operation and maintenance expenditures is

$$OM_t = F(S_t, SAC_t, t) \tag{8.4}$$

where SAC is the military strength in the area of conflict.[3] Thus, the operation and maintenance expenditures tend to be positively correlated with the strength of the active military force, the strength in the area of conflict, and time.

[2] The proposed model for this shock is based on work by Harvey Galper and Edward Gramlich, "A Technique for Forecasting Defense Expenditures," *Review of Economics and Statistics*, May 1968, pp. 143–155.
[3] With no direct U.S. intervention, the value of this variable is zero (or low if there are U.S. troops in the area prior to the conflict).

The economic models for each category of procurement expenditures take the form[4]

$$PRO_t^j = F^j(OBA_{t-x})$$ (8.5)

where OBA_{t-x} are funds obligated for procurement category j in past time periods. Procurement expenditures are related to past obligations by a distributed lag. The time pattern of the lag structure is a function of a timing coefficient, a capacity utilization factor, and military strength. Initially, all procurement expenditures can be aggregated so a single lag structure may be used.

The research, development, test, and engineering expenditures and the construction and family housing expenditures are also related to past obligations by a lag structure similar to that for procurement expenditures. However, it is proposed that rather than attempting to predict values for $RDTE$ and CH and for civil defense, revolving and management accounts, and military assistance expenditures separately, the referee announce the combined change in the amount of expenditures so that

$$\Delta Z \equiv \Delta(RDTE + CH + CD + RMA + MA).$$ (8.6)

8.2.3
Relating Military and Nonmilitary Shocks to
World Trade Expenditures
Both nonmilitary and military shocks can affect world trade; the former directly and the latter indirectly by disrupting production and transportation that affect world trade patterns.

The Wharton-EFU model disaggregates imports into three types: (1) crude and manufactured food products, (2) nonfood crude materials and semimanufactured goods, and (3) goods and services other than food products, raw materials, and semimanufactured goods. Each of the import equations contains a price index of the appropriate type as an explanatory variable. Because the trade variables are indices, a series of weights must be defined; thus, let W be the weight that the commodity has in a price or quantity index and let its superscript indicate which index and its subscript which country; that is, W_j^k would be the weight of country j imports in commodity category k. These definitions give a basis for relating a price or quantity change for a specific country's commodity to changes in a price or quantity index.

[4] The categories of procurement are vehicles, weapons, and ammunition; aircraft; missiles; ships; electronics and communications; and other.

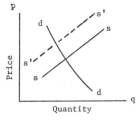

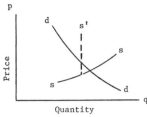

a. A shift in the supply curve   b. A capacity limit to the supply curve

Figure 8.1.   Changes in supply curves resulting from an international shock.

Defining the appropriate exogenous or explanatory variables is the first step in specifying economic models; it is then possible to use current work in international world trade to obtain estimates of the parameters. Figure 8.1 represents typical supply-demand curves for a commodity. In a simple economic model, a trade disruption is assumed to shift the supply curve as shown in Figure 8.1a since a smaller quantity is available at any price.[5] Alternatively, a trade disruption may change the shape of the supply curve and make it inelastic beyond a limit established by remaining capacity, as shown in Figure 8.1b. Thus, the resulting change of a commodity's price is a function of the shape of supply-demand curves. Let α and μ be the price flexibility and elasticity of the supply curve; that is, α is the percentage change in price resulting from a one-percent change in quantity demanded, and μ, the inverse of α, is the percentage change in quantity offered for a one-percent change in the price offered. Then, let β and η be the corresponding flexibility and elasticity of the demand curve.

Let S be a measure of the relevant substitutability between exports and their domestic use; let X^* be an index of U.S. exports and X be an index of U.S. imports; let P^* be the export price index and P be the import price index; and let Q be the production of the commodity. The superscript $k = 1, 2, 3$ denotes one of three commodity classes, and the superscript c denotes a specific commodity within a commodity class. The subscript $j = 1, 2, \ldots, n$ denotes one of n distinguishable geographic areas, the subscript a denotes the United States, and the subscript w denotes the rest of the world. Variables without superscripts refer to the sum over all

[5] Models, such as that developed by Bella Balassa and M. D. Kreinin in "Trade Liberalization Under the 'Kennedy Round': The Static Effects," *The Review of Economics and Statistics*, vol. 69 (May 1967), pp. 125–137 might be used to relate tariff changes to primary model variables.

Table 8.4   Economic Models for Shocks That Effect International Trade†

Shock	Dependent Variable	Index Weight	Independent Variable
Foreign	ΔX_j^k	W_c^k	$Q_j^c, \Delta Q_j^c, S_j^c$
Production	ΔX_w	$W_{j,k}^w$	ΔX_j^k
Change	ΔP^k	W_j^k	$\alpha_j^k, \beta_a^k, \Delta X_j^k$
	ΔP_w	W_k^w	ΔP^k
Tariff	ΔP^k	W_c^k	$P_a^c, \Delta T_a^c, \mu_j^c, \eta_a^c$
Barrier:	μ_j^c	—	$X_j^c/Q_j^c, S_j^k$
Domestic	ΔX_w	$W_{j,c}^w$	$\eta_a^c, \Delta P^c$
	ΔP_w	W_c^w	ΔP^c
Tariff	ΔP^*	$W_{j,c}^*$	$P_j^c, \Delta T_j^c, \mu_a^c$
Barrier:	μ_a^c	—	$X_a^c/Q_a^c, S_a^c$
Foreign	ΔX_w	$W_{j,c}^w$	$\mu_a^c, \Delta P^*$
	ΔP_w	W_c^w	ΔP_c^*
Nontariff	ΔP^k	W_c^k	X_a^c, β_a^k, R_a^c
Barrier:			
U.S. import	ΔX_w	$W_{j,c}^w$	R_a^c, X_a^c
quota			
Nontariff			
Barrier:	ΔX_w	$W_{j,c}^w$	R_j^c, X_j^c
Foreign	ΔP^*	$W_{j,c}^*$	$X_a^c/X_j, X_j^c, R_j^c, \alpha_a^c$
import quota			
Monetary			
Revaluation	$\Delta P^k; k = 1, 2, 3$	W_j^k	$\alpha_a^c, ER_j, \Delta ER_j, S_j^k, S_a^k$
	ΔX_w	W_j^w	$\Delta P^k, \eta_a^k$

† Notation: variables are W = index weight, α = price flexibility of supply, μ = price elasticity of supply, β = price flexibility of demand, η = price elasticity of demand, ER = exchange rate, R = quota, T = tariff, S = substitutability between export and domestic use, X^* = export quantity, X = import quantity, P = price, and Q = production quantity. Super or subscripts are j = geographic area, k = commodity class, c = commodity, a = U.S. index, w = world index, and $*$ = export.

geographic regions. (The subscripts and superscripts are different for the index weight variable explained earlier.) Thus, U.S. exports X_w^* equal

$$\sum_{j=1}^{n} X_j^*$$

and U.S. imports equal

$$\sum_{k=1}^{3} \sum_{j=1}^{n} X_j^k.$$

The various international shocks would then shift or change the shape of supply or demand curves by changing production quantities Q, tariffs T, establishing quotas R, or changing the exchange rate ER. The variables discussed in the above paragraphs are used in the economic models for the six international nonmilitary shock categories and for the world trade effects of the four military shocks that, in addition to increasing defense expenditures and military manpower, may change foreign production. The ten models are summarized in Table 8.4.

Table 8.5 indicates which exogenous variables and auxiliary model(s) are affected by each shock discussed in this section. This table represents the communication between the referee and the computer model; if the model requires absolute amounts and the referee inputs percentage amounts (for example, tariffs), the computer program requires the base figure so necessary conversions can be made.

Formulation of the economic model is an intermediate step toward making the model operationally useful in the game. One possible approach is to use models already developed by others (for example, the Balassa-Kreinin model cited in Footnote 5). Another approach is to estimate statistical models for the specific shocks of interest.

8.3
Auxiliary Models for Domestic Strikes

Domestic labor disputes also disrupt the normal flow of economic events; a steel strike is a good example. In the months immediately prior to negotiations, inventories will be increased as a hedge against a possible strike, and imports may increase as users seek to maintain foreign supply sources. Even if a strike does not occur, inventories will be depleted after the settlement is reached. In the event of a strike, inventory depletion may continue until stocks are drawn below normal levels; in this case, rebuilding of inventories will occur after the settlement. Auxiliary models can be

Table 8.5   Exogenous Variables for the International Shock Auxiliary Models

Shock Category	Range of Variations in the Exogenous Variables Change in Military Strength or Expenditure (thousands of men or \$billions)					Change in Foreign Production (%)
	ΔS	ΔSR	ΔSAC	ΔOBA	ΔZ	$\Delta Q_j^e/Q_j^e$
International Military						
No direct U.S. intervention:						
Small amount	10	0	0	5	5	100
Large amount	100	100	0	20	10	100
Direct U.S. intervention:						
Small amount	50	50	50	10	5	100
Large amount	200	200	100	50	10	100

	Tariff Change (%)		Quota Change (%)		Change in Foreign Production (%)
	Foreign $\Delta T_j^e/T_j^e$	U.S. $\Delta T_a^e/T_a^e$	Foreign $\Delta R_j^e/X_j^e$	U.S. $R_a^e/X_j^{*,e}$	$\Delta Q_j^e/Q_j^e$
International Nonmilitary					
Unilateral tariff change	100	100	—	—	—
Bilateral tariff change	100	100	—	—	—
Nontariff change	—	—	100	100	—
Supply restriction	—	—	—	—	50

	Monetary Devaluation (%)
International Nonmilitary	
Monetary devaluation:	ΔER_j
Reserve country	50
Nonreserve country	50

developed to relate inventory, imports, and (for example, in the case of an auto strike) consumption variables to strike variables. The strike variables would include a "build-up" variable to represent the time prior to negotiations, a strike variable to represent the duration of the strike, and a rebuilding variable for the period after the strike is terminated. Predicting the occurrence or duration of a strike or military conflict is, of course, beyond the scope of economic analysis; some investigators have, however, attempted to analyse these events.[6]

[6] See W. Horvath, "A Statistical Model for the Duration of Wars and Strikes," *Behavioral Science*, vol. 13, no. 1, (January 1968), pp. 18–28; also L. F. Richardson, *Statistics of Deadly Quarrels* (Pittsburgh, Pa.: Boxwood Press, 1960).

9

An Appraisal of the Procedure and Its Potential Applicability

9.1
Models, Games, and Their Relationships

This final chapter is an attempt to appraise the usefulness of the procedures developed and illustrated in the previous eight chapters.

9.1.1
Macroeconomics and Policy Making

In 1964, Edwin Kuh presented a paper with the intriguing title "Econometric Models: Is a New Age Dawning?" Kuh predicted a future in which "governmental economic expertise will rely more on econometric capability for analyzing alternative policy implications instead of current primary dependence on the expert back-of-the envelope calculation."[1]

One goal of the adaptive modeling procedure is to create the environment in which this future can be realized. If econometrics is to be used in formulating policy, then the environment must be such that policy makers can understand the underlying structure of the various available models, can examine the results that will be brought about by alternative theoretical structures and/or alternative exogenous events, and can investigate the implications of the relevant policy choices.

Figure 9.1 illustrates the general relationships between macroeconomic theory, models, and policy making. In the period from Keynes to, say, 1960, the primary connection was line C.[2] Policy makers, or their chief advisers, generally used the theory to create implicit, nonformal, models. Thus, they would turn to "pump priming" or fiscal stimulus to increase economic activity. A more rigorous evaluation of alternatives (that is, how much of what kind of stimulus was required to achieve a specific unemployment rate) had to wait until the development of quantitative models.

During the 1950s, the development of computers, advances in data collection and statistical techniques, and the advent of economists well grounded in mathematics and statistics, created an environment from which came statistically estimated models of the economy. This, then, was a new repository for theory and a mechanism by which specific decisions could be quantitatively evaluated. Thus, a new linkage between theory and policy, lines A and B in Figure 9.1, was created. But there are a number of

---

[1] Edwin Kuh, "Econometric Models: Is a New Age Dawning," (Papers and Proceedings of the 77th Annual Meeting of the American Economic Association), *American Economic Review*, vol. 55, no. 2 (May 1965), p. 365.
[2] For an interesting history of this relationship, one that dates its beginnings prior to Keynes, see Herbert Stein, *The Fiscal Revolution in America* (Chicago: University of Chicago Press, 1969) 526 pages.

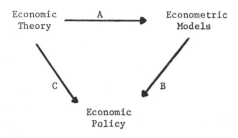

Figure 9.1.   Possible relationships between theory, models, and policy.

reasons why the linkage is not as effective as it might be. Adaptive model-ing procedures provide a means for circumventing these difficulties.

The first set of problems relate to the difficulties inherent in developing adequate econometric models. (See line A in Figure 9.1.)

Theoretical limitations are perhaps the most important obstacles; the lack of comprehensiveness and precision in many theoretical constructs has forced econometricians to develop their own theory. Economic theory frequently lacks adequate descriptive content about behavior and insti-tutions and provides only general guidance. Econometricians began to develop models based "more and more closely on attributes which theory originally had perceived dimly or not at all."[3]

Data limitations are a second formidable obstacle. Lawrence Klein has stated his belief that better theory and better data will contribute "much more to the improvement of empirical econometric results than [will] more elaborate methods of statistical inference."[4]

Another problem, one inherent to all the social sciences, is that the historical data frequently do not provide information about the effect of many variables. Generally, any variable that has remained constant in the recent past will not appear in an econometric model; that is, estimation of the model structure will yield a parameter that is not different from zero. Thus, if the variable is expected to change in the near future, the econo-metric model may not be useful; only theory can suggest the algebraic sign and magnitude of the parameter.

[3] Edwin Kuh, *Econometric Models*, p. 362–363.
[4] Lawrence R. Klein, "Single Equation vs. Equation System Methods of Estimation in Econometrics," *Econometrica*, vol. 28 (October 1960), p. 867.

Theory, however, supported by special studies[5] may provide the necessary relationships for an auxiliary model to be used in the adaptive modeling procedure. While this may not be an appropriate econometric procedure, it is a scientific procedure as long as the predictions are testable.

For, as Fox and Thorbecke point out, statistical techniques applied to aggregate time-series data, do not exhaust our knowledge of the economic system; "in much econometric literature the estimation of models of an economy has been treated as a problem primarily of probability theory and statistics . . . but the concept of the structure of an economy is independent of and logically prior to techniques for measuring that structure."[6] The adaptive procedure utilizes available knowledge about the economic structure.

Another set of problems that limit the application of economic theory to policy making is the lack of incentives for economists to engage in policy-oriented research. Model development, as a result, frequently followed academic interests rather than policy needs. As a result, important relationships between policy instruments and goals were ignored. Thus, monetary instruments were slighted until the recent FRB-MIT model was developed with support from a policy-making organization. The lack of incentives is related to the policy maker's general unfamiliarity with the larger models and the difficulty inherent in manipulating them. If policy makers create a demand for the product, economists will turn, in far greater numbers, to research that is relevant to policy makers. For, as Jacob Marshak points out in the foreword to Carl Christ's text: "The standards of the economist's profession require that his empirical results be useful for practical policy."[7]

The adaptive modeling procedure can be designed to help bridge the gap between the economist and the policy maker. It will help the economist understand the environment in which policy is made while making the economist's product relevant and useful to policy makers. Casting the adaptive modeling procedure in the form of a game, as was demonstrated

---

[5] Guy H. Orcutt and A. G. Orcutt, "Experiments for Income Maintenance Policies," *American Economic Review* (September 1968) pp. 754–772, is an example of the intended type of study.

[6] K. A. Fox and E. Thorbecke, "Specification of Structures and Data Requirements in Economic Policy Models," *Quantitative Planning of Economic Policy* (Washington, D.C.: Brookings Institution, April 1965), p. 45.

[7] Carl Christ, *Econometric Models and Methods* (New York, N.Y.: John Wiley & Sons, 1966), p. viii.

in Chapters 6 and 7, should create a situation in which such a bridge can be built.

The procedure focuses attention on the relevant variables and changes. The environment is one that resembles many real decision-making exercises in which an individual, acting as a referee (the devil's advocate), asks proponents of various alternatives to defend their proposed courses of action under various, generally adverse, conditions. The similarities between the serious business of economic models and games may be more important than their differences. This is especially true for the adaptive modeling procedures.

9.1.2
Terminology of Games and Models

Differences between the terminologies used to describe games and models are likely to become less meaningful as conversational-mode computing replaces batch processing. The correspondence among terms frequently used to describe games and models indicates their conceptual similarity.

GAMING TERMINOLOGY

A game has rules that describe what moves are allowed, who can make them, when they can be made, what information is available to the players, and so forth. Such rules describe the set of all possible moves and the conditions under which they can be made (for example, the king in chess can move one space in any direction); for a single game, a collection (subset) of moves is selected from the set of all possible moves. In a game like chess, the subset of moves made is small compared to the set of all possible moves the player may make; similarly, an adaptive modeling procedure attempts to reduce the number of alternative situations a decision maker must consider.

The players (or sides) in a game are referred to as persons. For example, chess is a two-person game, poker may be an n-person game, and roulette may be a two-person game (the man against the wheel). In the many-person games against nature, such as those described in the pilot and prototype adaptive procedures (Chapters 6, 7, and 8), the decision maker plays against nature as represented by a referee and a random-number generator.

Payoffs are a part of most games. In a zero-sum, two-person game, one person gains what the other loses: as might be expected, this class of games is the most suitable to be analyzed by game theory. The payoff in a game like chess may be a simple bet. On the other hand, the payoff function may be more complex: It may determine the payoff amount as a function of the number of required moves or as a function of performance (for example, the scoring function in the pilot and prototype procedures).

Games may also be characterized by the information available to the players. In chess, both players are fully and exactly aware of all previous moves, but future moves are known by both with a great deal of uncertainty; however, each player can generally specify what his response would be to any particular move that his opponent might make. In other words, while he cannot specify his future moves explicitly, he can write them as a function of his opponent's action (and his own previous responses).

By definition, a move is a decision, and a strategy is a set of decision rules. The player uses a strategy function to map the position on the board at point t into his response at point $t + 1$; the decision maker may use a decision rule (for example, the linear programming algorithm) to map a given state of the world into his response.

The player is unable to foretell his opponent's reaction; the decision maker, in addition to being unable to predict values that will be assumed by uncontrollable variables, is frequently uncertain of the data reflecting past and current performance.[8] The proposed adaptive procedures reflect this uncertainty and thus may resemble kriegspiel (a chess-like game in which information about the opponent's previous moves is incomplete) more than chess.

One subset of rules specifies the conditions under which a game is terminated (a checkmate or a stalemate in chess); in the pilot and prototype procedures, this rule corresponds to the planning horizon.

MODEL TERMINOLOGY

The descriptive terms of the game—rules, moves, persons, payoffs, information, strategy, and termination—may also be used to describe the elements of the model (see Table 9.1). In the model, the relationships (or constraints) are analogous to the rules of the game; for example, an aggregate production function, with a given labor force and capital stock, limits the economy's output. Models (and the real world) are often analogous to two-person games; government is on one side and the economic uncertainties (that is, nature) is on the other. Each player selects his move from all those possible; nature selects a path from all possible paths.

---

[8] The problem of measuring past and current performance is dealt with in Oskar Morgenstern, *On the Accuracy of Economic Observations* (Princeton, N.J.: Princeton University Press 1963).

Table 9.1   Comparison of Game and Model Terminology

Games		Models	
Defining Term	Examples from Chess	Defining Term	Example from Decision Models
Rules	Description of moves allowed the king, queen, . . . , pawn	*Constraints*	The model's equations and parameters; limits for alternative choices
Moves	Set of moves selected from allowed moves	*Decisions or plans*	Set of instrument values selected from all possible alternatives
Person	Player	*Decision maker*	Referee, policy player, decision maker
Payoff	Simple bet (win or lose) or number of moves required to win	*Objective function*	Scoring function to measure performance
Information	Moves known by the two players:*	*Degree of certainty*	Predicted values of uncontrollable variables

	Past	Future
Player 1		$\otimes$
Opponent 2		$\times$

Games		Models	
Strategy	Move at point t:† $\text{Move}_t = F_s \, (\text{board})_{t-1}$	*Decision rule*	Relationships between controllable and uncontrollable variables
Termination	Checkmate or stalemate	*Planning horizon*	Finite or infinite

* Notation: $\sqrt{}$ indicates knowledge with certainty; X, unknown; $\otimes$, known as a strategy function of an unknown.
† Here F_s is the strategy function.

One important distinction between the adaptive modeling game described in this book and most traditional games (such as chess) is the asymmetry of each player's moves. For example, in a chess game the same rules apply to all players, but in the prototype procedure one set of instruments may be controlled by the government, another by industry, a third by consumers, and so forth.

Many-person, nonzero-sum games are described in this book. One group of players represents government decision makers; certain instruments are available to them, and they are guided by a particular objective function that measures their payoff. The other player, or referee, represents nature who, with a random-number generator, chooses the values of certain uncontrollable variables.

The adaptive modeling components described for the growth and stabilization problems determine the state of the economy and the value of the resulting payoff functions. The moves are made each period, therefore the primary models must be of the dynamic difference-equation type. A round is the action that takes place in a single time period; it consists of the series of moves by all players and the results estimated by the model (for example, a round is analogous to both halves of an inning in a baseball game). A game is the sequence of rounds for a specific number of periods (for example, nine time periods, or rounds, are analogous to the nine innings required to complete a baseball game).

In the adaptive modeling procedure, the players, who assume roles of economic policy or decision makers, and the game referee, who introduces exogenous changes, provide a degree of realism that is generally lacking, as are the conditions of uncertainty when an econometric model is run through periods of time in a stable environment. Repeated runs of an econometric model (allowing for changes in both input data and parameters) can produce alternative forecasts but not the decision analyses.

To support real decision making, adequate primary models must generate realistic, accurate results. Chapters 4 and 5 use familiar input-output models; the interindustry coefficients are periodically estimated by the Office of Business Economics.

The prototype procedure of Chapter 7 employs a well-known, well-tested primary model; an additional role, that of the monetary policy maker, is added by using a submodel of the monetary sector. Thus, players, who take over the functions of some of the actors in the real decision-making process, are able to act in an environment of realistic relationships. The decision-making roles could easily be more disaggregated by including roles representing consumers, investors, and commercial bankers; in such cases, the functions of the model could be replaced by players who operate within an expanded set of rules of play. The use of an input-output model as a disaggregating auxiliary model may also be considered so that the implications of alternative decisions on specific industries can be evaluated. These are but a few additions that could be useful in the prototype procedure described in Chapter 7.

The objective of this research is not to develop recreational or educational devices but rather to aid in policy and decision making. The pilot and prototype procedures do provide an opportunity to use the game concepts experimentally to induce implicit objective functions of the players; however, the primary goal is decision analyses by simulating the decision-making process. Thus, the developed procedures are, hopefully, prototypes to operational procedures that can be installed in the real decision-making process.

9.2
Appraisal of the Adaptive Modeling Procedure

The analogy between decision makers using an adaptive modeling procedure and architects using a house plan was developed in Chapter 2. One goal of this book is to develop a procedure for the economic planner that is as flexible as the architect's tools; however, because the economic planner's problem is more complex, his tools are necessarily more complicated.

The analogy can be extended by noting that both architectural and economic plans must ultimately be implemented if the planning is to be more than an academic exercise. In neither case is the implemented plan likely to be optimal, but hopefully it will be satisfactory. The planning tools, in both cases, must be judged in comparison with available alternatives; thus, the proposed procedures must be compared with current decision-making procedures and, if the comparison shows that the adaptive procedure provides better decisions, it is of value.

The adaptive procedure attempts to make progress toward three goals: determination of the policy maker's objective function, statistical decision analysis, and relating to the political decision-making process. By removing the objective (or scoring) function and observing the response of various players to alternative economic situations, one can proceed toward the first goal. Whether progress is made with any particular procedure depends on the realism of the environment created, on the design of the experiments, and on the specific individuals playing the game.

The procedure contains a decision analysis framework so that progress can be made toward the second goal. In the classical adaptive case of statistical decision analysis, the decision maker learns about unknown probability distributions as he gains experience and receives information concerning past events. In the adaptive modeling procedure, he learns about the multivariate responses of the composite (primary and auxiliary) model to selected exogenous events and instrument values.

Finally, the question remains: Can the suggested adaptive procedure relate to, and become part of, the real-life political decision-making process? No doubt, adaptive models conforming to the specifications outlined in this paper can be constructed; their relevance to real-world problems will, however, depend on how well the composite model and the selected exogenous events capture the underlying economic reality.

The procedure can be evaluated in terms of the following descending scale in which each step includes a wide range of qualitative opinions:

1.

The procedure accomplishes the initial objective—enhancing the usefulness of economic models by applying the logic of decision analysis to the real problems of economic decision making.

2.

The procedure may increase the usefulness of econometric models by efficiently using computer technology (for example, rapid turn-around, time-sharing) and by facilitating the communication between economists and decision makers (for example, members of Congress) who are not familiar with economic models.

3.

The procedure may be useful as a supplement to (or partial replacement of) a traditional course or as a training device for a potential administrator in an educational setting.

Hopefully, Steps 1, 2, and 3 can be achieved. If an evaluation reveals that the first step is not achieved, it may be an indication that the procedure does not effectively synthesize decision analysis with economic models or that decision analysis has little meaning in practical situations. If any of the steps are achieved, the appropriate area of application must be determined; the procedure may be most productive in areas of socio-economic planning (for example, development of urban-system designs) for which current models are yet unsatisfactory and for which accepted premises may be internally inconsistent. The ultimate determination of the procedure's usefulness will be determined from empirical evidence obtained from decision makers who use (or ignore) it.

Bibliography

Abrams, John W.; Wroe Alderson; Stafford Beer; Warren G. Bennis; William M. Evan; Murray A. Geisler; Fred Hanssmann; and Donald E. Ladd.
"Commentary on 'The Researcher and the Manager: A Dialectic of Implementation." *Management Science*, vol. 12, no. 2, October 1965.

Abromovitz, Moses.
Inventories and Business Cycles with Special Reference to Manufacturing Inventories. New York, N.Y.: National Bureau of Economic Research, 1950.

Ackley, Gardner.
Macroeconomic Theory. New York, N.Y.: The Macmillan Company, 1961.

Almon, Jr., Clopper.
The American Economy to 1975. New York, N.Y.: Harper & Row, 1966.
————. "Consistent Forecasting in a Dynamic Multisector Model," *The Review of Economics and Statistics*, vol. 45, May 1963.

Arrow, Kenneth.
Social Choice and Individual Values. Cowles Foundation Monograph No. 12. New York, N.Y.: John Wiley & Sons, 1951.

Balassa, Bella, and M. D. Kreinin.
"Trade Liberalization Under the 'Kennedy Round': The Static Effects," *The Review of Economics and Statistics*, vol. 69, May 1967.

Barna, Tibor, ed.
Structural Interdependence and Economic Development. New York, N.Y.: St. Martin's Press, 1963.

Bellman, Richard.
Adaptive Control Processes, A Guided Tour. Princeton, N.J.: Princeton University Press, 1961.

Bellman, Richard, and R. Kalaba.
Dynamic Programming and Modern Control Theory. New York, N.Y.: Academic Press, 1965.

Bergson, A.
"A Reformulation of Certain Aspects of Welfare Economics," *Quarterly Journal of Economics*, vol. 52, 1938.

Braithwaite, Richard B.
Scientific Explanation. New York, N.Y.: Harper & Row, 1960.

Brown, Richard G., and R. F. Meyer.
"The Fundamental Theorem of Exponential Smoothing," *Operations Research*, vol. 9, 1961.
————. *Statistical Forecasting for Inventory Control.* York, Pa.: Maple Press, 1957.

Carnap, Rudolf.
Logical Foundations of Probability. Chicago, Ill.: University of Chicago Press, 1950.

Carter, A. P.
"The Economics of Technological Change," *Scientific American*, April 1966.

Chakravarty, S.
"Optimal Programme of Capital Accumulation in a Multi-Sector Economy," *Econometrica*, vol. 33, no. 3, July 1965.

Charnes, Abraham; Jacques Dreze; and Merton Miller.
"Decision and Horizon Rules for Stochastic Planning Problems: A Linear Example," *Econometrica*, vol. 34, no. 2, April 1966.

Chenery, Hollis Burley.
"Interindustry Research in Economic Development," *American Economic Review*, May 1960.

Christ, Carl.
Econometric Models and Methods. New York, N.Y.: John Wiley & Sons, 1966.
_____. "A Short-Run Aggregate-Demand Model of the Interdependence and Effects of Monetary and Fiscal Policy with Keynesian and Classical Interest Elasticities," *American Economic Review*, vol. 58, May 1967.

Colm, Gerhard.
"Economic Stabilization Policy," Sidney S. Alexander and others, eds., *Economics and the Policy Maker*. Washington, D.C.: The Brookings Institution, 1959.

Darling, Paul C., and Michael Lovell.
"Factors Influencing Investment in Inventories," James S. Dusenberry and others, eds., *The Brookings Quarterly Econometric Model of the United States*. Chicago, Ill.: Rand McNally & Company, 1965.

De Leeuw, Frank, and Edward Gramlich.
"The Federal Reserve–MIT Econometric Model," *Federal Reserve Bulletin*, vol. 54, January 1968.

Dolbear, Trenary; Richard Attiyeh; and William Brainard.
"A Simulation Policy Game for Teaching Macroeconomics," *American Economic Review*, vol. 58, no. 2, May 1968.

Domar, Evsey David.
"Capital Expansion, Rate of Growth and Employment," *Econometrica*, 1946.

Dorfman, R.; Paul Samuelson; and Robert Solow.
Linear Programming and Economic Analysis. New York, N.Y.: McGraw-Hill Book Co., 1958.

Duesenberry, James S.; Gary Fromm; Lawrence Klein; and Edwin Kuh, eds.
The Brookings Quarterly Econometric Model of the United States. Chicago, Ill.: Rand McNally & Company, 1965.

Edwards, Ward, and Paul Stovic.
Seeking Information to Reduce the Risk of Decisions. Ann Arbor, Mich.: The University of Michigan, August 1962.

Evans, Michael K.
"A Postwar Quarterly Model of the United States Economy, 1947–1960." Unpublished dissertation, Brown University, 1963.

Evans, Michael, and Lawrence R. Klein.
The Wharton Econometric Forecasting Model. Philadelphia, Pa.: University of Pennsylvania, 1967.

Ferber, R.
A Study of Aggregate Consumption Functions. Technical Paper No. 8, National Bureau of Economic Research, Inc. New York, N.Y.: Basso Printing Company, 1953.

Ferguson, Charles E.
"Inflation, Fluctuations and Growth in a Dynamic Input-Output Model," *Southern Economic Journal,* vol. 28, no. 3, January 1962.
———. *A Macroeconomic Theory of Workable Competition.* Durham, N.C.: Duke University Press, 1964.

Fox, K. A., and E. Thorbecke.
"Specification of Structures and Data Requirements in Economic Policy Models," *Quantitative Planning of Economic Policy.* Washington, D.C.: The Brookings Institution, 1965.

Fox, Peter D.
"A Theory of Cost-Effectiveness for Military Systems Analysis," *Operations Research,* vol. 13, no. 2, March–April 1965.

Friedman, Milton.
"The Role of Monetary Policy," *American Economic Review,* March 1968.

Fromm, Gary.
"Econometric Models and Defense Policy," unpublished paper presented at the Symposium on the Role of Economic Models in Policy Formulation, Washington, D.C., October 20–21, 1966.
———. "An Evaluation of Monetary Policy Instruments," unpublished paper presented at the Annual Econometric Society Meeting, San Francisco, California, December 1966.

Fromm, Gary, and Paul Taubman.
Policy Simulations with an Econometric Model. Washington, D.C.: The Brookings Institution, 1968.

Galper, Harvey, and Edward Gramlich.
"A Technique for Forecasting Defense Expenditures," *Review of Economics and Statistics,* May 1968.

Goldberger, Arthur.
Econometric Theory. New York, N.Y.: John Wiley & Sons, 1963.

Gruchy, Allen G.
Modern Economic Thought. New York, N.Y.: Prentice-Hall, Inc., 1947.

Gurley, John, and Edward Stone Shaw.
"The Growth of Debt and Money in the United States 1800–1950: A Suggested Interpretation," *Review of Economics and Statistics,* August 1957.
———. *Liquidity and Financial Institutions in the Postwar Period.* Joint Economic Committee Study Paper No. 14. Washington, D.C.: U.S. Government Printing Office, January 25, 1960.

Hadley, G.
Linear Programming. Reading, Mass.: Addison-Wesley Publishing Co., 1962.
———. *Non-linear and Dynamic Programming.* Reading, Mass.: Addison-Wesley Publishing Co., 1964.

Harrod, Roy Forbes.
"An Essay in Dynamic Theory," *Economic Journal,* March 1939.

Henderson, James M., and Richard E. Quandt.
Microeconomic Theory. New York, N.Y.: McGraw-Hill Book Co., 1958.

Hickman, Bert G., ed.
"Introduction," *Quantitative Planning of Economic Policy.* Washington, D.C.: The Brookings Institution, 1965.

Holt, Charles C.
"Linear Decision Rules for Economic Stabilization and Growth," *Quarterly Journal of Economics,* February 1962.
———. "Quantitative Decision Analysis and National Policy: How Can We Bridge the Gap?" *Quantitative Planning of Economic Policy.* Bert C. Hickman, ed. Washington, D.C.: The Brookings Institution, 1964.

Hotelling, Harold.
"The General Welfare in Relation to Problems of Taxation and Railway and Utility Rates," *Econometrica,* vol. 6, 1938.

Horvath, William.
"A Statistical Model for the Duration of Wars and Strikes," *Behavioral Science,* vol. 13, no. 1, January 1968.

Howard, Ronald A.
"Foundations of Decision Analysis," *System Science and Cybernetics*, vol. 55c-4, no. 3, September 1968.

Johnston, John.
Econometric Methods. New York, N.Y.: McGraw-Hill Book Co., 1963.

Jorgenson, Dale.
"Anticipations and Investment Behavior," James S. Dusenberry and others, eds., *The Brookings Quarterly Econometric Model of the United States*. Chicago, Ill.: Rand McNally & Company, 1965.

Kaplan, Richard J., and Robert Newman.
Studies in Probabilistic Information Processing. Santa Monica, Calif.: Systems Development Corporation, October 1964.

Keynes, John Maynard.
A Treatise on Probability. 2d ed. London: The Macmillan Company, 1929.
_____. *General Theory of Employment, Interest, and Money*. New York, N.Y.: Harcourt, Brace & World, 1936.

King, William H.
"On the Nature and Form of Operations Research," *Operations Research*, vol. 15, no. 6, November–December 1967.

Kirschen, Etienne S.
Economic Policy in Our Time. Amsterdam: North-Holland Publishing Co., 1964.

Klein, Lawrence R.
"The Efficiency of Estimation in Econometric Models," *Essays in Economics and Econometrics*. R. Pfouts, ed. Chapel Hill, N.C.: University of North Carolina Press, 1960.
_____. "Single Equation vs. Equation System Methods of Estimation in Econometrics," *Econometrica*, vol. 28, October 1960.
_____. *An Introduction to Econometrics*. Englewood Cliffs, N.J.: Prentice-Hall, Inc.,1962.
_____. "A Postwar Quarterly Model," *Models of Income Determination*, vol. 58, Studies in Income and Wealth. Princeton, N.J.: Princeton University Press, 1964.

Klein, Lawrence R., and Ronald G. Bodkin.
"Empirical Aspects of the Trade-Offs Among Three Goals: High Level Employment, Price Stability, and Economic Growth," *Inflation, Growth, and Employment, Commission on Money and Credit*. Englewood Cliffs, N.J.: Prentice-Hall, Inc., 1964.

Klein, Lawrence R., and Michael Evans.
"Wharton Economic Newlsetter," *Wharton Quarterly*, Winter 1968.

Klein, Lawrence R., and Arthur Goldberger.
An Econometric Model of the United States 1929–1952. Amsterdam: North-Holland Publishing Co., 1955.

Klein, Lawrence R., and R. J. Roll.
An Econometric Model of the United Kingdom. Oxford, England: Basil Blackwell & Mott, 1961.

Klein, Lawrence R., and Yoichi Shinkai.
"An Econometric Model of Japan 1950–59," *International Economic Record*, January 1963.

Klein, Lawrence R., and Robert Summers.
The Wharton Index of Capacity Utilization. Philadelphia, Pa.: University of Pennsylvania, 1966.

Koopmans, Tjalling C.
"Measurement without Theory," *Readings in Business Cycles*. Homewood, Ill.: Richard Irwin, 1965.

Kuh, Edwin.
"Econometric Models: Is a New Age Dawning?" (Papers and Proceedings of the 77th Annual Meeting of the American Economic Association), *American Economic Review*, vol. 55, no. 2, May 1965.

Leontief, Wassily W.
"Quantitative Input and Output Relations in the Economic System of the U.S.," *Review of Economics and Statistics*, August 1936.
————. *The Structure of the American Economy 1919–1929*. Cambridge, Mass.: Harvard University Press, 1941.
————. *Input-Output Economics*. New York, N.Y.: Oxford University Press, 1966.

Lerner, Abba P.
The Economics of Control. New York, N.Y.: The Macmillan Company, 1946.

Liebenberg, Maurice; A. Hirsch; and J. Popkin.
"A Quarterly Econometric Model of the United States: A Progress Report," *Survey of Current Business*, vol. 46, May 1966.

Lipsey, Richard G.
"The Relation Between Unemployment and the Rate of Change of Money Wage Rates in the United Kingdom, 1862–1957: A Further Analysis," *Economica*, vol. 27, no. 1, February 1960.

Lipsey, Richard G., and Kelvin Lancaster.
"The General Theory of the Second Best," *Review of Economic Studies*, vol. 24, 1956.

Lovell, Michael.
"Manufacturers' Inventories, Sales Expectations, and the Acceleration Principle," *Econometrica*, vol. 29, no. 3, July 1961.

Machol, Robert E.
"On King's Note," *Operations Research*, vol. 15, no. 6, November–December 1967.

Magee, John F.
"Decision Trees," *Harvard Business Review*, July–August 1964.
_____. "How to Use Decision Trees in Capital Investment," *Harvard Business Review*, September–October 1964.

McCarthy, Michael D.
"On the Aggregation of the 1958 Direct Requirements Input/Output Table," unpublished paper. Washington, D.C.: The Brookings Institution, June 1965.

Merriam, C.
"Social Welfare Expenditures, 1964–1965," *Social Security Bulletin*, (reprint) October 1965.

Morgenstern, Oskar.
On the Accuracy of Economic Observations. Princeton, N.J.: Princeton University Press, 1963.

Miyasawa, Koichi.
"Information Structures in Stochastic Programming Problems," *Management Science*, vol. 14, no. 5, January 1968.

Nagar, A. L.
"Stochastic Simulation with the Brookings Econometric Model," unpublished paper presented at the December 1966 Econometric Meeting, San Francisco, California.

National Center for Health Statistics.
Conceptual Problems in Developing an Index of Health. Washington, D.C.: U.S. Government Printing Office, 1965.

National Goals Research Staff.
Toward Balanced Growth, Quantity with Quality. Washington, D.C.: U.S. Government Printing Office, July 1970.

Naylor, Thomas, and others.
Computer Simulation Techniques. New York, N.Y.: John Wiley & Sons, 1966.

Nerlove, Marc.
"A Tabular Survey of Macro-Economic Models," *International Economic Review*, vol. 7, no. 2, May 1966.

Novick, David, ed.
Program Budgeting. Cambridge, Mass.: Harvard University Press, 1965.

Office of Business Economics.
"The Transactions Table of the 1958 Input-Output Study and Revised Direct and Total Requirement Data," *Survey of Current Business*, September 1965.
————. *Survey of Current Business*, vol. 48, no. 12, December 1968.

Orcutt, Guy H.; M. Greenberger; J. Korbel; and Alice Rivlin.
Microanalysis of Socioeconomic Systems. New York, N.Y.: Harper & Row, 1961.

Orcutt, Guy H., and A. G. Orcutt.
"Experiments for Income Maintenance Policies," *American Economic Review*, September 1968.

Packer, Arnold H.
"Applying Cost-Effectiveness Concepts to the Community Health System," *Operations Research*, vol. 16, no. 2, March–April 1968.
————. "Simulation and Adaptive Forecasting as Applied to Inventory Control," *Operations Research*, vol. 15, no. 4, 1967.

Parzens, Emanuel.
Modern Probability Theory and Its Application. New York, N.Y.: John Wiley & Sons, 1964.

Patinkin, Don.
Money, Interest, and Prices. New York, N.Y.: Harper & Row, 1965.

Perry, George L.
"The Determinants of Wage Rate Changes and the Inflation-Unemployment Trade-Off for the United States," *The Review of Economic Studies*, vol. 30, no. 4, October 1964.
————. *Unemployment, Money Wage Rates, and Inflation*. Cambridge, Mass.: The MIT Press, 1966.

Pfouts, Ralph W.
"Artistic Goals, Scientific Method and Economics," *Southern Economic Journal*, April 1967.

Phelps, Edmunds.
"The Golden Rule of Accumulation: a Fable for Growthmen," *American Economic Review*, vol. 51, September 1961.

Phillips, A. W.
"The Relation Between Unemployment and the Rate of Change of Money Wages in the United Kingdom, 1862–1957," *Economica*, vol. 25, no. 4, November 1958.

Popper, Karl.
Conjectures and Refutations: The Growth of Scientific Knowledge. New York, N.Y.: Basic Books, 1962.
————. *Logic of Scientific Discovery.* New York, N.Y.: Harper Torchbooks, Harper & Row, 1965.

Raiffa, Howard.
"Bayesian Decision Theory," R. E. Machol and P. E. Gray, eds., *Recent Developments in Information and Decision Processes.* New York, N.Y.: The Macmillan Company, 1962.

Raiffa, Howard, and Robert Schlaifer.
Applied Statistical Decision Theory. Cambridge, Mass.: Harvard Business School, Division of Research, 1961; Paper. Cambridge, Mass.: The MIT Press, 1968.

Rasche, Robert, and Harold Shapiro.
"The FRB-MIT Econometric Model: Its Special Features," *American Economic Review,* May 1968.

Richardson, L. F.
Statistics of Deadly Quarrels. Pittsburgh, Pa.: Boxwood Press, 1960.

Robinson, Joan.
The Economics of Imperfect Competition. London: Macmillan & Co., 1933.

Samuelson, Paul.
Foundations of Economic Analysis. New York, N.Y.: Atheneum, 1965.

Samuelson, Paul, and Robert M. Solow.
"Analytical Aspects of Anti-Inflation Policy," *American Economic Review,* vol. 50, no. 2, May 1960.

Saunders, B. S.
"Measuring Community Health Levels," *American Journal of Public Health,* vol. 54, no. 7, July 1965.

Savage, Leonard J.
The Foundations of Statistics. New York, N.Y.: John Wiley & Sons, 1954.
————. "Bayesian Statistics," R. E. Machol and P. E. Gray, eds., *Recent Developments in Information and Decision Process.* New York, N.Y.: The Macmillan Company, 1962.

Schlaifer, Robert.
Probability and Statistics for Business Decisions. New York, N.Y.: McGraw-Hill Book Co., 1959.

Schum, David A.; Irwin L. Goldstein; and Jack F. Southland.
The Influences of Experience and Input Information Fidelity upon Posterior Probability Estimation in a Simulated Threat-Diagnosis System. Columbus, Ohio: Ohio State University Press, April 1965.

Shubik, Martin.
Strategy and Market Structure: Competition, Oligopoly and the Theory of Games.
New York, N.Y.: John Wiley & Sons, 1959.

Shultze, Harry.
Statistical Laws of Supply and Demand. Chicago, Ill.: University of Chicago
Press, 1928.
_____. *The Theory and Measurement of Demand.* Chicago, Ill.: University
of Chicago Press, 1938.

Simon, Nancy W.
"Personal Consumption Expenditures in the 1958 Input-Output Study,"
Survey of Current Business, October 1965.

Solow, Robert M.
"A Contribution to the Theory of Economic Growth," *Quarterly Journal
of Economics,* February 1956.
_____. "Technical Progress, Capital Formation, and Economic Growth,"
American Economic Review, Papers and Proceedings, May 1962.
_____. "Substitution and Fixed Proportions in the Theory of Capital,"
Review of Economic Studies, vol. 29, June 1962.

Sono, Masazo.
"The Effect of Price Changes on the Demand and Supply of Separable
Goods," *International Economic Review,* vol. 2, no. 3, September 1961.

Stein, Herbert.
The Fiscal Revolution in America. Chicago, Ill.: University of Chicago
Press, 1969.

Strotz, Robert Henry.
"The Empirical Implications of a Utility Tree," *Econometrica,* vol. 25,
April 1957.

Suits, Daniel B.
"Forecasting and Analysis with an Econometric Model," *American
Economic Review,* March 1962.

Theil, Henri.
Optimum Decision Rules for Government and Industry. Chicago, Ill.: Rand
McNally & Company, 1964.
_____. "Linear Decision Rules for Macrodynamic Policy Problems,"
Quantitative Planning of Economic Policy. Bert Hickman, ed. Washington,
D.C.: The Brookings Institution, 1965.

Tinbergen, Jan.
*Statistical Testing of Business Cycle Theories, Business Cycles in the United
States of America 1919–1932.* Geneva, Switzerland: League of Nations,
1939.
_____. *Central Planning.* New Haven, Conn.: Yale University Press, 1964.

Trustman, Stanley.
Methods of Estimating Production Capacity for the PARM System. Research
Triangle Park, N.C.: Research Triangle Institute, June 1966.

U.S. Bureau of the Budget.
Special Analyses of the Budget of the United States, Fiscal Year 1971. Washington,
D.C.: U.S. Government Printing Office, 1970.

U.S. Congress. Joint Economic Committee.
*1967 Joint Economic Report. Report of the Joint Economic Committee, Congress
of the United States, on January 1968 Economic Report of the President Together
with Statement of Committee Agreement, Minority and Other Views.* Senate
Report No. 73, 90th Congress, 1st Session. Washington, D.C.: U.S.
Government Printing Office, 1967.

U.S. Congress, Joint Economic Committee.
Twentieth Anniversary of the Employment Act at 1946: An Economic Symposium,
89th Congress, 2nd Session, February 23, 1966.

U.S. Congress Joint Economic Committee.
Hearings 90th Congress, First Session, June 27–29, 1967. Washington,
D.C.: U.S. Government Printing Office, 1967.

U.S. Council of Economic Advisers.
Economic Report of the President 1968.
Washington, D.C.: U.S. Government Printing Office, January 1968.
———. *Economic Report of the President 1971.*
Washington, D.C.: U.S. Government Printing Office, February 1971.

U.S. Department of Health, Education and Welfare.
An Index of Health-Mathematical Models. Washington, D.C.: U.S. Government Printing Office, 1965.

U.S. Department of Health, Education, and Welfare.
Reference Facts on Health, Education, and Welfare. Washington, D.C.: U.S.
Government Printing Office, January 1966.

U.S. Department of Labor.
Projections 1970. Washington, D.C.: U.S. Government Printing Office,
December 1966.

U.S. Office of Management and Budget.
Budget of the United States Government, Fiscal 1972. Washington, D.C.: U.S.
Government Printing Office, January 1971.

Von Neumann, John, and Oskar Morgenstern.
Theory of Games and Economic Behavior. Princeton, N.J.: Princeton University Press, 1944.

Wald, Abraham.
Sequential Analysis. New York, N.Y.: John Wiley & Sons, 1947.
_____. *Statistical Decision Functions.* New York, N.Y.: John Wiley & Sons, 1950.

Webster's Seventh New Collegiate Dictionary.
Springfield, Mass.: G. & C. Merriam Company, 1965.

Index

Ackley, Gardner, 111–112
Arrow, Kenneth, 56

Bayes' theorem, 16–17, 27, 36
Bellman, Richard, 18, 26–27, 28, 37
Bergson, A., 68–69
Braithwaite, Richard B., 48, 50, 51
Brookings Institution, 83

Cambridge conditions, 69
Capital, 76, 85–86, 87, 90, 120–122, 143, 151–152, 175
Capital/output ratios, 78, 117–118, 122, 134–136, 145
Carnap, Rudolf, 17
Chernoff, H., 16
Chiang, C. L., 60–61
Cowles commission, 51
Cost effectiveness, 57–68
Consumption, 91–93, 134, 137, 141, 151, 152

Decision analysis, 1, 6–7, 16–22, 30. See also Decision making
Decision making, 10, 12, 13–16, 31, 38–39, 53–55, See also Decision analysis
in dynamic environment, 10, 77–78
and exogenous event library, 195–196
and games, 214–219
macroeconomic, 67–75
microeconomic, 57–67
processes of, 26–30
and resource allocation, 79, 86–87, 87–90, 120–137, 141
and stabilization problem, 155, 163–164, 178–181, 184–185, 193–194
and uncertainty, 5–6, 35–37
Demand. See Supply/demand
Decision tree approach, 18
Domar, Evsey D., 110–111, 133
Duesenberry, James, S., 22
Dynamic case, 10, 15–16, 109–146, 163–167, 187–194. See also Uncertainty

Einstein, Albert, 51
Employment, 3–4, 69–70, 97, 132–134, 138, See also Labor; Unemployment
Evans, M. K., 175

Fox, K. A., 212
Friedman, Milton, 22
Fromm, Gary, 24–25, 73

Gauss, Carl Friedrich, 49
Great Britain, 23
Gross national product (GNP), 121–122, 151, 157, 175, 184
Growth rate, 69–70, 157–158, 163

Harrod, Roy F., 110–111, 133
Health care, 57–67
Holt, Charles, C., 7–8, 24, 53

Imports, 92, 94–95, 97, 204–207, 209
Inflation. See Prices
Information systems, 14–15, 33, 159–163, 173, 183
Interest rates, 151, 176–177, 179–180, 194
Inventories, and exogenous event library, 207–209
and resource allocation, 87, 90, 104–105, 117, 139, 143, 173
and stabilization problem, 177
Investment, and resource allocation, 93, 118–120, 139, 141, 143
and stabilization problem, 151, 175

Japan, 23
Johnston, John, 195

Keynes, John Maynard, 17, 21–22, 51, 137, 210.
Keynesian multiplier, 133
King, William H., 7
Klein, Lawrence, 6, 23, 46–47, 175, 211
Koopmans, Tjalling C., 7, 51
Kuh, Edwin, 210

Labor, and exogenous event library, 207–209. See also Employment; Unemployment
and resource allocation, 76, 85–86, 87–90, 97, 100–101, 117–122, 135, 139, 143, 145
and stabilization problem, 152
Lagrangean multiplier, 56
Leontief, Wassily W., 76, 112–113, 115–116

Lerner, Abba P., 68–69

Machol, Robert E., 7
Markovian system, 18
Marshak, Jacob, 212
Massachusetts Institute of Technology, 38. *See also* Models
Miyasawa, Koichi, 18–19
Model building, 8, 14, 24, 25, 29–31
Models, 5–8, 25, 31, 34, 49–50, 54–55, 69, 80–81
  Balassa-Kreinen, 207
  Brookings, 6, 23, 24–25, 174
  concepts of, 11–16
  Domar, 110–111
  econometric, 8, 14, 22–25, 36, 172
  FRB-MIT, 174, 176, 212
  Harrod, 110–111, 133
  Keynesian, 21–22, 31, 133, 147, 175
  Klein, 20, 23, 175
  Klein-Goldberger, 23
  Leontief, 80–81, 112–113, 115–116
  macroeconomic, 34–35, 174
  OBE, 174
  Phelps, 111
  Solow, 111
  Suits, 23–24, 174
  von Neumann, 112
  Wharton-EFU, 6, 8, 23, 172, 175, 176, 178–179, 181, 189, 196, 204
Modigliani, 22
Moses, L. E., 16
Multiplier analysis, 23, 24, 29
Monte Carlo studies, 46–47

National Income Accounts, 23
Netherlands, 20, 25

Orcutt, Guy, 6–7
Output, and exogenous event library, 207
  government influence on, 3–4
  and resource allocation, 80–86, 88–90, 91–95, 97, 115–116, 134–136, 137
  and stabilization problem, 152
  and welfare economics, 68–69

Pareto optimality, 63, 65, 69
Phelps, Edmund S., 111, 115

Phillips curve, 71–73, 153
Policy making, 1–2, 4–5, 8, 12, 23, 53–57, 70
  and games, 216–219
  and macroeconomics, 210–213
  and resource allocation, 76–77, 90, 91–92, 93, 95–96, 99–100, 101, 139–141, 143–145
  and stabilization problem, 165, 172–173
Popper, Karl, 48, 49, 50–51
Prices, 70, 71–73. *See also* Shadow prices
  and resource allocation, 89–90, 91, 93–95, 104
  and stabilization problem, 152–153, 157–158, 163, 175, 180
  and welfare economics, 70–73
Probability, 16–22, 27
Production. *See* Output

Resource allocation (dynamic case), 110–146
  and capital, 120–122, 143
  and capital/output ratios, 118–120, 122, 125, 134–136, 145
  and consumption, 134, 137, 141
  and decision making, 141
  and dynamic problem, 77–78
  and employment, 132–134, 138
  and government expenditures, 133
  and GNP, 121–122
  and inventories, 117, 120–122, 139, 143
  and investment, 118–120, 120–137, 139–141, 143
  and labor, 117–122, 135, 139, 143, 145
  and output, 115–116, 120–121, 134–137
  and policy making, 139–141, 143–145
  and shadow prices, 120–122, 123, 134–136
  and supply/demand, 115, 133, 143, 145
  and uncertainty, 137
Resource allocation (static case), 76–109
  and capital, 76, 85–86, 87, 90
  and capital/output ratios, 78
  and consumption, 91–93
  and decision analysis, 86–87
  and decision making, 79, 87–90
  and employment, 97
  and government expenditures, 93
  and imports, 86, 92, 94–95, 97

Resource allocation *(continued)*
and information systems, 95–96
and inventories, 87, 90, 104–105
and investment, 93
and labor, 76, 85–86, 87–90, 97, 100–101
numerical example of, 100–101
and output, 80–86, 88–90, 91–95, 97
and policy making 76–77, 90, 91–92, 93, 95–96, 99–100, 101
and prices, 89–90, 91, 93–95, 104, 108–109
and shadow prices, 76, 78, 96
and static problem, 77
and supply/demand, 78–85, 90–95, 103–105
Resource allocation (static-dynamic case), 139–146

Samuelson, Paul, 48
Saunders, B. S., 61
Schultze, Harry, 22
Shadow prices, 28, 76, 78, 108–109, 120–122, 123–125, 134–136, 139
Shubik, Martin, 38
Simon, Nancy, 101
Solow, Robert M., 111, 114–115, 142–143
Southeast Asia, 36
Stabilization problem, 8, 147–194
and capital, 151–152, 175
and commercial banking, 173, 179
and consumption, 151, 152
and decision making, 155, 163–164, 178–181, 184–185, 193–194
and Department of Defense, 172, 173, 178–179, 193
and dynamic environment, 163–167, 187–194
and government expenditures, 151, 153, 172, 179, 180, 183
and Federal Reserve Board, 172, 180
and gross national product (GNP), 151, 157, 175, 184
and growth rate, 157–158, 163
and information systems, 159–163, 173, 183
and interest rates, 151, 176–177, 179–180, 194
and inventories, 175, 177
and investment, 151, 175

Stabilization problem *(continued)*
and labor, 151–152
and policy making, 165, 172–173
and prices, 152–153, 157–158, 163, 175, 180
and supply/demand, 175, 180
and taxes, 152, 155, 163, 172, 180, 183, 194
and transfer payments, 151, 155, 163, 194
and uncertainty, 62, 165, 173, 194
and unemployment, 152, 157, 163, 175, 180, 181–183
Static case, 76–109
Static-dynamic case, 139–146
Strategy, 10, 15–16, 28, 37–38
Suits, Daniel B., 23–24, 174
Sullivan, D. F., 60, 61–62, 63
Supply/demand, and exogenous event library, 205–207
and resource allocation, 78–85, 90–95, 95–96, 103–105, 115, 133, 143, 145
and stabilization problem, 175, 180

Taubman, Paul, 25, 73
Taxes, 4, and stabilization problem, 152, 155, 163, 172, 180, 183, 194
Theil, Henri, 19–21, 25, 26–27, 70, 71, 73
Thorbecke, 212
Tinbergen, 1, 3, 8, 20, 22, 71
Transfer payments, 151, 155, 163, 194

Uncertainty, 35–37. *See also* Dynamic case
and decision making, 5–6
and model building, 13–14, 30–31
and resource allocation, 137
and stabilization problem, 16, 165, 173, 194–196
Unemployment, 210
and stabilization problem, 152, 157, 158, 163, 175, 180, 181–183
and welfare economics, 70, 71–73
U. S. Government, budget, 3–5
and centralized planning, 1, 3
Department of Defense, 172, 173, 178–179, 193, 202–204
economic impact of, 3–5
Employment Act, 1946, 3, 21, 69

U.S. Government *(continued)*
  expenditures, 4–5
    cost effectiveness of, 57–67
    and resource allocation, 93, 133
    and stabilization problem, 151, 163,
      172, 179, 180, 183
    Federal Reserve Board, 34, 173, 180.
      See also Models
    Federal Reserve System, 179
    macroeconomic goals of, 23, 68–71
    National Bureau of Economic Research,
      51
    and national income, 3–4
    Office of Business Economics, 83, 101,
      216
    Department of the Treasury, 172, 178
  Utility theory, 55–57, 59, 63–64

van de Boggard, 25
Vietnam, 36
Vining, 7
von Neumann, John, 112

Walrusian system, 77
Welfare economics, 68–75